TRAVEL AND TOURISM
International Approach

TRAVEL AND TOURISM
International Approach

Dr. K.N. Patel

ADHYAYAN

ADHYAYAN PUBLISHERS & DISTRIBUTORS
NEW DELHI (INDIA)

Published by
ADHYAYAN PUBLISHERS & DISTRIBUTORS
4378/4B, 105, J.M.D. House, Murari Lal Street
Ansari Road Darya Ganj, New Delhi - 110002
Ph.: 011-23263018, 011-23277156, Fax: 011-23280028
Email: adhyayanpublishers@yahoo.com

TRAVEL AND TOURISM International Approach

Edition 2010
ISBN 978-81-8435-226-9

Printed in India

Published by Harish Chandra Yadav for Adhyayan Publishers & Distributors, Laser Typeseting at A.V. Rao and Printed at Tarun Offset Printers, Delhi

Preface

Travel and tourism one of the world's largest foreign exchange earner among industries, provides employment directly to millions of people worldwide and indirectly through many associated service industries. A very wide industry, it includes government tourism departments, immigration and customs services, travel agencies, airlines, tour operators, hotels etc. and many associated service industries such as airline catering or laundry services, guides, interpreters, tourism promotion and sales etc. Travel and tourism enterprises include major internationals with a workforce of thousands, to the small private travel agent with a handful of employees.

In India, travel and tourism, as an industry, has been somewhat slower to take off than in many other places. However, with increasing worldwide interest in travel, and with the government's encouragement of its activities, it is undergoing massive expansion and improvement. This forecasts a bright future for all those who choose to make a career of travel and tourism.

This book presents a new and refreshing approach to the study of contemporary tourism and how it is conceptualised and endorsed. An extremely student-friendly and accessibly written text, it provides a useful introduction to some of the key emerging issues and inevitable difficulties which arise when defining tourism as a coherent industry and a singular packaged product. The book is structured sensibly into nine chapters, and each chapter sequentially reflects a contemporary aspect of tourism aimed at enhancing the reader's understanding of the interrelationships between tourists, tourism suppliers, destinations and the variety of experiences created. This text will be an essential reading for anyone related to travel and tourism.

Author

Contents

1

Introduction to Travel and Tourism

There is no agreed upon definition of tourism. The term may refer to anyone who travels or it may specify reasons for travelling such as sightseeing, visiting friends, educational or cultural trips, participating as visitors at special events, shopping expeditions, rest and relaxation or others. Tourism professionals may consider it tourism only if there is an overnight stay or if the destination of travel is more than a specified distance from the traveller's home, such as fifty miles. Generally, there is also the implication that such travel is not part of a daily routine.

Definition of "international tourism" was recommended by Council of Nations' League; in 1953 it was adjusted by Statistics Commission of United Nations, which admitted definition of "international visitor". 1967 m. This commission ratified definitions of "visitor", "tourist" and "excursionist". In 1993, Statistics Commission of United Nations in its 27th session ratified "Tourism statistics recommendations", which were prepared by World Tourism Organisation. Tourism forms and categories, descriptions of the main tourism definitions, tourism supply and demand classification, Standards of International Classification of tourism activity (SICTA) were described in it.

Primal definition "traveller" is described as "any person who travels from one place to another irrespective of trip's purpose and kind of transport. "Visitor" is "any person who travels to another place outside his/her usual environment for a period not exceeding 12 months and whose main purpose of visit is other than the exercise of an activity remunerated from within the place visited".

According to forms of tourism visitors are divided into international visitors and domestic visitors. According to duration of a visit – to same-day visitors and tourists (visitors who stay at least one night in a collective or private accommodation establishment in the country visited).

In recent years, increasing attention has been paid to the management and marketing of tourism, hospitality, and leisure, which have been widely recognised as very important sectors of the service economy. However, a different approach to the management and marketing of tourism, hospitality, and leisure services than to that of physical goods is required.

Tourism has a number of different definitions. It is very difficult to pinpoint a definition that would give a meaningful and adequate explanation of tourism, because the concept is fragmented, wide-ranging, and multidimensional. Historically, the concept of tourism was first developed in the period between the two world wars.

Tourism was defined as a sum of relations and phenomena resulting from the travel and stay of nonresidents, in so far as [travel] does not lead to permanent residence and is not connected with any permanent or temporary earning activity. Since 1942, the concept of tourism has been broadened by including various forms of business and pleasure travel.

McIntosh, Goeldner, and Ritchie defined tourism as a short-term movement of people to places other than their normal place of residence and work, including the activities of persons travelling to and staying in locations outside their places of residence and work for not more than twelve months, for the purpose of:

(1) leisure (recreation, vacation, health, study, religion, and sport); and

(2) business, family, mission, and meetings.

Several characteristics of tourism may be identified based on the analysed definitions:

1. Two main elements:
   (a) movement, which refers to the journey (travel) to and from a destination (the dynamic element of tourism); and

(b) the overnight stay outside the permanent residence in various destinations (the static element of tourism)

2. Movement to and from the destination is temporary (temporary change of residence), short-term, with intention to return
3. Destinations are visited for purposes other than taking up permanent residence or employment
4. The activities tourists engage in during their journey, and the stay outside the normai place of residence and work, are distinct from those of the local residents and working populations of the places visited The review of various definitions also illustrates a number of conceptual problems in defining tourism. There is no agreement on how far an individual has to travel, how many nights the individual has to stay away from home, or what activities must be engaged in, etc. There are also cross-national differences in defining the concept of tourism.

Four groups of participants are involved and are influenced by tourism:

(1) tourists,
(2) businesses providing goods and services that the tourist market demands,
(3) the government of the host community, and
(4) the host community.

McIntosh, Goeldner, and Ritchie defined tourism as the sum of the phenomena and relationships arising from the interaction of these four groups in the process of attracting and hosting tourists and other visitors. These groups cooperate to accomplish a set of goals at the micro and macro levels within constantly changing legal, political, economic, social, and technological environments.

Categories of Tourism

In relation to a given country, the following forms of tourism can be distinguished:

— *Domestic tourism*, involving residents of the given country travelling only within this country;

— *Inbound tourism*, involving non-residents travelling in the given country;

— *Outbound tourism*, involving residents travelling in another country.

These three basic forms of tourism can be combined in various ways to derive the following categories of tourism:

— Internal tourism, which comprises domestic tourism and inbound tourism;

— National tourism, which comprises domestic tourism and outbound tourism;

— International tourism, which consists of inbound tourism and outbound.

Tourism is the activities of persons travelling to and staying in places outside their usual environment for not more than one consecutive year for leisure, business and other purposes. There are three elementary forms of tourism in relation to a given area (e.g. region, country, group of countries) :

i) *Domestic tourism:* This is defined as comprising the activities of residents of a given area travelling only within that area, but outside their usual environment;

ii) *Inbound tourism*. This is defined as comprising the activities of non-residents travelling in a given area that is outside their usual environment;

iii) *Outbound tourism*. This is defined as comprising the activities of residents of a given area travelling to and staying in places outside that area.

Tourism is a comprehensive and extensive phenomenon. Tourism is demand led and influenced by many external factors. It generates physical and financial flows that have strong economic, socio-cultural and environmental impacts. To study the domain of tourism one must quantify and interrelate the various characteristics of tourism. In practice most tourism statistics take the transactors in the tourism process as their starting point, in particular visitors and direct supplier. Factors influencing tourism, the impact of tourism and the interrelation between supply and demand are usually tackled by integrating data from a great number of sources followed by model type analysis.

Characteristics of Tourism

It is generally agreed that tourism is fragmented. It is made up of various sectors or subindustries such as transportation, accommodation, attractions, amenities, catering, entertainment, eating and drinking establishments, shops, activity facilities (leisure and recreation), and many others. These sectors provide products and services for individuals or groups of tourists who travel away from home.

Consequently, tourism is an amalgam of the products and services that its various subsectors make available for tourists. The provision of these products and services depends on the linkages between various sectors and their mutual interactions. Tourism is the most wide-ranging industry, in the sense that it demands products from many sectors of the economy and employs millions of people in different sectors.

For example, airplanes and buses must be manufactured to transport tourists; computers must be produced to make hotel booking and airline reservations; steel, concrete, and glass are needed to build hotels and restaurants; fabrics are needed to make clothes; meat, wheat, and vegetables must be grown to feed visitors. No other industry has so many linkages and interactions with so many sectors of the economy, and delivers so many different kinds of products and services to its consumers.

Tourism is multidimensional. McIntosh, Goeldner, and Ritchie noted that tourism embraces virtually all aspects of human life and society. Tourism is a major economic activity of the travel, lodging, retail, entertainment subsector, and many other subsectors that supply tourist needs. It is a major sociocultural activity that provides different tourist markets with cultural experiences.

Tourism involves production, marketing, and consumption of numerous products such as car rentals, hotel rooms, meals, etc. It requires researching, planning, managing, and controlling tourist enterprises. It is about the location of tourist areas, their physical planning, and changes that tourism development brings to the landscape and community.

The industry depends on various intermediaries and organisations that perform tourism activities. Tourism also involves a historical analysis of tourism activities and various institutions. It is difficult to apply the concept of an industry to tourism in view of the special nature and complexity of the potential contributors to the tourism product.

Tourism is about activities and services. It is about the buying, selling, managing, and marketing of numerous activities and services, which range from renting hotel rooms, selling souvenirs, and managing an airline, to marketing special events. However, since these activities and services represent the supply in the market (tourists constitute the demand) and are part of the economy, they might be described as the tourism "industry".

There is a strong link between tourism and travel. Travel refers to the spatial displacement of people and the activities of people taking trips to places outside their residence for any purpose except daily commuting to and from work. Travel may be undertaken for tourism purposes, or other purposes such as migration, commuting, or exploring. It includes both business and convention tourism as distinguished from "pure" pleasure tourism. Thus, travel has wider meaning and application than tourism.

Hospitality is concerned with the provision of accommodation and catering services for guests. It also refers to the reception and entertainment of travellers, the way they are treated by industry employees (with empathy, kindness, and friendliness), and an overall concern for the traveller's well-being and satisfaction.

Tourists are not the only consumers of hospitality services; local residents also use them. Leisure is considered to be part of free time available to the individual after necessary work and duties are accomplished, to be spent at the discretion of the individual. It refers to the time free from obligations, filled with specific activities, without pressure of necessity.

The problem is, however, in distinguishing between work and leisure activities, and activities undertaken for the purpose of subsistence (e.g., eating). The same activities can be regarded as leisure and as obligations by different individuals. For instance, gardening can be regarded as a leisure activity by some people and as work by others.

Eating, shopping, social activities, and even sleeping may be considered as leisure rather than necessity. The difficulties in categorising leisure activities were illustrated by Cosgrove and Jackson in Mieczkowski. Consequently, what is viewed as leisure or work depends upon personality, traditions, and/or education of an individual or, as Shaw and Williams noted, upon the individual's attitude of mind, feelings, perceptions, or social position.

Tourism activity is only possible during time available for leisure. However, much of leisure time is spent at home or close to the place of residence; therefore, it is beyond the scope of tourism. Tourism can also be substituted for leisure (e.g., swimming while on vacation can be substituted for swimming in the local sport and recreation centre).

Moreover, vacation experiences may affect the expectations of leisure experiences at home. For example, experiences of playing golf can create the expectation that golf courses should be provided in every local recreation and leisure centre. Experiencing high-quality facilities in local recreation centres may create high expectations for vacation resorts.

Often, leisure is used synonymously with recreation. Recreation refers to the experiences and activities (or inactivities) undertaken during leisure time to recreate physically, psychologically, spiritually, and mentally after work in order to prepare the individual for future work. Recreation activities may include play, games, sports, cultural functions, informal education, sightseeing, entertainment, relaxation, and amusements, as well as travel and tourism.

Clawson and Knetsch in Mieczkowski argued that recreation is the attitude toward activities. An activity is recreation when it involves no feeling of obligation. Recreation is only possible during leisure time. However, not all leisure can be regarded as recreation (e.g., studying, visiting parents). The same activities may be regarded as recreation by one individual yet work by another.

The assessment of what activities are recreational depends on the individual's attitudes and feelings. For example, sport activities can be viewed as recreation, or as a job in professional sports. Tourism is a form of recreation. Recreational tourism is the most significant part of tourism. However, tourism includes elements such as business tourism, which cannot be classified as recreation.

Recreation also involves elements such as urban recreation, which cannot be classified as tourism. Further, tourism can occur within work time (business tourism) whereas recreation occurs during leisure time. Some forms of tourism, such as health tourism, pilgrimages, and visiting friends and relatives are often not associated with recreation.

Also, tourism is always associated with temporary change of residence and overnight stay outside the permanent residence. In contrast, most recreation occurs at home within the local community. In addition, the purchase of recreation equipment often requires financial expenditures that otherwise could have been allocated to tourism and travel. Also, tourism has far more significant commercial implications for the economy than recreation, which is often provided for, free of charge, by the government or social organisations.

Further, tourism does not require learning special skills, as opposed to recreation, which may require the acquisition of special skills such as sport skills. In short, the concepts of tourism, hospitality, and leisure are different, although they are related. Tourism and hospitality are concerned with the provision of goods and services; leisure is a concept of time; and recreation is a concept of activity. Much tourism takes place during leisure time. Recreation is often the main purpose for participation in tourism. All these concepts are characterised by very complex relationships in the creation and delivery of their services to tourists.

The Manila Declaration on World Tourism was agreed in 1980 at the World Tourism Conference, convened by the World Tourism Organisation (WTO) with the participation of 107 delegations of States and 91 delegations of observers.

The Declaration touches upon all aspects and roles of Tourism and considers the responsibility of States for the development and enhancement of tourism in present-day societies as more than a purely economic activity of nations and peoples.

The Declaration acknowledges that tourism as an activity which is essential to the life of the Nations and recognises the right to annual paid holidays.

The Declaration continues by saying that Tourism is a very important factor in national economies, that domestic as well as tourism from abroad should be expanded and that it represents a great source of employment, as well as a source of mutual knowledge and understanding. Youth tourism should also be encouraged.

Most importantly, point 18 of the Agreement recognises that "The satisfaction of tourism requirements must not be prejudicial to the social and economic interest of the population in tourist areas, to the environment or, above all, to natural resources which are the fundamental attraction of tourism, and historical and cultural sites".

In the practice of tourism, spiritual elements must take precedence over technical and material elements. Governments should mobilise the means of education and information at their disposal; preparation for tourists, travellers and holiday could usefully form part of the process of youth education and training.

Recreation and Tourism

Tourism has been the fastest-growing component of world economy for the past decade. Continuing growth in recreation and tourism is likely, although in the near future, the rate of growth may be slower than was the case in the early 1990s. Recreation and tourism is not just fun: it is both big business and an often-cited component of individual well-being. In terms of economic importance, travel and tourism is estimated to account for more than 10 percent of world economic activity; in the United States, travel and tourism is estimated to account for more than 12 percent of gross domestic product, and more than 13 percent of employment.

Although the importance of recreation and tourism is widely acknowledged, estimates of its scale and relative importance continue to be debated largely because recreation and tourism are not conventional economic sectors with routinely-reported statistics .

The growth of recreation and tourism as an economic activity may present opportunities for some communities to adjust to reductions in production and employment in timber and other commodity sectors. In some cases, recreation and tourism has long been an under-recognised component of the natural resource-related economy. The difficulty of establishing precise definitions and the absence of consistent, explicit data on recreation and tourism as an economic sector complicates any effort to understand the economic dimensions and economic dynamics of these activities.

Although the recreation activity of residents does not, by itself, bring additional income into local economies, recreation opportunities and environmental amenities are often significant factors in determining migration (including the selection of retirement and second homes) and tourism. Consequently, resource management for amenity and recreation services is likely to affect the both the size and structure of the local economy. Equally important, tourism (recreation by non-residents) is often an export sector for local and regional economies. That is, tourism is part of the economic activities that provide new employment and income on which the secondary component of the local economy depends. However, there are divergent views on what constitutes the base of an economy. Leaving definitions aside, there is also uncertainty (and dispute) over the effects of land management activities on local economic structure.

What is important is that the net economic benefits of tourism, such as job creation, are comparable in principle to traditional economic base industries. There are obvious and possibly significant differences (as compared to commodity-based industries) in, among other things, wages paid and skills required. But part of the growing awareness of changing social and economic conditions is an acknowledgement of how economies have broadened and the need to understand the dynamic determinants of change.

Some communities facing declining comparative advantage in commodity production may have (or be able to develop) comparative advantage in supplying the services associated with recreation and tourism. Foreseeable changes in demographics, technology, and broad-scale economic conditions make it possible to imagine sustaining or even substantially increasing the contribution of recreation and tourism to state and local economies in the west.

Although the economic opportunities associated with recreation and tourism are important, especially for some rural communities, these opportunities vary widely. In addition, the scale and distribution of the economic benefits of this sector are not well understood. In the short term, any source of economic growth is typically welcome. However, over the longer term, increasing dependence on recreation and tourism may simply replace the cycles and impacts of commodity production and extraction-based industries with a different set of challenges, both for communities and for forest management and policy.

The increasing importance of recreation and tourism to communities especially tourism presents a set of social challenges that accompany the economic opportunities. Changes in the structure of local economies, and greater dependence on the provision of services (often in place of employment in extractive industries and manufacturing) contribute to fundamental changes in social conditions at the community scale. Some of these changes are the consequences of broad-scale trends; some of these changes are closely related to specific natural resource management policies and management decisions.

As compared to commodity goals for forest management, recreation and tourism may present greater challenges for collaborative decision-making and management. Whereas sustained commodity production is assumed to be synonymous with community stability, sustained policy and management support for recreation and tourism may contribute to profound and unwelcome changes in communities. For example, an emphasis on providing recreation services from forests may satisfy local goals for amenities and services, but increasing tourism (non-resident recreation) may lead to conflicts or reductions in the quantity or quality of services for residents.

Recreation and tourism development presents multiple pathways for most communities, and in few cases will these paths provide equivalent or identically distributed benefits. The policy and management challenges for federal resource management agencies are at least as complex as those associated with management for commodity production. Consideration and comparison of local, regional, and national interests, in the context of broad-scale policy objectives as well as national and international trends is required, but the metric for doing this remains unclear.

It is difficult to describe and quantify how individual perceptions of well-being are affected by the quantity and mix of opportunities for leisure activities and the trade-off with opportunities for other types of economic development. We do know that environmental aesthetics and opportunities to appreciate them are important components of well-being, and that there is a wide range of preferences associated with management for aesthetics.

Environmental aesthetics include scenery and associated opportunities to recreate in natural resource based settings. There is considerable evidence, including survey data, to suggest that quality of life issues are taken quite seriously by many residents of Alaska. Therefore, forest management is further challenged to satisfy complex, often intangible, but nevertheless critically-important social objectives.

Increasing recognition of the economic and social importance of recreation and tourism must be accompanied by recognition of the need to formulate and evaluate public policies affecting this sector and its prospective future development. National Forests have long been recognised for their role in providing opportunities for a variety of outdoor recreation activities. In the country as a whole, and especially in the west, National Forests are a dominant provider of a variety of nature-based, dispersed recreation services.

Present and future forest policies affecting types, locations, and levels of recreation use are likely to have effects on human communities as well as on forest ecosystems that are at least as profound as the effects of decisions regarding commodity programs. In order to be effective, forest planning should consider recreation and tourism both as an economic sector and as a social activity. In both the short term and over the long term, forest policies and management have affected the timing and direction of many of the economic adjustments associated with recreation and tourism. Some of the effects of forest policy and management have been intended, and some have been unintended; the consequences of policy and management have not been uniformly positive. Documenting this activity and its relation to natural resource conditions and management is increasingly important for sound public policy making.

As at present, the future will provide a variety business opportunities, and there is likely to continue to be variety in scale and type of operations; although competition is likely to increase, interdependence and cooperation may also increase. Information technology in advertising and marketing for businesses, and technology in equipment will play an increasingly important role for both businesses and individuals. The transportation system and policies regarding access will be key considerations that will shape the future, in terms of both scale and type of activities.

There is potential for, perhaps even the likelihood of increasing conflict among recreation users seeking widely divergent experiences; the likelihood will be reduced but not eliminated by increasing the capacity of the recreation infrastructure.

Among the developments they highlight are a degree of uniformity in the bundle of services packaged for tourists (tourism is becoming a commodity, with accompanying cost and price-based competition); and a counter-trend toward niche marketing for places and firms. Economies of large scale and a variety of developments in transportation enable the former; developments in information technology enable the latter.

Much of the concern about contemporary land management planning can be characterised as the need to better understand the extent to which it is possible to simultaneously achieve economic, social, and natural resource policy objectives. In the past decade, increasing attention has been given to the need to emphasise protection and restoration of ecosystem services in place of commodities; there is also greater emphasis being given to other natural resource-based services, such as recreation. In many places, increasing recreation and tourism development is almost inevitable given prospective economic changes (both structural change and income growth) and demographic changes. This leads to two fundamental questions. First, is the growth of recreation and tourism likely to contribute to sustainable community development? Second, what are the tradeoffs between recreation use and the biophysical conditions of an ecosystem?

Recreation and tourism is a significant economic sector and a component of the quality of life. Therefore, resource allocation decisions affecting the -'physical plant' of recreation and tourism will be important. The physical plant must be seen to include the infrastructure (campgrounds, cabins, roads, trails, etc.) and the landscape in which it exists. Increasingly, management and policy choices will reflect trade-offs between accommodating (or even promoting) recreation and tourism and other objectives of forest management, as well as trade-offs among types of recreation and tourism activity. Understanding both the reality and dimensions of these possible tradeoffs are future research questions.

There appear to be divergent trends between recreation (resident) and tourism (visitor) activities. Economic and demographic factors will contribute to increases in the relative importance of tourism (visitor activity) within the recreation and tourism mix.

In general, trends in recreation and tourism use and demand appear to have slowed across a number of activities in the late 1990s as compared to rapid growth in the early part of the decade. Various measures of recreation and tourism use support this conclusion, but the data are insufficient to draw long-term implications from this observation. Among the possible explanations for slowing of the rates of increase in tourism are: local and national economic and demographic trends, cycles and competition in the tourism industry and capacity constraints in some activities or key infrastructure. Capacity constraints include both physical limitations and psychic limitations based on perceptions of the quality of acceptability of experiences.

Concepts of carrying capacity for recreation activities are not well understood; therefore, managing for maximum numbers of users is likely to require greater attention to quality issues.

Continuing growth in recreation and tourism is likely, although in the near future, rates of growth may be slower than was the case in the early 1990s. In the future, recreation and tourism activities are, on average, likely to be shorter in duration and more intense, in keeping with broader social and economic trends. This is likely to lead to increased opportunities for commercially-mediated activities. At the same time, continuing evolution and competition in the commercial recreation and tourism sector will, itself, contribute to innovation and efforts to exploreand createmarket opportunities. The result is likely to be continued increases in demand for management decisions that support commercial activities. Competition within the commercial sector, and competition between commercial users and the general public will continue and increase.

TOURISM DEMANDS

Tourism is primarily a demand-side oriented concept, i.e. oriented by those persons engaging in tourism. These persons are called visitors. The term 'visitors' comprises tourists and same-day visitors. The term visitor describes: "any person travelling to a place other than that of his/her usual environment for less than twelve consecutive months and whose main purpose of travel is other than the exercise of an activity remunerated from within the place visited".

The three fundamental criteria that appear sufficient to distinguish visitors from other travellers are as follows:

i) the trip should be to a place other than that of the usual environment,

ii) the stay in the place visited should not last more than twelve consecutive months,

iii) the main purpose of the visit should be other than the exercise of an activity remunerated from within the place visited.

The usual environment - The usual environment of a person consists of the direct vicinity of his/her home and place of work or study and other places frequently visited. The concept of usual environment and therefore tourism, has two dimensions:

— *Frequency:* places which are frequently visited by a person are considered as part of their usual environment even though these places may be located at a considerable distance from the place of residence.

— *Distance:* places located close to the place of residence of a person are also part of the usual environment even if the actual spots are rarely visited.

Length of stay - usual residence: The second criterion is that visitors should not stay 12 consecutive months or more in the place visited. This is in fact an extension of the usual environment concept, since if a person resides within an area during 12 consecutive months, this area can be considered to have become his/her "usual environment". A person staying or intending to stay one year or more in a given area is considered a resident of that place and therefore not a visitor from the point of view of tourism statistics.

Resident in a country/in a place : for the purposes of international/domestic tourism statistics, a person is considered to be a resident in a country/place if he/she:has lived for most of the past year (12 months) in that country/place, or has lived in that country/place for a shorter period and intends to return within 12 months to live in that country/place.

The place/country of usual residence determines whether a person arriving in a region/country is a visitor or other traveller, as well as that person's origin. The underlying concept in the classification of international visitors by places of origin is the country of residence, not their citizenship/nationality. Foreign citizens residing in a country are assimilated to other residents for the purpose of domestic and outbound tourism statistics. Citizens of a country residing abroad who return to their home country on a temporary visit are included among non-resident visitors, though it may be desirable to distinguish them in some studies.

Remuneration from the within the place visited: The third criterion is that the main purpose of the visit should be other than the exercise of an activity remunerated from within the place visited. The term "remuneration" refers to payments which cover the reward for labour, i.e. wages and salaries (including payment in kind) and not travel allowances or small participation fees.

Origin and destination : trip and stay - Whatever form or category of tourism is studied, we can have an origin-based or a destination-based perspective. To distinguish the two it is recommended to use the term "trip" to describe tourism from the standpoint of the generating place or country (the origin) and "stay" to describe tourism from the standpoint of the receiving place or country (the destination or place visited). The "trip" covers the whole period during which the person engages in tourism, while the "stay" covers only part of it.

The volume and character of tourism depend on the point of measurement. To avoid double counting and ambiguity, the following conventions should be applied:

— Every tourism stay has only one corresponding origin of the trip, which is the actual place of residence of the visitor

— Every tourism trip can have several destinations but only one main destination;

— Every tourism trip has only one main purpose, which is the purpose in the absence of which the trip would not have taken place.

Destination: This is a significant place visited during a trip/stay. It may be defined as the farthest point away from home visited (distance destination), the place where the most amount of time is spent (main destination), or the place the visitor thinks of as the primary place visited (motivating destination).

Duration of a visit: The duration of a visit (stay or trip) is measured in the units of the number of hours for same-day visits, and of nights for staying visits. The duration is measured either in terms of time spent in the receiving place/country for inbound tourism (= Duration of the stay), or time away from the usual residence for outbound tourism (= Duration of the trip).

Main purpose of the visit: this is the purpose in the absence of which the trip would not have been made or the given destination would not have been visited.

Overnight visits: Short and long stays concern the activities of visitors who stay overnight in collective or private accommodation in the place (region, country) visited. An international tourist is an international visitor who stays at least one night in collective or private accommodation in the country visited. A domestic tourist refers to a domestic visitor who stays at least one night in collective or private accommodation in the place visited. An overnight stay may be defined differently depending on the statistical approach taken. From a destination-based perspective a person is counted as spending the night in a place visited only if the data of his/her arrival and departure are different. From an origin-based perspective a person spends a night on a qualifying trip if (a) the date of his departure and return are different, and (b) s/he sleeps in collective or private accommodation during his absence.

Same-day visits: Same-day visits concern the activities of visitors who do not stay overnight in collective or private accommodation in the place (region, country) visited. A same-day visitor is defined as a visitor who does not spend the night in collective or private accommodation in the place or country visited. An international same-day visitor is an international visitor who does not spend the night in collective or private accommodation in the place or country visited A domestic same-day visitor is a domestic visitor who does not spend the night in collective or private accommodation in the place visited The same criteria and delimitations as for visitors apply to same-day visitors.

To avoid ambiguity it is important to distinguish three types of same-days visits based on the place of departure and arrival:

— Round trips starting from the place of usual residence (and other places to which one is not a visitor)

— Round trips from a place at which one is an overnight visitor

— Stopovers as part of transit travel

Only visits of the first type, round trips starting from the place of usual residence, are classified as same-day visits from an origin-based as well as a destination-based perspective.

Visits of the second type are part of long/short overnight visits and will only be classified as a same-day visit from a destination-based perspective.

Visits of the third type differ from the other two types by the fact that the nights before and after the same-day visit are spent in different places, which are also different from where the transit stop takes place. They will only be classified as a same-day visit from a destination-based perspective.

To avoid double counting with overnight visits, data on the first type of same day visits should always be distinguished from the other two types.

The statistical unit to be measured in tourism demand surveys carried out in homes may be:

(i) A household whose tourism participation is reported by one respondent speaking for the visits made by all members of the household, or an individual selected randomly from within a household, responding only for him/herself, or an individual identified by quota controls set by an agency responsible for the conduct of a quota sample.

(ii) A visitors selected by a random or quota control procedure, or a travelling party. selected by a random or a quota control procedure. A travelling party is not necessarily the same as a household group.

The sampling for surveys in respondents' homes, as well as in destination surveys and at international arrival and departure points, should be of individuals aged 15 or over, selected at random or according to a quota control procedure. The tourism activity of children can be measured by asking the adults about the children's tourism habits.

Data on the volume of tourism:

(a) Estimates of the generation of tourism demand (percentage and characteristics of each country's population and number of people participating in tourism on one or more occasions).

(b) Estimates of the number of visits made by the population participating in tourism (domestic and outbound = national tourism).

(c) Estimates of the number of visits of non-residents received within a country (inbound visitors).

(d) Estimates of the number of visits generated by the residents of a country to other countries (outbound visitors).

Data on Visitor profile: Information on the visitor profile provides vital data for analysing the nature of tourism demand. It tells us who the visitors are, i.e. the personal characteristics of the visitor : sex, age, level of education, economic activity status; occupation, income, household composition. In order to analyse tourism demand (and its various market segments), it is important to link information on the personal characteristics of the visitor (profile) with information on the purpose, behaviour and habits of the visitor (characteristics of the visit).

Data on the characteristics of the trip, including purpose of visit: These data describe the trip itself and involve relating the variables to the classification of the purpose of the visit, duration of the stay, accommodation used, transport used, activities engaged in and destination types visited. They also cover the areas/destinations visited, months of departure and types of overall tourism product purchased - including use of packages/inclusive tours or independent travel.

Information on the purpose of the trip is useful in segmenting the tourism markets. In order to obtain a more accurate picture, it is useful to include the secondary purpose. Questions covering destination types, purpose of the visit and visitor activities are needed to calculate estimated participation in rural tourism, cultural or specific kinds of tourism markets.

The duration of the trip is a very important item of data : it is the most significant measure of the volume of the various tourism activities, such as accommodation; it is instrumental in establishing the maximum limit beyond which the trip is no longer considered to be part of tourism (one year); it distinguishes the tourist from the same-day visitor.

The means of transport has a strong bearing on visitor behaviour and expenditure. The mode of transport used refers to the mode used by the visitor to travel from his/her place of usual residence to the places visited. The main mode of transport used is defined as the conveyance used to cover the greatest distance. In many cases it is also interesting to know the secondary or other modes of transport which may have been used during the visit. Information on the distance covered to the destination and back is also a valuable variable, which can be linked to transport, energy and environment statistics. The classification breakdown of the distance covered may be finer for same-day visits than for short and long stays. Links with transport statistics on passenger mobility can provide useful information.

Data on tourism expenditure: Data on tourism expenditure form part of the processes involved in estimating the balance of payments and employment attributed to tourism. The approach may be different according to whether it is origin-based or destination based. In the first case, one would be interested in all the expenditures for the trip, including advance outlay necessary for the preparation and undertaking of the trip and travel-related outlays made in the place of residence after returning from the trip. From a destination-based perspective, the primary interest would be the expenditures made in the place visited. But this does not affect the variables or classifications as such.

To optimise the total resources devoted to measuring tourism activity, information on demand and supply should be co-ordinated. The services and products in demand can be linked to the supply of these by studying tourism expenditure and activities. This presupposes that demand statistics are recorded in detail and that the statistics on supply are compiled according to the tourism demand classifications. Two important tourism-related statistics in this field are services statistics and the commodity accounting of input-output accounts.

For some key statistical variables in countries with registration requirements and some form of voluntary or legal enforcement, important aspects of tourism demand may be measured indirectly through the statistics on tourism accommodation:

— estimates of the total number of visitors staying in commercial accommodation in a country or a particular destination may be derived directly through guest registrations;

— if the regulations covering accommodation registration require visitors to complete registration forms, or if international transport data can be supplemented with limited data available from immigration/emigration cards, supply-side data may also be used to help estimate purpose of travel (business/holiday etc.), size of travelling party, and place of residence or origin of visitors. Such methods only produce valid results, however, where strict controls are applied to the data collection process.

Demand for a country or region may be partly estimated through an analysis of passenger transport data. In each of the cases above, however, for the data to meet identified user needs for demand purposes, it is necessary to know what proportion of all tourism uses the supply of products and services offered. Such proportions can only be derived from surveys of overall demand.

Tourism Supply

The definition of tourism supply should result from the definition of tourism. Thus it can be defined as the supply of all assets, services and goods to be enjoyed or bought by visitors and occasioned by the journeys of visitors. Statistics on tourism supply may be approached in two ways :

— statistics on the production (structure) of enterprises etc., e.g. supply has been interpreted as activities of enterprises such as the supply of HORECA, transport and retail services;

— statistics on the results of such activities, i.e. products, which also may be services, consumed by visitors;

The general purpose of statistics on tourism supply is to assess the contribution of the tourism sector to a country's general socio-economic process and to identify the effects of tourism, distinguishing between direct effects and indirect or induced effects.

Some economic activities depend on tourism for their survival, e.g. tourist accommodation, travel agencies, long-distance passenger transport. Other activities such as restaurants and bars, car rental services, entertainment and attractions services also tend to rely strongly on tourism. The dependency of certain activities of enterprises on tourism may also depend on their location. Thus the supply of tourism activities comprises diverse economic activities, and presented as a sector is very heterogeneous, encompassing different activities some of which are directly dependent on tourism and others only partly.

To delimit and define in more detail tourism activities, the WTO has drawn up the International Standard Classification of Tourism Activities : SICTA. This classification was adopted by the Statistical Division of the United Nations and is based on the revised International Standard Industrial classification. SICTA remains at present a provisional classification. It attempts to distinguish between activities which receive their revenue primarily from tourism (labelled "T") and activities which have a partial relationship with tourism (labelled "P").

Many types of data can be observed from the activities of enterprises (production units) :

— Data on the unit itself, such as type of activity, size, legal status
— Data on the production factors, such as breakdown of fixed assets, labour
— Accounting data, such as the breakdown of turnover or value added
— Data on the output (goods and services) of the unit, expressed in physical quantities and distinguished according to the nature of the product and use of the production capacity
— Data on the prices and tariffs of goods and services sold.

Institutional statistics on the sectors of activities related to tourism generally fall within the framework of Enterprise statistics, so that direct reference can be made to other parts of the Eurostat Manual of Business Statistics, developed by the Statistical Office of the European Communities.

Supply of Tourism Products

The global product approach deals not only with products as direct results of economic activities but all products (diversions, goods and services) that are enjoyed or bought by visitors.

Tourism products may be considered as follows:

— Products (goods and services) consumed by visitors that can be described by a standard product classification such as the Central Product classification by Activities (CPA) or the CPC (Central Product Classification);
— natural assets of a location, such as mountains, beaches, lakes, etc. and weather conditions, the environment in general;
— attitude of the population to visitors, the lifestyle and culture of the receiving area

The products supplied represent more than tourism expenditure. Tourism expenditure is the counterpart of the majority of products having the shape of goods and services, although not every good or service has to be paid for by the consumer.

The use of assets (e.g. roads, historical areas, national park, nature) in many cases is free, in other cases visitors have to pay for the facility offered (a 'service'). In fact, most assets offer 'services' to their users or to the people enjoying them, regardless of whether visitors have to pay for them or not. Nevertheless, free 'services' of the type which benefit from the infrastructure of a country belong to the supply of tourism products. Free for the visitor does not mean that the free service is also free for the supplier ; the country has to spend money in order to maintain fresh air, etc. Because these types of products are hard to quantify, they are excluded from the statistical analysis.

To make the definition of the supply of tourism products practical, only products which can be identified in a standard product classification are taken into account. In defining the supply of tourism products, two considerations (representing two sides of the same coin) must be kept in mind:

— the supply of tourism products includes all products supplied to the visitor, including non-characteristic tourism products.

— products that are consumed by visitors may also be consumed by other types of consumer.

Therefore, when attempting to measure the supply of tourism products, one must attempt to identify the share of the product which is consumed by visitors.

The reporting unit that can best supply information about the product under review depends on the type of product to be observed. In general the following may be used as a reporting unit: enterprise, local unit, kind-of-activity-unit (KAU), local KAU, (local authorities) of a community, province etc. Since the observation unit is the product, the reporting unit should be asked to provide information on the breakdown of their activities according to kind-of-activity units or supply the breakdown by sales of products.

As tourism is basically a demand-oriented concept, the need to collect information from the demand side is essential in order to know the destination of goods and services produced and therefore complete the supply-side data. The demand of residents can be estimated by demand-side statistics, the total tourism demand within a certain country can be estimated via supply-side statistics. By deducting demand of residents from total demand, the non-resident tourism demand may be calculated.

Administrative data such as registers of enterprises and establishments maintained by the tax authorities, registers of establishments prepared by the CSOs, register of establishments maintained by health or licensing authorities, can be used to identify production units supplying tourism products and to obtain basic information on the production unit. In many cases, information relating to tourism products can be obtained directly from enterprises or other statistical units. Information on some types of facilities may be gathered through accommodation statistics. Information on certain tourism products may be derived from enterprise, transport, consumption statistics and statistics on prices.

Tourism Accommodation

A large share of short-term accommodation supply is taken up by tourists. The basic aim of tourism accommodation statistics is to measure the capacity and use of collective accommodation establishments and (if possible) of private means of accommodation. Tourist accommodation is defined as: "any facility that regularly provides overnight accommodation for tourists". It is important to distinguish facilities that commercially service the bulk of overnight stays away from the guest's usual environment and those providing occasional overnight accommodation. Thus tourist accommodation has been divided into two main groups:

— collective accommodation establishments and

— private tourist accommodation.

Collective Tourist Accommodation

Collective tourist accommodation is defined as an accommodation establishment providing overnight lodging for the traveller in a room or some other unit, but the number of places it provides must be greater than a specified minimum for groups of persons exceeding a single family unit and all the places in the establishment must come under a common commercial-type management, even if it is not for profit.

The major group "collective tourist accommodation establishment" is subdivided into three minor groups: hotels and similar establishments, specialised establishments, and other collective establishments. These minor groups are further subdivided into nine unit groups.

Hotels or similar establishments: This category is typified as being arranged in rooms, in number exceeding a specified minimum; as coming together under a common management; as providing certain services including room services and daily bed-making and cleaning of the sanitary facilities; as grouped in classes and categories according to the facilities and services provided; and as not falling in the category of a specialised establishments.

— *Hotels*: Comprises hotels, apartment-hotels, motels, roadside inns, beach hotels and similar establishments providing hotel services, including more than daily bed-making and cleaning of the rooms and sanitary facilities.

— *Similar establishments*: Comprises rooming and boarding houses, bed-and-breakfast establishments, tourist residences and similar accommodation arranged in rooms and providing limited hotel services, including daily bed-making and cleaning of the rooms and sanitary facilities.

Specialised establishments: This category is typified as being any establishment intended for tourists, which may be non-profit making; as coming under a common management; as providing minimum common services (not including daily bed-making); as not necessarily being arranged in rooms but perhaps in dwelling-type units, camp sites or collective dormitories; and as engaging in some activity besides the provision of accommodation, such as health care, social welfare, conferences or transport. This minor group consists of establishments that, besides providing accommodation, have another specialised function. This minor group is subdivided into four unit groups : health establishments, work and holiday camps, conference centres and accommodation in collective means of transport, which are described as follows :

— *Health establishments*: This unit group comprises health treatment and health care establishments providing accommodation, such as spas, thermal resorts, (mountain) sanatoria, convalescent homes, health farms, fitness resorts and other similar establishments.

— *Work and holiday camps*: This unit group comprises camps providing accommodation for holiday activities, such as agricultural, archaeological and ecological work camps, holiday camps, scout camps, riding and sailing schools, other sports centres, and other similar establishments.

— *Passenger transport*: This unit group consists of the accommodation with sleeping facilities associated with collective public transport and inseparable from it in terms of fare. It comprises cruise ships of all kinds (usually not using marinas to stay overnight), accommodation in scheduled passenger ships and sleeping-car and couchette accommodation in trains and motor coaches, and other accommodation in public or hired means of transport . This is a special category of accommodation in the sense that it is mobile.

— *Conference centres*: This unit group includes establishments offering accommodation and specialised in facilities for congresses, conferences, courses, vocational training, meditation, retreats, etc. The sleeping accommodation is generally only available to the participants of the specialised activities organised in or by the establishment.

Other collective establishments: This category is typified as being any establishment intended for holiday-makers, which may be non-profit making; as coming under a common management; as providing minimum common services (not including daily bed-making); and as not necessarily being arranged in rooms but perhaps in dwelling-type units, camp sites or collective dormitories. This minor group consists of establishments arranged as holiday dwellings, tourist campsites and social tourism accommodation.

— *Holiday dwellings:* This unit group includes collective facilities under common management, such as apartment buildings, clusters of houses or bungalows arranged as dwelling-type accommodation. Often tourist services such as recreational activities, canteen, laundry facilities and information services are provided.

— *Tourist campsites*: This unit group consists of collective facilities in enclosed areas for tents, caravans, trailers and mobile homes. All come under common management and provide some tourism services (shop, information, recreational activities, canteen, laundry facilities).

— *Other collective establishments*: This unit group comprises social and group tourist accommodation establishments and marinas. Social tourist accommodation includes youth hostels, tourist dormitories, group accommodation, holiday homes for the elderly, holiday accommodation for employees and workers' hotels, halls of residence for students and school dormitories and other similar facilities that come under common management, have a social interest and are often subsidised. Marinas are also included under this unit group. Marinas include boating harbours where boat owners can hire a permanent berth in the water or a place on the land for the sailing season or the year (long-term hire) and ports for passing vessels where sailors pay mooring per nights. At least some sanitary facilities are provided.

Private Tourist Accommodation

Private tourist accommodation comprises forms of accommodation that do not conform to the definition of collective tourist accommodation. These provide limited numbers of places for rent or free of charge. The major group "Private tourism accommodation" is subdivided into two minor groups and five unit groups. It is important to distinguish between the minor group "private rental accommodation" and "private non-rental accommodation", as the former generates lodging expenditures and an associated economic impact that the latter does not.

Private rental accommodation

— Rented rooms in family houses: The accommodation covered by this unit group differs from the boarding house in that the tourist stays with the family that usually lives in the home and pays rent.

— Dwellings rented from private individuals or professional agencies: This unit group comprises apartments, villas, houses, chalets and other dwellings rented or leased as complete units between households, on a temporary basis, as tourist accommodation.

Private non-rental accommodation: This minor group concerns lodging places offered free of charge to guests.

— *Owned dwelling*: This unit group comprises immobile units such as second homes/apartments, villas, houses, chalets, and other dwellings used by visitors who are members of the owner household. This group also includes dwellings incorporated in a time-sharing contract (owned by various people).

— *Accommodation provided without charge by relatives or friends*: The accommodation of this unit concerns tourists allowed by relatives or friends to use all or part of their home free of charge.

Other private accommodation: his unit group does not fit entirely into the major group of private tourist accommodation. It includes other types of accommodation such as tents, caravans, trailers, campers at non-organised sites (not placed in collective tourism accommodation) and vessels at unofficial moorings.

Because regional aspects and characteristics of the accommodation establishment itself are very important to the results of accommodation statistics, local kind-of-activity units (KAU) should be used as the basic statistical unit, e.g. the observation unit in accommodation statistics. Alternatively the local unit can be used as the basic statistical unit of tourism accommodation establishments. In some cases the enterprise and the local unit coincide, but it is quite common for one enterprise to comprise two or more establishments or facilities of the same kind or of a different kind. This is one reason why the tourism accommodation establishments classification used for tourism statistics described on the previous pages does not have a one-to-one relationship with activity or product classifications.

The supply and capacity of tourist accommodation concerns information on the number of establishments providing their services to tourists, and on the structure and quality of this supply. The use of tourist accommodation concerns information on guest flows.

Variables on the supply and capacity of tourist accommodation establishments:

(i) Number of establishments according to each type of accommodation

(ii) Overnight capacity, number of:

a) *Bed-places*: The number of bed-places in an establishment or dwelling is determined by the number of persons who can stay overnight in beds set up in the establishments, ignoring any extra beds that may be set up by customer request. The term bed-place applies to a single bed. A double bed is counted as two bed-places. This unit serves to measure the capacity of any type of accommodation. A bed-place is also a pitch or, in a boat, a mooring to accommodate one person. A pitch for a tent (if counted), caravan, mobile home and similar shelter, or a boat on a mooring, usually counts for 4 bed-places if the actual number is not known.

b) *Bedrooms*: A bedroom is a unit formed by one room or groups of rooms constituting an indivisible rental whole in an accommodation establishment or dwelling. Rooms may be single, double or multiple, depending on whether they are equipped permanently to sleep one, two or several people. The number of existing rooms is the number the establishment habitually has available to accommodate guests (tourists). If a room is used as a permanent residence (for more than one year) it should not be included. Bathrooms and toilets do not count as a room. This number should generally coincide with the number of units recorded in the establishment recorder. Apartments are a special type of room. They consist of one or more rooms and have a kitchen unit and own bathroom and toilet. Apartments may be with or without hotel services. Cabins, cottages, huts, chalets, bungalows, villas and summerhouses can be treated like bedrooms and apartments, i.e. to be let as a single unit.

c) *Pitch and mooring*: The majority of camp sites let pitches for tents, caravans, mobile homes and similar shelter to tourists who want to stay on a 'touring' pitch for only a couple of consecutive days or weeks, as well as to people who want to hire a 'fixed' pitch for a season or a year. Moorings on boats in marinas can be dealt with similarly to pitches. Hired fixed pitches and moorings for long-term rent (more than a year) may also be considered as private accommodation. It is advisable to obtain monthly data on the number of bed-places, bedrooms, pitches and moorings because they may change according to the season and are needed in order to calculate occupancy rates.

(iii) Months (or days) open during the year: This variable is necessary to get an impression of the seasonal aspects of the business, and to calculate the occupancy rates.

(iv) Services offered - Number of establishments offering: a) Restaurant services is the most important variable of services offered. Other variables may be: b)breakfast (buffet/other), c)lunch, d)dinner, e)bar services (only for staying guests / for other clients also), f) M2 conference rooms, g) swimming pool, h) sauna or solarium, i) sports facilities, j) (other) facilities for health treatment, k) shops, l) children's playgrounds / play room, m) laundry service, n) self-service laundry, o) self-catering kitchen, p) guarded or closed parking, q) amusement (e.g. dancing).

(v) Other quality criteria - Number of establishments with: a) Awarded quality classifications, e.g. stars, crowns, flags, etc. b) Bathrooms for individual use c) (Bedrooms) provided with heating and suitable for all-year accommodation. Other variables may be d) soundproof rooms, e) rooms provided with air conditioning, f) length of the majority of the beds, g) rooms with audio equipment and television.

(i) *Guest flows* - Numbers of arrivals and overnight stays:

a) Arrivals (or departures) of accommodation establishment guests

— by country of residence of the guest

— by month

A guest arrival/departure is defined as a person who arrives at/leaves a collective accommodation establishment or private tourism accommodation and checks in/out.

Because tourists arrive at and leave from an accommodation establishment within a relatively short time, there is statistically not much difference between the numbers of arrivals and departures. The arrivals of non-tourists (refugees, guests on medical referral, etc.) should be counted separately, if possible.

b) Overnight stays of accommodation establishment guests

— by country of residence of the guest

— by month

An overnight stay (or night spent) is each night that a traveller stays or is registered in a collective accommodation establishment or in private tourism accommodation, his or her physical presence there being unnecessary.

The overnights stays of non-tourists should be counted separately if possible.

(ii) *Average length of stay*: This variable is obtained by dividing the number of overnight stays by the number of arrivals (can calculate also according to country of residence of guests). It is more relevant at local and regional level because at country level, the effect of same persons spending nights in several places obscures the measurement.

(iii) *Purpose of the visit*: This can be counted either by number of guests or overnight stays.

(iv) *Variables on occupancy*: Occupancy rates give information on differences in use between various types of accommodation and, when measured on a monthly basis, indicate the seasonal patterns.

a) *Net occupancy rate of bed-places*: The net occupancy rate of bed-places in one month is obtained by dividing total overnight stays by the product of bed-places on offer and the number of days when the bed-places are actually available for use (net of seasonal or other temporary closures for decoration, police order, etc.) for the same group of establishments, multiplying the quotient by 100 to express the result as a percentage.

b) *Gross occupancy rate of bed-rooms*: The gross occupancy rate of bed-places in one month is obtained by dividing total overnight stays by the product of bed-places on offer and the number of days in the corresponding month (sometimes termed bed-nights) for the same group of establishments, multiplying the quotient by 100 to express the result as a percentage.

c) *Net occupancy rate of rooms (houses, pitches, moorings)*: For hotels and similar establishments, the room occupancy rate can be a better measure of capacity utilisation than bed occupancy because a room with a double bed is very often occupied by only one person. This is calculated by dividing the total number of rooms used during the month (the sum of the rooms in use per day) by the average number of rooms available for the month multiplying the quotient by 100 to express the result as a percentage.

d) *Gross occupancy rate of rooms (houses, pitches, moorings)*: This can be calculated in the same way as for bed-places.

Accommodation statistics figure partially as a second-best alternative to gain information on the demand side of tourism, especially on tourists from abroad. Results of accommodation statistics provide information on the use of accommodation, as well as on some variables of some categories of tourists (i.e. purpose of visit). In this way they give information on demand. Accommodation statistics data in one country provide additional information to demand-side tourism data of another country.

A solid connection can be found between accommodation statistics and services statistics on the horeca sector. Generally, accommodation statistics are census-based and services statistics are sample-based, but if both use the same address register, it is then possible to connect data on an individual basis and to interpret financial data on tourism. Important variables such as the proprietorship of the establishment, the number of persons employed, and general monetary variables can be obtained from business registers, services statistics, labour force surveys.

An updated register of names and addresses of accommodation establishments is extremely important. Guidebooks and tourism organisations are good sources of capacity, services offered and quality classifications. For commercial private accommodation, the intermediary agencies are an important source. For non-commercial private accommodation, housing registers, censuses and surveys may give information, e.g. the number of second homes.

As there is a strong interest in regional data, most European countries have census surveys for tourist establishments. For larger countries it is possible to use samples without losing much reliability at country level.Countries use different legal or statistical standards for excluding minimal-capacity tourist accommodation suppliers. The threshold is usually based on the number of rooms, (or pitches) or beds. The threshold chosen should be determined in such a way that at least 95% of all nights spent in the groups of accommodation establishments included in accommodation statistics are covered.

On some countries there are legal obligations for the guests to give information to the establishment. If there is no legal act that requires tourist to fill in registration forms, information can be obtained on a voluntary basis, or simply from the night registers of the establishment. In some countries businesses are required to fill out and send the questionnaires of accommodation statistics to the national statistical authority. When the replies are checked regularly and reminders sent to the establishments failing to send the data on time, high response rates are possible.

Tourism Expenditure

Tourism expenditure is defined as "the total consumption expenditure made by a visitor, or on behalf of a visitor, for and during his/her trip and stay at destination". This concept encompasses a wide variety of items, ranging from the purchase of consumer goods and services inherent in travel and stays to the purchase of small durable goods for personal use, souvenirs and gifts for family and friends. Tourism expenditure is not restricted to payments made during the visit. It also includes advance outlays necessary for the preparation and undertaking of the trip and travel-related purchases made in the place of residence after returning from a trip. These categories refer to payments for travel insurance, transport, the purchase of travel guides, etc.

There are certain types of outlays or acquisitions which are to be excluded from tourism expenditure. These are purchases for commercial purposes, capital-type investments or transactions (e.g., real estate, cars, boats, etc..), even if they may in the future be used for tourism purposes, and cash or donations made to private persons or institutions which do not represent payment for tourism goods or services.

Total tourism expenditure can be broken down from different perspectives :

— Domestic and international tourism expenditure;
— Within international expenditure, between transport fares and other types of expenditure;
— Expenditures on same-day visits and overnight stays;
— The products to which the expenditures relates.

Domestic tourism expenditures are defined as expenditures incurred as a direct result of resident visitors travelling within their own country of residence.

International tourism expenditures are defined as expenditures of outbound visitors in other countries, including their payments to foreign carriers for international transport (although for the sake of consistency with the Balance of Payments recommendations of the International Monetary Fund (IMF) it is recommended to classify these international fare expenditures separately). They should also include any other prepayments or payments made afterwards for goods and services purchased from the countries visited.

International fare expenditures are defined as all payments made to carriers registered abroad by any person resident in the compiling country.

International tourism receipts are defined as expenditures of international inbound visitors, including their payments to national carriers for international transport (although for the sake of consistency with the Balance of Payments recommendations of the International Monetary Fund (IMF) it is recommended to classify these international fare receipts separately). They should include any other prepayments or payments made afterwards for goods and services purchased from the country visited.

International fare receipts are defined as all payments made to the carriers registered in the compiling country of sums owed by non-resident visitors, whether or not they are travelling in that country.

Balance of Payments

Tourism expenditure in the Balance of Payments concerns international tourism expenditure. Expenditures by outbound travellers are generally a debit of the given country, while expenditures by inbound travellers in the country constitute a credit. The Balance of Payments includes tourism expenditure of international visitors (tourists and same-day visitors) within a defined accounting scheme with its own methodology established in the International Monetary Fund (IMF) Balance of Payments manual. In these recommendations, international tourism expenditure is covered by 2 items:

— Travel

— Other transportation, passenger services,

All tourist expenditures, except international fare payments (which is under passenger services) are included under the Travel item.

There are three basic concepts to be considered in international tourism expenditure: residence, visitor and tourism expenditure, since only the expenditure of resident visitors travelling abroad and that of non-resident visitors travelling to the compiling economy is to be taken into account.

Tourism statistics attempt to remain as consistent as possible with the IMF Balance of Payments recommendations. However, the IMF definition of its "Travel" item, i.e. the expenditure of international "travellers" is broader than that of the definition of tourism and the "visitor" in tourism statistics. This leads to two major discrepancies between what is included in the Travel item of the Balance of Payments and what is included in international tourism expenditure from the conceptual approach of tourism statistics :

— The IMF considers students and medical patients as residents of their economy of origin, even if their length of stay is over one year, and therefore includes their expenditure under "Travel". By contrast, such travellers are excluded from the visitor concept in tourism statistics because their length of stay exceeds one consecutive year, and their expenditures are therefore excluded from international tourism expenditure.

— The IMF includes expenditure of seasonal and border workers under "Travel". By contrast, the definition of the visitor in tourism statistics excludes seasonal and border workers because their main purpose is the exercise of an activity remunerated from within the place visited, and their expenditures are therefore excluded from international tourism expenditure.

From the Balance of Payments perspective, the Statistical unit to be considered differs according to the system used. For the Balance of Payments two broad approaches are used to measure travel expenditure:

(i) *The International Transaction Reporting System (ITRS).* This approach attempts to measure the instruments used to pay for the travel. It compiles information for the Balance of Payments on receipts and payments between resident and non-residents. In principle, in systems based on international receipts and payments data, the statistical unit is either the resident travelling abroad or the resident enterprise that pays non-residents for services to be provided to residents travelling abroad or is paid by non-residents for services provided during their stay in the country. Usually, this information is reported to the compiling organisation through the credit institutions (banks, savings banks, etc.) that effect their receipts and payments. In turn, these credit institutions report their transactions with foreign-currency notes and coin and the notes and coin of their own country surrendered to non-resident credit institutions.

(ii) *Enterprise surveys (ES) and additional surveys relating directly to visitors and their expenditure.* Enterprise surveys concern the collection of information on international transactions undertaken by resident enterprises. Such supply-or demand-side surveys attempt to measure the actual expenditure by travellers. In systems based on supply-side surveys, the statistical reporting unit is defined in "Statistical units" of Tourism Supply, i.e. the enterprise, local unit, etc. In systems based on demand-side surveys, the statistical reporting unit is defined in "Statistical units" of Tourism Demand, i.e. a household or individual in household surveys and a visitor or travelling party in surveys at international arrival and departure points or destinations.

To date there has not been a very close connection between international receipts and payments from the Balance of payments and tourism supply and demand statistics. A closer relationship between data obtained from the regular registration of exchange transactions by central banks and data obtained from surveys on tourism, and even the use of the latter to estimate, compare and check the former, would improve the overall quality of the data on international tourism expenditure. To improve the results, the following actions are recommended:

Short-term action

— Exchange of information between the various countries on both "Passenger transport" and bank note transactions on a uniform basis and use at EEA level.

— Unification of estimate and adjustment criteria.

— Increased use of tourism and transport statistics to check data quality or as a source for estimates and adjustments.

Long-term action

With the introduction of a common European currency in the near future, it will be impossible to obtain information on cash receipts and payments made between EU Member states, so that it is advisable in the future to replace the current data collection systems by other methods. In principle, the most obvious way seems to be to obtain information on Balance of Payments debits through household surveys. The exchange of information between EU Member States would provide each Member State with credit data in a similar way as between the United States and Canada. The remaining credits could be estimated through visitor surveys or other estimates, and information could also be exchanged with some other countries using a system similar to the one applied at EU level.

Tourism prices, costs and tariffs

Prices on tourism can be considered as:

— prices (including tariffs) of goods and services linked to tourism, the level of which influence tourism expenditure. The prices of these goods and services are related to the demand side of tourism and are consumer prices;

— prices of goods and services which determine the cost of tourism production. The prices of these goods and services refer to the supply side of tourism and are called either cost of production prices or input prices on tourism.

The level of prices paid by visitors is influenced by tourism demand. Increasing demand for goods and services related to tourism will have an impact on their prices. On the other hand, the level of prices of goods and services related to tourism affects tourism demand.

Prices related to goods and services of intermediate consumption for tourism activities, the remuneration of the factors of tourism production and the prices for goods and services contributing to fixed capital formation on tourism sector affect the cost of tourism supply. Although in many cases the real prices and changes are interesting to measure, this section will focus on price changes measured by constructing price indices which combine the different changes in prices of individual items in such a way that a single number can be used to indicate the overall change in prices.

The main variable considered here is Prices indices, and as such can be included as an economic variable for the tourism sector.

Price indices on tourism can be divided into the following two main categories:

(i) price indices from the demand side (consumer prices);

(ii) price indices from the supply side (cost of production).

Price indices on tourism from the demand side measure changes in prices over time of a given pattern of tourism expenditure, or compare the price level of tourism expenditure in space. Therefore, these indices can be subdivided into:

(a) inter-temporal (time) price indices, and

(b) inter-spatial (space) price indices.

Many inter-temporal price indices from the demand side can be constructed depending on the expenditure covered by each index. The inter-spatial price indices can be distinguished into:

— inter-regional price indices, which make comparisons of the price level of tourism expenditure between regions of a country, and

— international price indices, which compare the price level of tourism expenditure between countries.

A "Tourism Expenditure Price Index" can measure the price changes of total expenditure made by all visitors (residents and non-residents) in the economic territory of a country (region, area). Tourism price indices from the supply side measure changes over time of the cost of producing tourism products. The measurement of the changes in the cost of production for the tourism sector as a whole or by activity can be achieved by measuring changes in prices of the main cost elements. The main cost elements are:

— Intermediate consumption, which represents the value of the goods and market services consumed by production units during the course of the relevant period in order to produce goods and services related to tourism;

— Remuneration of factors of production;

— Depreciation of fixed capital. The measurement of the changes in this cost element is achieved indirectly by measuring the changes in prices of goods and services contributing to fixed capital formation.

Consequently, the following price indices from the supply side can be constructed :

(i) price indices of intermediate consumption, which measure over time changes in prices of a given pattern of intermediate consumption of production units engaged in tourism activities;

(ii) price indices of fixed capital formation, which measure over time the changes in prices of goods and services contributing to capital formation in tourism activities.

(iii) price indices of the production factors, which measure over time changes in the remuneration of factors of production engaged in tourism activities.

Tourism expenditure price statistics (demand side) refer to the prices of goods and services consumed by visitors. The consumption of visitors is a part of the final consumption of households. Many goods and services consumed by visitors are also consumed by non-visitors. All goods and services of households' final consumption are therefore to be carefully combined with the activity classification, following which products and services which are exclusively or partially consumed by visitors are to be identified.

Tourism price statistics from the supply side (costs and their price indices) will be calculated for activities which are mainly or partly dependent on tourism. The goods and services which constitute the intermediate consumption of each tourism activity, as well as the goods and services contributing to the fixed capital formation, will be classified according to the activity branches of the whole economy from which they come.

Tourism price indices from the demand side are closely linked with statistics on tourism expenditure. The results of tourism expenditure surveys, broken down by categories according to the visitors' place of residence (residents, non-residents) and purpose of travelling as well as by type of expenditure, are necessary for the calculation of the weighting scheme of tourism price indices from the demand side.

Surveys of tourism expenditure are usually conducted at rather long intervals (three or more years), and the estimation of tourism expenditure for the intermediate years is therefore achieved by using extrapolation methods based on time tourism price indices. The purpose of time tourism price indices from the demand side is to measure the changes over time in tourism expenditure due to price changes. Consequently, tourism expenditure and tourism price indices are interconnected variables. Comparisons in real terms of tourism expenditure between countries is achieved by using the space price indices from the demand side. The price level and its changes, measured by price indices, influence tourism demand. Additionally, the differences in real terms of price level between countries, measured by space price indices, influence tourism demand of the countries because these differences determine their competitive position.

Tourism price indices from the supply side are linked with surveys on enterprises, from which (surveys) cost production data (intermediate consumption, remuneration of the factors of production) as well as data referring to fixed capital formation can be derived. The results of surveys on the cost by activity are necessary for the estimation of the weights of the corresponding price indices. Moreover, as the above surveys are probably not conducted every year, the price indices are useful for estimation of the changes in several cost elements due to price changes, for the intermediate years. Finally, regardless of the periodicity of the costs surveys, the price indices from the supply side of tourism can be used for measuring the effect of price changes on the cost of production. Consequently, costs and price indices on tourism from the supply side are mutually connected.

Link with other statistics:

(i) Tourism price indices from the demand side are linked with the following statistics:

(a) Consumer Price Index refers to the prices of goods and services of households' consumption, a part of which is the consumption of resident visitors. Therefore, some goods and services included in the Consumer Price Index are related to tourism consumption, and their price indices can be used in the calculation of the Tourism Expenditure Price Index.

(b) Family Budget Surveys cover all the expenses of households, some of which are related to the expenditure of resident visitors.

(c) Survey of Purchasing Power Parities covers, among other things, private consumption, part of which refers to tourism consumption. Consequently, it includes some goods and services linked to tourism, the prices of which can be used in the calculation of international space price indices on tourism.

(ii) Tourism price indices from the supply side are linked with the following statistics:

(a) Input-Output tables, from which useful data concerning flows on tourism activities can be obtained and used in the estimation of the weights of the corresponding price indices.

(b) National Accounts can be taken into account especially for the index of gross fixed capital formation on tourism.

(c) Wholesale Price Indices. Some goods included in these indices refer to intermediate consumption or to gross fixed capital formation on tourism, and their price indices can be used for the calculation of the corresponding price indices on tourism.

(d) Construction Price Indices. Some constructions (buildings, public works etc.) refer to tourism, and the relevant individual price indices can be used in the calculation of Gross Fixed Capital Formation Indices on Tourism.

(e) Surveys on wages and salaries, provided they cover the tourism sector.

References

Bremner, Caroline (2010). "Trend Watch: Euromonitor International's Top City Destination Ranking". *Euromonitor International.*

Cooper, Chris; et al (2005). *Tourism: Principles and Practice* (3rd ed.). Harlow: Pearson Education.

Laidlaw, Katherine (19 April 2010). "Vacationing a human right, EU chief says". *National Post.*

Lennon, J. John; Foley, Malcolm (2000). *Dark Tourism.* London: Continuum.

2

Travel and Tourism: Emerging Trends

Each and every day around the world billions of people rise to engage in an economic pursuit. Whether that pursuit brings value beyond employment opportunities and shareholder returns is a question increasingly being asked by consumers, governments, and civil society— even business itself.

It is the good fortune of those of us in the Travel & Tourism (T&T)/ hospitality industries to have the opportunity to make a positive difference in the quality of life for so many, in so many ways.

What is apparent is that, since ancient times, the T&T industry has contributed immensely to the human experience. Well before modern student–exchange programs, Travel & Tourism provided first–hand educational experiences for youth. Long before any international summit of world leaders was convened, Travel & Tourism brought visionaries together to reach accords.

The T&T industry is not unique only in that it grew out of a very human desire to traverse the globe and come together in real time, but it remains unique today in that it is one of the world's greatest economic drivers. It provides employment opportunities at every experience level, from entry level jobs to lifelong careers, and it does this at a staggering rate: *one in every 10 workers worldwide is employed because of Travel & Tourism*.

Travel & Tourism accounts for 10 percent of world GDP, 8 percent of jobs, and 12 percent of global investment annually. It also has the highest potential for growth of any industry—currently running at more than 4 percent per year.

The resilience of Travel & Tourism shows how much it has become a necessary and vital element to the world. It is a force that can be slowed, but it simply cannot be stopped.

Travel & Tourism is becoming more and more appreciated by its host countries and communities. It is helping build economies emerging from poverty, conflict, and confusion while stimulating infrastructure development and secondary economic activity.

Indeed, Travel & Tourism fills a need and invigorates economies. Fulfilling market need and wealth creation is basic to any industry's survivability. *How* it fills this need is today the focus of enlightened societies, governments, and companies.

As World Economic Forum Chairman, Klaus Schwab correctly points out that "As state power has shrunk, the sphere of influence of business has widened. Companies get involved in the health of workers, the education of employees and their children, and the pensions that sustain them in retirement." Companies within the travel and hospitality industries have long recognised their potential impact on society.

Tourism in the Developing World

Tourism is a vital part of the global economy. Generating roughly $1 trillion in global receipts in 2008 (up 1.8 percent from 2007), international tourism ranked as the fourth-largest industry in the world, after fuels, chemicals, and automotive products. The breadth of international travel also has greatly expanded in recent years to encompass the developing world. In 1950 just fifteen destinations—primarily European—accounted for 98 percent of all international arrivals. By 2007 that figure had fallen to 57 percent. Tourism is a key foreign exchange earner for 83 percent of developing countries and the leading export earner for one-third of the world's poorest countries. For the world's forty poorest countries, tourism is the second-most important source of foreign exchange after oil.

The economic might of the tourist industry has helped transform societies, often for the better. Tourism has several advantages over other industries:

i) It is consumed at the point of production so that it directly benefits the communities that provide the goods.

ii) It enables communities that are poor in material wealth but rich in culture, history, and heritage to use their unique characteristics as an income-generating comparative advantage.

iii) It creates networks of different operations, from hotels and restaurants to adventure sports providers and food suppliers. This enables tourist centers to form complex and varied supply chains of goods and services, supporting a versatile labor market with a variety of jobs for tour guides, translators, cooks, cleaners, drivers, hotel managers, and other service sector workers.

iv) It tends to encourage the development of multiple-use infrastructure that benefits the host community, including roads, health care facilities, and sports centers, in addition to the hotels and high–end restaurants that cater to foreign visitors.

With these benefits in mind, the United Nations has identified the development of tourism as one of the methods poorer countries might use to meet the Millennium Development Goals (MDGs). For the first MDG—alleviating poverty—the merits of tourism are evident. It can provide jobs and generate income for communities that, in some cases, lack viable alternative means of employment. With its tendency to produce flexible labor markets and offer diverse working opportunities, tourism can also help realise a second MDG, that of promoting gender equality. In Mali, the World Tourism Organisation's Sustainable Tourism for Eliminating Poverty (ST-EP) program has supported an effort to train the female artisans of Djenne, one of Mali's oldest and most visited towns. If carefully managed, tourism can also be an important part of promoting a sustainable environment, another of the MDGs. Frangialli identified tourism's potential for not only protecting the natural environment, but also "preserving historical, archaeological, and religious monuments; and stimulating the practice of local folklore, traditions, arts and crafts, and cuisine." Finally, as tourism by definition involves the transfer of people, culture, and ideas, it is ideally placed to foster effective global partnerships, the eighth MDG.

In addition to advancing development goals, some have credited tourism with helping to build and sustain peace. Among them is

Wangari Maathai, the Nobel laureate and founder of the Green Belt Movement, who highlights tourism's potential as "a great vehicle for peace promotion."

That said, while tourism can bring positive benefits, good does not necessarily follow. And holiday destinations, tragically, have become a popular target for terrorists, who want to maximise civilian casualties and publicity for their actions. In recent years, Mumbai, Bali, Sharm el-Sheikh, Dahab, Mombasa, and Casablanca have come to be associated as much with mass bombings and killings as with tourism.

Ecotourism

While conventional mass tourism often negatively affects host environments, other forms of tourism have emerged in recent decades that are more sensitive to their surroundings and offer tangible benefits to the local labor force. These newer forms of tourism have come to be known as ecotourism, an umbrella term best defined as responsible travel to natural areas that conserves the environment and improves the well-being of local people. These include geotour ism, pro-poor tourism, sustainable tourism, responsible tourism, and travellers' philanthropy. They are united by the simple idea that tourism should offer a benefit—and not incur a cost—to the host community. They reflect the desire of many holiday goers to give something back to the places they visit, or at the very least, avoid doing them harm. Costa Rica led the way in developing the ecotourism concept, followed closely by Ecuador, Tanzania, Kenya, and Nepal.

Case Studies

Kenya, Nigeria, and India are three developing countries with tourism industries at different stages of matur it y. Kenya has a long established and highly successful tour ist sector cater-ing to the conventional and ecotourism markets. As the table demonstrates, international tourism is a lucrative source of income for Kenya, accounting for 2.24 percent of the nation's gross domestic product (GDP) in 2006. India has several tourist centers but, given its vast size, it has yet to realize tourism's economic potential. International receipts from tourism made up just 0.35 percent of its GDP in 2006.

A mixed picture emerges. In Kenya, which has had a longer time to finesse its strategy, ecotourism is starting to bring about the progress that Honey describes. Conservationist David Western, the author of a study of Kenya's tourism industry, explains how Kenya learned from some of the mistakes it made when it began building its safari-based tourism industry. He discusses how Kenya became the first country in Africa to establish both an ecotourism society and a framework for assessing the social and environmental impact of resort developments. Most important, he shows how Kenyan communities have benefited directly from tourism by running their own wildlife conservation areas. However, the picture he paints is not overwhelmingly rosy. While pockets of good practice exist, a fair share of Kenya's tourism tramples on local customs, is indifferent to conservation, and fails to pass on economic benefits to host communities. In her analysis, Adeleke argues that, while tourism may well promote peace, peaceful conditions have to be in place before tourism can thrive. The lack of peace and security, she argues, is the main reason why Nigeria has been unable to persuade foreigners to visit its many cultural and natural attractions. For Adeleke, Nigeria faces a catch-22 scenario, whereby tourism has the potential to promote peace and development but can only take root in areas where peace and development are already present.

The third case study offers a reminder that tourism is not a magic bullet with the ability to transform developing countries for the better. Aditi Chanchani of Equations, an Indian nongovernmental organisation (NGO) that promotes good practice in the tourism industry, shows that her country has a lot of work to do in developing a sustainable tourism model that delivers benefits to local communities.

Although Kenya, Nigeria, and India differ significantly in how they have sought to develop tourism, it is possible to draw some common lessons from their experiences. The first is that certain levels of peace and economic development are preconditions for tourism. But tourism, in turn, can strengthen existing conditions of peace and development. However, everything depends on the way it is managed. Ecotourism could provide a blueprint for managing this process, as it not only builds entrepreneurial skills at a local level but also links community members to the larger world in ways that cre-ate knowledge, understanding, and appreciation of other peoples.

Ecotourism exposes communities to a social network and gives them both a reason and the skills to manage social networks in order to benefit themselves; the knowledge and communication linkages that tourism creates, for their part, depend on and promote fair practices, stability, and peace.

Kenya

East Africa is a natural destination for tour ist s, boasting the richest and most var ied con-centration of wildlife on the continent. Kenya spotted the potential for tourism quickly, opening its first national park in 1947 and building a flourishing industry based around the safari. Unplanned and unsympathetic development, however, led to Kenya becoming the "Costa Brava of the wildlife world," by the 1990s, providing mass tour ism commonly associated with the resorts of the Spanish coast.

Although progress has been patchy, Western concedes that Kenya's ecotourism has been able to deliver concrete benefits to its people. Involving local communities is one of its central tenets. Ordinary Kenyans also have been involved in developing tourism in their areas, and through programs such as Parks Beyond Parks, have been given the lead role in managing and conserving wildlife areas in their own communities. As a result, tourism has helped provide employment and alleviate poverty, the first of the United Nations' MDGs. The stronger focus on ecotourism has also aided Kenya's progress toward achieving another MDG, that of environmental sustainability.

One of the most important advantages of tourism, according to Western, is that it tends to have a snowball effect, generating revenue in indirect ways. Donor countries are more likely to give aid and support to nations that their citizens visit, and where tourists beat a path, businesses and NGOs often follow. Although difficult to quantify, this hypothesis merits further study.

In his explanation of the growing importance of ecotourism, Western gives most of the credit to individual travelers rather than the Kenyan government. Ecotourism, he argues, ref lec ts "the traveler 's urge to do good." This enables ecotour ism to "grow spontaneously through contagious social responsibility, rather than by rules and regulations and policies." In Western's v iew, more can be done to capitalise on the w illingness of individual travelers to give something back to the communities they visit. The best model for tourism, he argues, should combine the responsible approach of ecotourism with travelers' philanthropic impulse to contribute to developing their holiday destinations. While there is a clear risk that such projects could fuel a dependency culture, they are a powerful way of directing wealth to communities in a virtually unmediated way. Kenya's experience demonstrates that tourism can positively affect development and help lay down the building blocks of peace, provided it respects of the environment, works closely with host communities, and harnesses the philanthropic impulses of overseas visitors.

Nigeria

The story of Nigeria's tour ism industry is one of unfulfilled potential, according to Adeleke. Theoretically, the country is tailor made for tourism: Its 370 ethnic groups give it a rich cultural heritage and it is blessed with natural wonders, unique wildlife, and a very favorable climate. Nigeria did not establish an official tourist board until 1976 and only in the 1990s did it formulate a national tourism policy. Most foreign visitors come to Nigeria for business or family visits.

What is the reason for this oversight? According to Adeleke, the enabling environment for tourism simply does not exist. For tourism—particularly international tourism—to flourish, a nation needs to be peaceful and safe. For most of its post independence history, Nigeria has been a byword for political instability, violence, ethnic rivalry, and crime. The challenges of marketing its tourist credentials are laid bare by the U.S. State Department advisory for the country, which gives even the most intrepid traveler pause. U.S. citizens are warned of the dangers of "violent crime in Lagos and other large cities as well as on roads between cities," the prevalence of "armed muggings, kidnappings and carjackings," and the risk of ethnic conflict. They are urged to avoid "all but essential travel" to the Niger Delta, the scene of years of violence among local citizens, international oil companies, and the Nigerian military. Clearly, however, tourism cannot gain a foothold in societies that are prone to conflict and instability.

Moreover, to thrive, tourism requires more than just an absence of conflict. Adeleke points to several other structural problems within

Nigeria that complicate efforts to build a strong tourism sector. Poor infrastructure is a particular barrier. Nigeria is a large country with a small and badly maintained road network. Tourists would struggle to travel between different regions. Parts of the country, such as the Niger Delta, are almost completely cut off. Poverty hinders domestic tourism, but even those who have the means have not developed a culture of travel. Another important barrier to tourism is the absence of organisation and institutional capacity at a national level. The government does not even possess reliable figures on the numbers of international arrivals to and departures from the country. Corruption is another serious deterrent, as it undermines government efficiency, deters potential investors in the tourism industry, and scares off visitors.

Addressing the Challenges

If tourism is to achieve its full potential as a force for promoting peace and prosperity, several challenges must be addressed:

i) *Bad neighborhood effect:* The case study of Nigeria shows that peace and security are pre-conditions for a thriving tourism sector. Travelers are risk averse and do not wish to spend their vacation feeling anxious about their personal safety, mindful of their belongings, and wary of being ripped off.

ii) *Investments:* Solid infrastructure is another precondition for any country wishing to estab-lish a tourism industry. Poor countries need to prioritise the search for capital investment to help them build the roads, airports, hotels, and leisure facilities needed to attract visitors in large numbers. Investments in human capacity are equally important.

iii) *Regulations and standards:* The India case study demonstrates that tourism needs to be subject to robust laws and regulations if it is to benefit local communities and prevent them from being exploited. Laws must protect the environment from overdevelopment and safeguard the land, property, and livelihoods of communities affected by tourism.

iv) *Structural leakages:* Developing countries must try to capture more tourism spending and limit leakage if they are to maximise their revenues from tourism. An international hotel chain that opens up in a developing country may create jobs in the local community, but it repatriates the profits.

v) *Ecotourism, not tourism numbers:* Governments need to emphasise implementing the sound principles and best practices of ecotourism rather than fixating on increasing tourism numbers. High-quality ecotourism can bring more revenue and decrease the harmful social and environmental effects of uncontrolled mass tourism.

vi) *Strategic oversight* Tourism cannot grow into a thriving sector of the economy without constructive leadership from the national government. Too many countries fail to reap the rewards of tourism because of poor planning, poorly thought-out strategies, and fragmented policies. Strategic oversight includes everything from overall budget planning and encouraging outside investment to educating host communities.

Tourism is a thriving global industry with the power to shape developing countries in both positive and negative ways. The tour ism sector has remained robust despite the transnational challenges posed by terrorism, health pandemics, and the global financial crisis. In 2007, international tourist arrivals passed 900 million; the United Nations predicts they will reach the 1 billion mark by 2010. It is up to developing nations to seize the economic opportunities that foreign visitors present, and some countries have proved more adept than others at doing so. Kenya has developed a lucrative tourism sector, powered in recent years by ecotourism, and some local communities have benefited directly through social and economic development. In Nigeria, structural weaknesses, insecurity, and poor leadership have locked the country out of the benefits that tour ism can offer.

The three case studies demonstrate that while tourism can be a force for good—both in alleviating poverty and helping to cement peace—much depends on the way the sector is planned and managed. Tour ism can only achieve the above goals if it respect s the environment and places host communities at the center of the development process. Responsibility lies with the governments of developing nations to ensure that tour ism grows in a sustain-able manner. But, as the case study of Kenya shows, individual tourists also have a part to play. As the driving force behind the ecotourism movement, they have shown that the choices they make as consumers can determine whether tourism takes a path that helps or hinders development in poorer countries.

Growth of Tourist Destinations

To understand the growth of a tourist destination it is necessary to comprehend the elements that relate and hence influence the increase of tourists to a place. To study a tourist destination it is important to view it as part of a tourism system as the one proposed by Leiper. While describing the components of the system such as the Traveller Generating Regions (TGR), the Transit Routes (TR) and the Tourist Destination Regions (TDR) one must analyse them under the influence of diverse environments. Tourism growth in a specific destination cannot be comprehensively understood unless the other regions, TGRs and TRs, as well as the environments influencing in each region are studied.

Human society as any other animal or plant species relates in complex ways among each other and with other species. To isolate a relationship, an environment or a component from another for further study obeys only to the need to simplify reality to understand it better and theorize.

The following argument evolves around the idea of understanding, in a very superficial manner, the tourism system of the Americas region as called by the World Tourism Organisation. The Americas region covers North America, Central America, the Caribbean and South America. While the Americas' tourism system is dissected into its three geographical components, the focus of the essay remains on the environments of the system and how these affect tourism and at the same time how tourism affects the environments at each geographical component.

Americas Tourism System

Forecasts for international tourist arrivals in the Americas show that there will be 282.3 million in 2020. This represents an annual growth rate of 3.9 per cent over the period 1995–2000, a little below the world average of 4.1 per cent.

Traveller Generating Regions

Traveller Generating Regions (TGRs) are the places where trips begin. where people who will later be described or counted as tourists start their journey". The TGRs for the tourism system of the Americas are countries of the same Americas, mainly from North America and South America. This kind of travel is called intraregional by the World Tourism Organisation. Intraregionl tourism "refers to arrivals of residents of any country of a particular region to any other country of the same region".

The second biggest TGR to the Americas is Europe with 15,901,000 international tourist arrivals. The most significant subregions were Western, Northern and Southern Europe with 7,161,000, 5,064,000, 2,236,000 international tourist arrivals respectively. The WTO calls this kind of tourism long-haul travel. Long-haul travel "refers to arrivals of residents of countries of one particular region to any country of any other region than their own".

It is important to analyse now the environments of the TGRs and how these determine the increase in the flow outbound tourist. Three main factors "time, affluence and freedom of movement are necessary predisposing circumstances for tourism to take place". These three circumstances, without taking motivations to travel, are the same environments mentioned by Leiper if we translate free time as a the social environment regarding labour rights, money considered as the economic environment and freedom of movement as a political environment. The possibility of travel could not be understood by isolating one environment for example economics.

Adding to these environments Burton concludes that one of the most important factors triggering international tourism is the climate (1991). "The main tourist flows in both Europe and North America are north-south to the warmer and more reliable climates". This can be the strongest environment regarding tourist arrivals to Mexico and the Caribbean. Other factors mentioned by Burton are: distance between countries, attractions, communications, relative costs, cultural links, and political factors.

Complementing the above mentioned factors Leiper presents the following factors that determine the size and characteristics of a traveller flow from a TGR: size population, gross economic prosperity, distribution of income and wealth, spare time, demographic characteristics, motivations as tastes and preferences, constraints on travel, transport facilities, fares and other prices, exchange rates, and promotion.

The economic environment at the TGR's for intraregional tourism of the Americas, mainly coming from the United States with its recession following the Gulf War of 1991 explains why "the Americas underperformed the global average. The economic situation in the regional TGR's added up with the environments prevalent in the TDR's, as will be discussed further on, has been a reason why the World Tourism organisation's forecasts for 1990–1998 international tourist arrivals were inaccurate "around 5 million higher in 1995" and 13 million higher in 1998.

Transit Routes

This is an intermediate zone where the principal travel activity of tourism occurs, distinct from visit activity in destinations. The factors that contribute to the growth of a TR must increase its efficiency. An efficient TR is a path where access is easy for large numbers of travellers. The factors mentioned by Leiper are: travel time, fares and other travel costs, availability of a carrier and other transport facilities, capacity, frequency of services on public carriers, changes in transit, discomfort, reliability, attractions around the way, and stopover points. Though some other environment can be inferred such as geography, affecting the travel time. Nowadays another two environments are relevant to consider in TRs: security and health. Further research is necessary to unravel the TRs of the Americas region and then analyse its environments.

Tourist Destination Regions (TDR)

TDRs according to Leiper are places where "a person chooses to stay a while in order to experience some feature or characteristic", hence "become, temporarily, tourists" and as a consequence "counted in statistical surveys or estimates as tourists". According to the WTO the main TDRs for the Americas were North, Caribbean and South America with 73.9%, 12.9% and 10.8% respectively for 1995 international tourist arrivals.

Some features and conditions are presented by Leiper on how TDRs become popular such as: attractions, accessibility, tolerance, security, life-support and comfort systems, cost and benefit advantage, and information diffusion. As it can be observed some factors relate to the normal service and product offering of tourism enterprises or the infrastructure and uniqueness of the destination. On the other hand, it is observed that environments are mentioned such as security. Security can cover such issues like health, terrorism, crime and political stability. "Competition and incidents that affect the safety of tourists are the two greatest challenges for the America's tourism administrators to overcome" . Accessibility and cost can be two reasons why South America remains a third regional destination in the past. These two reasons relate to the geographical location and the economic-political environment of the destination. Though the common assumption would be that South America's growth in the future, because of these two environments, would not be very strong other environments might be working, because according to the WTO South America will become the second biggest TDR of the Americas taking over the Caribbean for the year 2020.

The WTO in its Americas report pinpoints several "factors determining Americas prospects" from which environments can be recognised such as technology, security and safety economic crisis, health and water. Some remarks by the WTO regarding how environments affect tourism and the prospects of growth in the Americas are very illustrative. "Outbreaks of disease, such as cholera, yellow fever and typhoid, which are particularly common in South America, have a temporary impact on tourists to worldwide destinations". "Natural disasters require substantial rebuilding before tourism can re-commence". "The end of several civil wars in Central America has produced a boom in tourism" a specific example of this was the signing of the peace treaty in 1996 in Guatemala.

The Americas region is the second most important TDR in the world. Growth is estimated for the region to establish at around 3.9 percent according to the WTO. Statistics and forecasts can draw a picture of what can happen concerning number of tourists, but other question stay unanswered, where do they come from and what causes this growth. Through this approach a better insight was gained on the tourism dynamics of the Americas region and also addressing the question presented to us, should Leiper's environments be considered in isolation when trying to understand the growth of a destination?

Destination growth cannot be understood unless the generating and transit regions to that destination are included in the analysis. The instruments by which to analyse those regions TGRs, TRs and TDRs are the environments that affect each one of them and as a result the whole of the tourism system. Environments cannot be considered in isolation to understand destination growth. The simplest analysis in one environment will sooner or later relate to another environment.

Implications for researchers and also managers are important with relation to this tourism system approach. "Effective managers must not only have very good knowledge of the region where they are personally based, but they should also be outward looking and knowledgeable about places away from their own area which are linked to it in significant itineraries". Further analysis is required to understand the tourism system of certain type of tourism, such as the so called alternative tourism. A detailed tourism system of alternative tourism for America would deliver significant information for marketers and managers of ecotours, for example.

Business Engagement

In the early 1990s, the perceived value of—and actual activity around—global engagement on the business stage was limited. Since the 1990s, individual stakeholders, media, nongovernmental organisations, and others have increasingly called for companies to act in a socially responsible way.

Though lagging a bit behind other parts of the world, Americans' expectations of their corporations' social responsibility practices are shifting. A recent study by Fleishman-Hillard-USA and the National Consumers League shows the impact that business engagement efforts have in the mind of Americans today.

Among the findings is the fact that Americans expect corporations to be engaged in their communities in ways that go beyond just making financial contributions. Defining exactly what that means to the various stakeholders and where corporate responsibility stops and government or civil society's responsibility starts is challenging.

Being acknowledged as "socially responsible" has become a goal of global corporations. Many find themselves searching for a consistent and sustainable framework for global engagement. It is clear that global citizenship can reinforce the positive role of business in society and enhance profitability in the long term.

Investors, too, have a growing interest in this trend. In recent years, the Johannesburg Stock Exchange, for example, has provided its users with a socially responsible investment index.

One of the greatest philanthropic efforts to further economic development is, quite simply, to provide a job. For Carlson, an American-founded company today operating global brands, providing jobs and economic growth to nearly 200,000 people all around the world and business operations in more than 150 countries, the development of social entrepreneurship and global corporate citizenship is a fundamental part of everyday activity. The ability to create such economic growth results in an improved economy for both the company and the world in which it does business.

Even outside the T&T industry we find examples of a new approach to business partnerships. A case in point: Woolworths' CEO Michael Luscombe has made it clear that the retail giant will "positively discriminate" toward suppliers and business partners with a responsible business practice in place.

Today, one would be hard pressed to find a global T&T company that is not engaged in socially responsible activities beyond job creation. From corporate philan–thropy and social investment to proper corporate governance and transparency, these have become *de rigueur* for companies that desire to carry their brands into the future. There is no turning back on these issues.

Global Citizenship: The Model for the Future

The great French philosopher Alexis de Tocqueville observed that "In democratic countries knowledge of how to combine is the mother of all other forms of knowledge; on its progress depends that of all the others."

We need new models that combine the best of society to improve society as a whole—models in which business, governments, and civil societies understand and respect each others' roles and unique capabilities and boundaries. Thoughtful leaders need to find the beneficial intersection of business, government, and the social society.

In a recent issue of *Foreign Affairs*, Klaus Schwab has taken an interesting look at the issues around global corporate social responsibility and has suggested the way in which corporations—and the world—need to address this new age of integrative thinking. He breaks down the issue of business engagement into five key areas: corporate governance, corporate philanthropy, corporate social responsibility, corporate social entrepreneurship, and global corporate citizenship.

By looking beyond the board room in order to contribute to global solutions, Carlson has discovered that it is the integration of all five of these factors that yields the greatest opportunity for impact and results for employees, customers, partners, and the communities in which business operations flourish. Integrative global citizenship suggests that companies must not only be engaged with their stakeholders, but that they must also see themselves as stakeholders along side governments and civil society.

With corporate leaders thinking across broad business sectors and developing public–private partnerships to solve social problems, the T&T industry can help provide for the stable development of democratic societies. A stable economy decreases the risk of negative choices such as gang activity, terrorism, and sex trafficking.

In looking at corporate social responsibility, Michael Porter, a Harvard Business School professor, and Mark Kramer, managing director of FSG Social Impact Advisors, wrote in the *Harvard Business Review* that corporations must engage in global issues while understanding that the business community cannot on its own solve global problems such as poverty, poor education, and inadequate health care. The key is to find the proper niche for each entity to do what it does best to support corporate social responsibility.

On an enterprise wide context, an innovative way to work the issues of social responsibility into an integrative global citizenship model can be illustrated through the diagram shown in Figure 1.

Education

At the earliest stages, philanthropic and volunteer efforts should be aimed at youth at risk. With financial support to organisations such as the US Big Brothers/Big Sisters and the Knowledge Is Power Program (KIPP), companies are addressing the need for quality early education and safety nets for our future generations.

The impact of educational social responsibility at the post–secondary level is worthy of note, as well. Financial support to universities and training institutions helps to build that pipeline for men and women who will find new prosperity within the T&T industry.

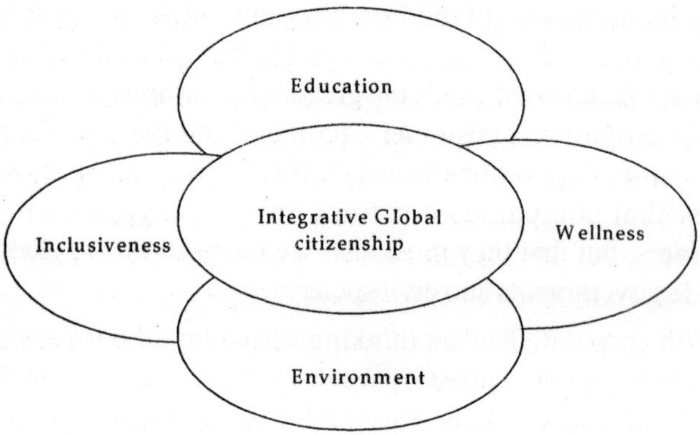

Figure 1. Integrated global citizenship model

For example, supporting industry focused training programs at the high school level such as that offered by the United States–based Academy of Hospitality & Tourism enables students to gain an understanding of the connections that exist between their education and the workplace. With more than 500 travel related companies participating as business partners, the academy fosters the personal, analytical, technical, and communications skills needed for a career path in hospitality and tourism.

Inclusiveness and Social Issues

As part of this new integrative model, the advancement of women and the protection of children from sexual exploitation in the T&T industry should be the hallmarks of Travel & Tourism–related companies' social responsibility programs.

Women

Social entrepreneurship and engagement for women is part of a best practices effort within global companies to expand roles for women. Carlson Women's Advisory Board, for example, pulls leading women from the local community into the Carlson culture for a best practices sharing of ideas and inspiration.

Within the T&T industry, the past 20 years have seen a significant increase in the participation of women. The industry has also been a major factor in the war on poverty in the lives of women, in particular. For most developing countries it is the largest single export and major driver of jobs, investment, and economic transformation. However, it is clear across the industry that at the executive level there continues to be a dearth of women in top roles.

The *Global Gender Gap Report 2007*, developed by the World Economic Forum's Women Leaders Programme and supported by corporate partners, including Carlson, intends to provide a guide for assessing successful policies that help improve conditions for women around the globe both within the industry and beyond.

The latest scores of the *Gender Gap Report* reveal that, globally, progress has been made on narrowing the gap between men and women in these key areas, but more work is to be done to create truly inclusive societies.

From a purely financial perspective, efforts to support organisations such as Athena International help to support and celebrate women leaders from all sectors of society.

Children

In pursuit of helping young people at risk, non–profit organisations such as the World Childhood Foundation are dedicated to serving the most vulnerable children in the world: street children, sexually abused and exploited children, children trafficked for sexual purposes, and institutionalised children, with a particular focus on girls and young mothers. The World Childhood Foundation supports more than 100 programs in 14 countries. Prevention, intervention, and education are hallmarks of these programs, which are found in urban, suburban, and rural areas over the world.

The growing clout of the ECPAT International program to combat child sex tourism is a testament to the impact that industry-related social responsibility programs can have on the lives of children around the world. As a result, there is greater awareness about the root causes of the problem and work is being done to decrease the risk of trafficking and child sex tourism involving the most vulnerable among us.

The ECPAT Code of Conduct was initiated by ECPAT Sweden in 1998 in cooperation with Scandinavian tour operators and the UN World Tourism Organisation. Carlson was among the first and very largest North American travel company to sign the ECPAT Code, demonstrating its increasing awareness and commitment to banning the exploitation of children within the company, the industry, and the communities in which Carlson operates.

The Code encourages companies adopting it to commit themselves to:

i) Establish an ethical corporate policy against sexual exploitation of children;

ii) Educate and train personnel to create awareness of the problem and be more aware of possible signs of the exploitation in both the country of origin and travel destinations;

iii) Introduce a clause that repudiates sexual exploitation of children in common contracts with suppliers;

iv) Develop information and awareness-raising materials such as catalogues, brochures, posters, in-flight films, ticket slips, and home pages;

v) Provide information to local "key persons" at the destinations; and

vi) Report annually on the implementation of these criteria.

The protection of women and children, along with efforts at creating greater self-esteem and social power, must continue to be an aim—and by product—of the T&T industry.

Wellness

Health care and wellness issues are at the forefront of policy dialogues around the globe. Discussions at the local, state, federal, and international levels are guiding business and providing opportunities for integrative solutions to one of society's greatest challenges.

In 1988, leading Minnesota business leaders developed the Buyers Health Care Action Group. This group is recognised throughout the United States for its innovative, leadingedge approach to healthcare purchasing.

The introduction of innovative wellness programs into the workplace demonstrates a company's commitment to employees and their lives. Innovative leaders should continue to find ways to approach and affect these kinds of social and economic challenges facing the world today.

Environment

The T&T industry is not immune from the growing focus on global warming and the environmental impact of human actions and development. In fact, innovative leaders in the industry have long promoted socially responsible development practices, particularly in emerging markets.

Destinations around the world are under pressure to create carbon–neutral experiences. Tourism is not shrinking from its responsibilities, but rather is actually responding through proactive behaviour changes, technology, and policy development.

Discussions at the 2008 annual meeting of the World Economic Forum spotlighted the efforts of the industry thus far on the issue of climate change. A set of proposed recommendations will be developed and shared within the Gleneagles Dialogue at the 34th G8-Summit in Toyako, Japan, in July of 2008.

Travel companies are helping clients to address environmental issues by enabling travellers to make well-informed decisions concerning their carbon footprint. A "carbon calculator" used at the time of booking allows business travellers to calculate and compare the carbon cost of transportation options. Post–trip reporting enables travel managers to track carbon dioxide emissions and ultimately neutralise their impact through carbon offsetting.

Other examples of integrative thinking around the environment are reflected in Rezidor™'s Responsible Business Program. In the Europe, Middle East, and Africa (EMEA) hotel market, Rezidor has pioneered solutions to the issues around responsible water consumption, decreased non-recyclable waste output, and reduced CO_2 emissions.

Integrated Leaders

To move forward in an accelerated fashion, we must teach our future leaders how to think and act effectively across sectors. How can this be accomplished when, in fact, most educational systems around the world are separated by discipline? One may study business, public affairs, political science, non–profit management, or social sciences. Think of it: poverty, climate change, terrorism, disease, and corruption cannot be neatly "ascribed" to any one discipline for study, nor can they be wholly "assigned" to government, business, or society to solve on its own.

As pointed out in a Booz Allen Hamilton study, "Leaders everywhere no longer express as much confidence about the future as they once did.... The methods and tools that helped them succeed in the past no longer work. The challenges they face—such as global competitiveness, health and environmental risks, or inadequate infrastructure—can no longer be solved by their organisations alone. And when they try to reach beyond the boundaries of their own corporation, government agency, or nongovernmental organisation, there is no clear pathway to success.

Those who are schooled and eventually employed in a particular sector, such as travel or hotel management, are often sorely unaware of the drivers, roles, and leverage of the other sectors within this mega community. Each graduate of these tracks emerges with his or her own model of thinking, interpretation, and problem solving; this model is not by nature aware or inclusive of other sectors—in fact, it might even be combative.

In his book, *The Opposable Mind: How Successful Leaders Win Through Integrative Thinking*, Roger Martin, dean at the Toronto School of Business, points out that "We often don't know what to do with fundamentally opposing models. Our first impulse is to determine which is 'right' and by the process of elimination, which is 'wrong.'… by forcing a choice between the two, we disengage the opposable mind before it can seek a creative resolution."

Carlson has chosen to contribute to the development of a new kind of leader who can better affect these solutions through the Center for Integrative Leadership, a joint initiative between the Carlson School of Management and the Hubert H. Humphrey Institute of Public Affairs at the University of Minnesota in the United States.

To accomplish this, the Center convenes thought leaders and practitioners from diverse disciplines to consider and propose new models and methods for dealing with such complex issues as economic development, health care, social issues, and international terrorism. The Center for Integrative Leadership seeks to develop a new model—one focused on the cross-boundary, coalition–building, and global approach to make a great contribution to the university, business and society at large.

In this increasingly complex and interrelated world, one must find a way to develop and engage the "opposable mind" in the problem solving of these challenges that demands intense and thoughtful cross–sector collaboration.

In the 21st century, a new vision of leadership is needed more than ever. Leaders from every sector must integrate knowledge and talent from individuals in the private, not–for–profit, and government sectors to advance the common good.

The importance of value–based leadership from the boardroom on down, and from the farthest reaches "in the field" and back up, is critical.

There are actions that the industry can take right now that are relevant to the challenges of today and will have an immediate effect; there are also actions that can be taken to ensure that the T&T industry remains effective and relevant for generations to come. The industry must take responsibility for what can be controlled and resolve to work intelligently across sectors to create new solutions to improve the common good.

Above all, integrative global citizenship in travel, tourism, and hospitality asks organisations to be mindful that actions today provide a window through which to glimpse the world of tomorrow. Certainly, the future always comes from the past and it will be here sooner than anyone dreamed possible.

Tourism and Travel Sketch

We would like to take this chance to welcome readers to this new journal and sketch out some of its aims at what we think is an exciting and challenging time for work on tourism. The main impetus for founding a new tourism journal was that in our view and in the minds of many key contributors to the tourism field, tourism studies had become stale, tired, repetitive and lifeless. At a time when John Urry has just launched his *Sociology Beyond Societies – Mobilities for the Twenty-First Century* when Anthony Giddens' 1999 Reith Lectures were called 'Runaway World' and when the subject of the 2000 *Theory Culture & Society* conference in Finland was cosmopolitanism, it seems almost impossible not to see tourist studies as one of the most exciting and relevant topics in these transnational times. And yet, it is not. The first trouble with tourism studies, and paradoxically also one of its sources of interest, is that its research object, 'tourism' has grown very dramatically and quickly and that the tourism research community is relatively new. Part of this trouble is that tourist studies has simply tried to track and record this staggering expansion, producing an enormous record of instances, case studies and variations. One reason for this is that tourist studies has been dominated by policy led and industry sponsored work so the analysis tends to internalise industry led priorities and perspectives.

Part of this trouble is also that this effort has been made by people whose disciplinary origins do not include the tools necessary to analyse and theorise the complex cultural and social processes that have unfolded. How many schools of tourism hire the specialist skills of social and cultural theory? Most researchers have become dependent on a relatively small core of 'theorists' whose work has tended to become petrified in standardised explanations, accepted analyses and foundational ideas.

This is related to a second trouble, that our understanding of tourism has become fetishised as a thing, a product, a behaviour but in particular an economic thing.

A third trouble leads on from this, in the way tourism is framed for study. Studies have generally been restricted to a vision of tourism as a series of discrete, localised events, where destinations, seen as bounded localities, are subject to external forces producing impacts, where tourism is a series of discrete, enumerated occurrences of travel, arrival, activity, purchase, departure, and where the tourist is seen as another grim incarnation of individualised, 'Rational Economic Man, forever maximising his solid male gains'. While there is necessarily a role for thinking of typologies, the obsession with taxonomies and 'craze for classification' seems often to produce lists that 'represent a tradition of flat–footed sociology and psychology' which is driven by 'an unhappy marriage between marketing research and positivist ambitions of scientific labelling'.

Despite the poverty of tourism theory, Eric Cohen has observed that there is on the one hand a wide variety of conceptual and theoretical approaches to tourism which have yet to be rigorously tested, as well as the proliferation of field studies which lack an explicit theoretical orientation and therefore contribute little to theory building. It appears, therefore, that there is a need for a journal which contributes consistently to the development (and testing) of theory in the area of tourism and related studies, and which provides a platform for the development of critical perspectives on the nature of tourism as a social phenomenon. We also need to examine the wider ramifications of tourism mobilities and sensibilities. Tourism is no longer a specialist consumer product or mode of consumption: tourism has broken away from its beginnings as a relatively minor and ephemeral ritual of modern national life to become a significant modality through which transnational modern life is organised. Tourism is now such a significant dimension to global social life that it can no longer be conceived of as merely what happens at self-styled tourist sites and encounters involving tourists away from home. The new agenda for tourism studies needs therefore to reflect this growing significance.

Departure Points

Without wishing to determine a specific agenda ourselves, we want to suggest a few recent developments, and persistent gaps, by way of demonstrating the enormous scope and potential for tourist studies. We most certainly do not seek to develop a sense of theory as an invariant model. We do not seek to model tourism as if it were a more or less constant cultural phenomenon the archetypal villain of this misconception is perhaps the widely taught *resort cycle model,* or the 'coercive conceptual schema' of tourism impact studies. Nor should we believe that tourism could continue to play the same role in cultural and economic life as it always has. In a globalising world, tourism can be disturbed and warped, as it too becomes a disturbing and warping force.

Locating Practices

Tourism studies has had a problematic relationship with the process of defining and regulating tourism. Tourism studies has often privileged the exotic and strange, reflecting anthropological legacies, to speak of dramatic contrasts between visitors and locals. Of course, this can produce dramatic insights—such as MacCannell's argument that 'Cannibal Tours' are less about seeing supposed cannibals than tourists cannibalising the exotic —but it also tended to down play the banal in tourism—such as the gendered domestic family life that also travels and the 'ordinary' tourist. Tourist studies has tended to reproduce an academic hierarchy of values that is homologous to the social hierarchy of travellers and tourists. Tourist studies needs to deal reflexively with the social arena of which it itself is a part, in the prestige and values developed through travel writing, the parallels of travel to study, travel to learn and enjoy, travel to study other travelling and so forth. The proliferation of discourses about destinations and travel takes a range of forms, and tourism seems one of the pre–eminent cases of discourse shaping knowledge of the world but it seems that the urge to create a purified language of commentary risks cutting us off from the lay and popular knowledges produced through tourism. So often the analyst flips from Benjaminesque flâneur to his figure of the 'brooder', the pre–eminent melancholy subject, who dwells on fragments, clouded by a tormented sense of occluded significance dwelling in insignificant things. We need both to consider the 'doing–knowledge' of tourists and the academic knowledge of studies—as where Trinh likens anthropology to formalised 'gossip', or Hutnyk dissects the viral spread of knowledge about Calcutta as 'Indobabble' and rumours. One way forward may be to deexoticise the activity from what other people do when they are somewhere else.

Tourism is at least part of the way we now perceive the world around us, wherever we are and whatever we do. It is a way of seeing and sensing the world with its own tool kit of technologies, techniques and aesthetic sensibilities and pre–dispositions. There are a number of dimensions to this that warrant further attention. To begin with, this tourism of everyday life might be seen rather like the expansion of flânerie: no longer confined to the cosmopolitan sensibilities of the emergent modern capital cities, most people are now alerted to, and routinely excited by, the flows of global cultural materials all around them in a range of locations and settings. The repertoires for this appreciation and taste are drawn from travel and tourism but, owing perhaps to the greater speed and extent of the circulation of peoples, cultures and artifacts, we find the distinction between the everyday and holiday entirely blurred. How will traditionalist mentalities, that defend localised cultures from a feared global erosion, configure with the tourism of the everyday? How does the sedentary tourism of the everyday influence the pattern of occasional and mobile tourisms and travel? Can a point be reached where the in bound flows of goods, peoples and cultures the ebbs and flows of a global world exceed the differences and pleasures that are typically experienced by travellers and tourists? Is it possible, then, for tourism to flow in reverse? Rich tourists from the west may view the glimpse of yet another poor peasant culture with profound indifference. However, the sight of rich Americans or Germans may be intensely pleasurable and produce great excitement in a peasant village. Constant flows of young tourists through a town may profoundly alter the local pattern of courtship and sexuality such that locals seek a romantic encounter with tourists and not just the other way around.

The implicit patterns of victim and perpetrator may need rethinking, so that we retain a sense of income and power disparities but develop more enhanced senses of the relationships between, say, how the bar workers of Thailand construct their roles and the tourists who may be clients or (guiltily) consuming a spectacle. Or it may be we need to acknowledge the inversions of, say, Bali, for so long associated with eroticised bare-breasted Balinese women, where the young men are now 'Kuta cowboys', trading sexual favours with female visitors and 'today it is the Balinese, dressed from head to foot, who come to contemplate the generously exposed breasts of the foreign women'. Tourism may be less of a one-way street than the all-engulfing westernising tidal wave it sometimes seems.

Second, since the 1980s when the Fordist economy collapsed leaving regional labour markets in tatters and increasingly attracted to the notion of developing tourism, the ensuing proliferation of tourist attractions has meant that more or less *everyone* now lives in a world rendered or reconfigured as interesting, entertaining and attractive for tourists. The majority of people are now part of the market aimed initially at visiting outsiders. More or less everyone lives in a region where this proliferation of local tourist development has altered the pattern and impact of leisure in profound ways. Paradoxically, 'local' people are now more exposed to the archaeologies of tourism to more knowledge about their locality, their past, geography, economy, literature, nature and so on. And because it is more meaningful to them, it may have all sorts of political and cultural ramifications. The unintended consequence of this may be to intervene in the construction of local identity: to constantly create and recreate a sense of belonging, past, place, culture and ownership. It may be, then, that we need to move away from a notion of 'authentic place', corrupted by tourism and rather towards 'cultural involution', loosely invoked, where tourism promotes local awareness.

Thus, the tourism of everyday life is not simply a function of changing local cultures caught in the stream of globalising flows or the touristification of localities. Tourism is not necessarily exogenous to localities. Indeed, the idea of local and threatened culture may be intensified or created through a cultural tourism that needs an object to visit. Scrupulous studies have suggested that while tourism does very often produce undesirable effects, it is not enough to see that 'cultural changes arising from tourism are produced by the intrusion of a superior sociocultural system in a supposedly weaker receiving milieu'. So, although most of us may not go to most of the places advertised, and for the majority, the 'holiday of a lifetime' is but a brief moment amid a succession of more mundane tourism experiences, the touristic gaze and imaginary shape and mediate our knowledge of and desires about the rest of the planet. The proliferating discourses of tourism can reduce places to interchangeable snapshots that circulate, giving the impression of culture coming in 5 × 4 glossy packages. More strongly, Meltzer makes the case for the performative creation of place through reflexive awareness.

World of Flows

The routinisation of touristic sensibilities in everyday life is also created by enhanced spatial flows of people a shift from cultural tourism to touristic culture. In addition to the increased flow of goods, information and culture in a globalising, post Fordist society, the highly flexible and mobile nature of contemporary labour markets means that more people are also becoming more routinely mobile. We live in a world where commuting has grown, where more people work for fewer large companies or groups of companies, and where such organisations routinely switch their personnel between work sites. In addition, profound global economic restructuring produces flows of people from economic backwaters to economic hubs in search of work. While migration has been a constant feature of modernity, globalising trends have increased the flows and normalised it. It can no longer be considered such a shattering blow to have to leave one's natal soil: many people believe it is now a necessary part of life. As migration becomes normative, it takes on an air of excitement as stories circulate of the life to be had in other locations, perhaps there are choices where migrants look for more than simply work opportunities rather like tourists. It is a state that Clifford has characterised as one of 'discrepant cosmopolitanism', where it is far more than the traditional elite who are travelling.

However, it is too easy to lightly appeal to an 'existential homelessness' or modern nomadism, when there are so many stark and salutary reminders of the pain and terror, and obstacles to mobility, associated with forced migrations and flight from poverty and fear. Mobility remains a relative privilege, but one that is becoming more widespread. Metaphors of mobility have a long intellectual history and one that has often worked to emphasise visual command over the landscape by a male traveller. The figures of the independent traveller as observer and the academic as interpreter need unpacking, as they are so often based upon the solitary male wanderer freed from domestic responsibilities, free to look but apparently not to be looked at, free to experience what they choose, when even popular guides indicate how profoundly gendered these assumed practices and the persona of the traveller are. However, in various forms of tourism it seems that some of the fixed polarities of home and away, feminised and male domains may be blurring.

In the *Tourist Gaze* Urry uncritically assumed that the tourist gaze was predicated on a circularity of mobility, of 'travelling to' and 'returning home'. However, in some recent work on refugees in Australia, Julian et al. for example, discovered that these migrants reported feeling a *mix* of homesickness and sadness with a very clearly touristic sense of excitement in living in a new place, particularly where this was compounded by being in a bustling touristic centre. More than just the excitement of being able to gaze, these refugees were able to meet new people, taste new foods and, for Hmong women, long used to Thai refugee camps, enjoy the intense pleasures of regular car driving. In other words, perhaps tourism should search for links with other mobilities such as commuting, mobile labour markets, migration and Diasporas. From the seemingly unlikely connections to refugees, we should think across to what Inglis calls 'suburban gypsies'. Moreover, there are small but significant numbers for whom the tourist destination has become the everyday and the home. Neither category of tourist or home can remain unchanged through these practices. Increasingly tourism workers, émigrés and various groups of more or less permanent resident tourists are creating novel transnational communities sustained through the networks of tourism. We also need to include the timeless and placeless non–places of transit. Like brochures, most theorisation has skipped lightly over the transitional spaces within tourism, of waiting, of bureaucracy and boredom – the airports, the buses, the hotel lobbies and so forth.

The excitement of mobilities in these highly mobile times, structured as they are by the language and practice of tourism, is that they generate new social relations, new ways of living, new ties to space, new places, new forms of consumption and leisure and new aesthetic sensibilities. It is surely to this wider sociology and geography of tourism that future research must itself move.

Embodying Tourism

All of the above disturbs our notion of tourism. Until relatively recently the view that tourism is dominated by visualism, based as it was on the centrality of the visual to modernity and the proliferation of visual technologies was very compelling. Urry's concept of the tourist gaze is critiqued by Dean MacCannell in this issue, ostensibly for its singularity, its putative subjective freedom, its alleged demand for difference and its dependence upon sign construction and sign posting. MacCannell suggests a more reflexive tourist, with a sceptical second gaze, interested in the minutiae of everyday life and often dismissive or scathing of touristic offerings. MacCannell may be correct when he hints that our knowledge is often an artefact merely of theory–bound questions. But MacCannell's critique may take us further than a second gaze and question the continuing basis of tourism in the visual.

We would not want to undermine the significance of the visual or of the tourist gaze itself. However, tourism is not confined to visual repertoires of consumption. The article by Kevin Markwell in this issue begins to put together the way photography as a practice combines with the exertions of climbing mountains, group bonding and framing encounters with nature. Activities other than gazing were cut down to the bare minimum so as to increase the number of separate gazes that could be clocked up in their brief sojourns away from work. But this changed quite dramatically, beginning in the 1980s. Tourism became sensually more diverse, tasting foreign food was encouraged; key words in brochures centred on experience and discovery 'as opposed to mere sight seeing'.

And contact is not merely visual, it is going beyond the visual just as 'action' and 'experience' go beyond the physical passivity of visual tourism into *kinaesthetic* sense *and flow*. More than just emphasising the body, these pursuits also resituate the practices of observation creating new visual registers perceptible through, say, the speeding encounter of power boats, helicopters and skydiving. At least some major areas of tourism show that tourists are seeking to be *doing something* in the places they visit rather than being endlessly spectatorially passive. While so many technologies of travel have been based around body containers, insulating the spectator, there are increasing numbers of what Prato and Trivero call body–expanding technologies. There have long been hill walking holidays and the like, but increasingly the body has become the object and centre of a range of tourism experiences from bungee jumping to white–water rafting. Tourist studies was always aware of the sexual and erotic component of tourism but it is only relatively recently that the visualism of the erotic has given way to a study of more explicitly embodied, sexualised tourism. Johnston raises a series of questions around Sydney's Mardi Gras parade, where what is clearly an assertion of gay identity and a challenge to heteronormal space also becomes an exotic spectator event for a straight audience. Meanwhile, some initial explorations of sexual tourism offer surprising findings: some male sex tourists seek tenderness, love and affection denied them through normative attempts to find sex partners at home or through commercially pressured prostitution. In sum, it seems that tourism studies must investigate the sensual, embodied and performative dimensions of change in tourism cultures. If Urry's point about the importance of difference and pleasure still being central to tourism is taken on board, then taste, touch, smell, sound and kinaesthesia are just as capable of delivering a touristic experience, especially since these are still in the process of 'discovery' and development. Tourist studies have perhaps too readily colluded in writing the body out of tourism. As Johnston argues 'Tourism studies, and most social research, tends to base its research on a universalised, contained, rational, and self-knowing subject.' Echoing the brochure world where bodies are either perfect or invisible, we risk also down playing tourism as actually involving fleshy, baggy bodies that are tired, get 'Delhi belly', burn and peel, or otherwise intrude on the pristine representations of tourism.

Indeed, it is not just bodily pleasure that have often been down played but pleasure *tout court.* A legacy of one-too-many jibes about fieldwork in exotic locations, or fears of being trivialised, have given a sometimes desperately earnest tone to tourist studies. Reading the literature it would be hard to get a real sense that perhaps the central feature of tourism is pleasure, fun and enjoyment. We lack a language that can speak to the enjoyment and pleasure of tourism or track our perhaps archetypal subject, *homo ludens.* As it is, it seems through methods that too often elicit answers visitors believe they should give, through to academic writing whose subject less passive prose denudes life from experiences, we engage in the social reproduction of seriousness. We need to be able to say tourism matters because it is enjoyable, not in spite of it. Beyond overtly sexualised tourism, we also need to be able to articulate the libidinal economy of desires around more general tourism. Yes, we may well interrogate the tropes of sexualised 'natives' but there are many less focused desires in tourism. More than just a 'territorialised hedonism', as Löfgren termed it, it creates landscapes and practices shot through with promiscuous energy and a range of desires many conflicting with each other.

Untidy Tourists

The centrality of vision to conceptions of tourism also distinguishes the viewing subject from the signifying object, with the result that tourist studies to date has been mainly interested in the subjectivities of tourism on the one hand and its social and symbolic construction on the other. The objects of tourism themselves have been left out of the picture, as if only useful as carriers of social and cultural meaning. This distinction between objects and things has come under more scrutiny by theorists in recent years, and some argue that it is impossible to separate out the thingness of objects from their social and cultural content; that there is such a thing as *the social life of things,* as they play critical roles in the unfolding of cultural events and processes and that many things formerly considered merely 'things' are more properly hybrids of the human and non–human. These observations will have a profound influence on tourist studies. Against the view that tourism and the production of a tawdry tourist art facture operate to undermine and flatten local cultural traditions, it was found that the tourist bark cloth, as both a thing and one of the most important social exchange goods in Fiji, played a critical role in the efflorescence of Fijian identity and traditional exchange practices. Even thinking about the pre-eminent visual and representational practice of photography, it is clear that this is not just promoting or affirming an image of places, but also about things circulating around and with tourists.

Tourism is entirely populated by hybrids, and future investigations in tourism will need to enumerate and analyse their potencies. In Urry's *Sociology Beyond Societies*, the meaningfulness of such work is laid out clearly in a chapter entitled 'Travellings' various tourism hybrids are highlighted, the railway, the automobile the airport. Following Lury, he further distinguishes tripper *objects* from *tourist objects*. Following Pickering he also observes that the more we interact with objects, such as computer driven things, as if they were agents, the more 'such artefacts will themselves exhibit some of the characteristics of unpredictable agency'. From the strangely interesting pebbles children insist on bringing back, to brochures and ticket stubs, there are hosts of objects whose significance is less their formal qualities than their numinous relationship with a distant place and memorable experience.

These hybrids also serve then to decentre tourism, highlighting elements such as off–site markers, expectations and memories. Tourism stops being parcelled away into discrete places and times, and becomes distended and distantiated. Too often it has been seen as composed of presences whereas instead we might look at the virtualities, the absences that permeate tourist events. As winter draws in, millions of us begin wondering, dreaming and possibly planning. We read novels, guidebooks, watch programmes of greater or lesser solemnity, all of which produce for us a phantom landscape which guides our understanding of the one we eventually see. As Barbara Kirshenblatt–Gimblett put it, when, say, faced with a heritage landscape where some historic event occurred: 'The production of hereness in the absence of actualities depends increasingly on virtualities'. And afterwards we will pull out the slides or pictures of the trip, swap anecdotes, display (or hide) souvenirs. Much of the everyday thinking about tourism, much of its meaning and significance then resides far outside a week or fortnight away. Activities are undertaken with an eye to a future audience back home, one we hope to impress or amuse. Most clearly in the language of 'doing Italy', it seems the experience is less a moment lived for itself and more that we aspire 'to have been' there or 'to have done that'. Meanwhile, formal pictures taken circulate, accumulate and are recycled, so documentary becomes calendar fodder, which becomes postcards, which in turn illustrate books.

The notion of hybridity muddies up not only the location of the visitor experience but also other much used concepts in tourism that have had a seemingly unjustifiable run of clarity. 'Nature', as Raymond Williams reminds us, 'is one of the most complex words in the English language'. And yet it would not appear so to read almost every paper on the subject of nature tourism, in which both the object 'nature' and the desire for 'nature' are given quite unproblematically and uncritically. Typically, nature is uncritically confused or conflated with 'environment'; typically in much tourism studies it is uncritically assumed that the agendas and values of environmentalism and especially the sciences of environmentalism and ecology are by definition those for the study of nature tourism. Beardsworth and Bryman's article in this issue seeks to grapple with these questions but there is much work that remains. It is unlikely that the answers to these questions will fall out of yet another site case study. Rather, more theoretically informed historical, economic and cultural analysis needs to be done and the net needs to include broader societal trends and processes, to address how, as Jane Desmond argues, 'tourism is not just an aggregate of commercial activities; it is also an ideological framing of history, nature and tradition; a framing that has the power to reshape culture and nature to its own needs'. Ideologies of spectacular display or of seeing nature *in situ* frame what might best be collectively called varieties of 'species tourism'. In the shaping and display of bodies say the eroticisation of Hawaiian surf boys and hula dancers we can see the inscription of social categories through supposedly biological markers. These studies suggest that symbolic categories are not just representations but are performed, repeated and changed through tourist practices.

REFERENCES

Honey, Martha (2008). *Ecotourism and Sustainable Development: Who Owns Paradise?* (Second ed.). Washington, DC: Island Press.

Nowaczek, A. (2010). "Ecotourism: Principles and Practices" *Annals of Tourism Research* 37.1: 270-271.

Randall, A. (1987). *Resource economics, Second Edition.* New York, USA: John Wiley and Sons.

Wilkerson, Chad (2003). "Travel and Tourism: An Overlooked Industry in the U.S. and Tenth District". *Economic Review* 88 (Third Quarter): 45-72.

3

Role of Information Systems in Tourism Industry

Despite unfulfilled business and stock market expectations, in some sectors such as the travel and tourism industry on-line transactions are rapidly increasing. This industry is the leading application in the b2c arena. The travel and tourism industry is witnessing an acceptance of e-commerce to the extent that the structure of the industry and the way business is conducted is changing.

In the year 2002 European on-line bookings increased by 53 percent, accounting for about 3,5 % of all consumer spending in this domain, whereas in the US this number is about 11 %. 64 Mio. Americans researched their travel options on-line and 32 percent of US travellers have used the Internet to book travel arrangements. Forecasts state that by 2007 30% of all transactions in the European tourism domain will be done via the Internet, at least in the German speaking countries. This importance of e-commerce can be explained by the features of the industry, but it highlights also another issue, not less important: e-commerce and especially the Web are not only transaction and business oriented, it is also a medium of curiosity, of creating communities or having just fun, all of which may or may not result into business. Especially the tourism product has to do with emotional experiences; it is not just business.

The travel and tourism industry is a global (and a globalisation) industry, with very specific features:

i) Travel and tourism represents approx. 11% of the world wide GDP.

ii) T here will be one Billion international arrivals in the year 2010. And tourism grows faster than the other economic sectors.

iii) It represents a cross-sectoral industry, including many related economic sectors such as culture, sport or agriculture, where over 30 different industrial components have been identified that serve travellers.

iv) This explains the industry's heterogeneity, and due to its SME structure it has a huge importance for regional development.

v) The supply and the demand side form a worldwide network, where both production and distribution are based on cooperation.

vi) The product is perishable, complex and emotional:

   a) A hotel bed not sold for one night represents a lost income. Suppliers are in a risky situation, which can be reduced if access to information is available;

   b) The tourism product is a bundle of basic products, aggregated by some intermediary.

   c) Vacations are emotional experience structures that involve cognitive and sensory stimulations as well as affective responses to certain events.

Tourism is an information based business, the product is a "confidence good"; an a priori comprehensive assessment of its qualities is impossible. Tourists have to leave their daily environment for consuming the product. At the moment of decision-making only a model of the product, its description, is available. This characteristic of tourism products entails high information search costs and causes informational market imperfections. Consequently, the industry has comparably long information and value chains.

On the supply side we denote with "primary" suppliers enterprises like hotels, restaurants, etc., which are mostly SMEs. One should note that with respect to a functional differentiation these companies are at the same level as the "big" players like airlines. Tour operators can be seen as product aggregators, travel agents act as information brokers, providing final consumers with the relevant information and booking facilities. CRS/GDS, stemming from the airline reservation systems already developed in the 60s, include also other products such as packaged holidays, or other means of transport.

Whereas the intermediaries on the right side can be seen as the "professional" connection between supply and demand the left side is relevant for the management, planning and branding of a destination. Normally, these entities have to act on behalf of all suppliers within a destination and are not engaged in the booking process.

New Business Landscape

The Web facilitates new ways to meet changing consumer behaviour and to reach new market segments, leading to an "informatisation" of the overall tourism value chain. This allows different strategies to generate value:

i) *Value extraction*: increases efficiency and reduces costs, e.g., automation of processes or outsourcing to clients such as self check in of hotel guests or airline passengers.

ii) *Value capturing:* client and sales data are used to support the marketing.

iii) *Value adding*: a linear combination of products / services to create richer product bundles.

iv) *Value creation*: the focus is on network effects, e.g., tourists within a destination participate in service definition and planning.

Such strategies allow for the design of new products and services, enlarging the range of options to customise and to configure products. IT and, more importantly, improved organisational procedures lower the price of customisation, enabling individualised offerings based on mass-customisation. On the other side, configuration points at the bundling of different product or service components to integrated offerings.

Given the dynamics of the sector and the emerging already very competitive electronic market, nearly all stakeholders have implemented their Internet strategy. Travel and tourism has also become the playing field for new entrants, either start–ups or companies from the media and IT sector. Since tourism is an information–based business, it fits well with their respective background.

The overall trend points towards a further specialisation and an ongoing deconstruction of the value chain paralleled by an integration of players and products. Companies will compete and cooperate at the same time, boundaries within the industry are blurring. All types of market players are affected:

i) Tourists will be addressed by more players, and as they accept the Web as a booking channel, they will also play a more active role in specifying their services.

ii) Travel agents will see a diminishing power in the sales channel, as a consequence they will put more emphasis on consulting and complex products.

iii) Internet travel sites, as platforms with bundling of offerings will enhance by providing new market functionality and technology.

iv) Destination management organisations will develop cooperation models within destinations and they will occupy a new role as consolidator and aggregator.

v) Tour operator will blur the boundaries between individual and packaged tour, based on mass--customisation and flexible configurations.

vi) CRS / GDS show an "INTEL inside" marketing strategy for major tourist Web sites to increase their transaction volume, and they also move into direct sales for the retail segment

vii) Suppliers will support electronic direct sales, increasing again price competition as well as price differentiation, and they will redefine customer processes.

This development leads to an evolution of the market best described as an ongoing interaction of concentration versus the simultaneous entering of new players. The related increased complexity, however, generates the need for new services such as providing transparent access or price comparisons. This enforces the design and deployment of more specialised services. Such a process will quite naturally create new business opportunities, accelerating competition and putting even more emphasis on technical innovation.

The IT Scenario

The described business scenario is based on flexible network configurations and the further integration of consumers into internal business processes. Adding the tourist life cycle–taking into consideration the mobility aspect of travellers one can draw the following simplified figure of linking tourists' life cycles with companies' business processes.

Obviously, processes cross company borders, leading to distributed b2b2c applications, requiring cooperation between companies, and supporting also mobile communication with the consumer. Such a future business scenario is based on the assumption that technology based on a common pervasive infrastructure will become transparent, invisible for the consumer; information will be available at home, the work place and during travel. Given such a "holistic" approach interleaving business and technology perspectives, what are specific requirements when looking at the user machine interaction?

User Requirements

One could look at the human computer interaction as a variant of the famous Turing test: as a competition between a human and an intelligent travel system. Even if one thinks of it as an engineering task, and not as a cognitive science test, it poses hard questions:

i) A simple problem like inquiring a flight from location A to B, with specific price and time constraints, complemented by a specific hotel, with similar constraints. In this case linking to a predefined database or to one of the CRS/GDS would be sufficient, if one ignores interoperability issues.

ii) A complex problem which involves background knowledge of a specific traveller, e.g., the problem of travelling to Milan only when Milan plays. This needs the modelling of knowledge about the Italian city of Milan, the inference that in this case Milan refers to AC MILAN, the timing regarding soccer tournaments. And other background knowledge might be needed such as specific weather conditions or cultural activities. In fact, the "leisure" domain might cover nearly all domains of daily life. Here wrapping techniques, learning accurate extraction rules and also adapting to structural changes in sites, are needed. Other non-trivial tasks within this context are

a) Conversation with its semantic and pragmatic aspects,

b) Identification of problem domains,

c) Search and information retrieval with the related evaluation,

d) Negotiation including additional and even unsolicited offers, both having cooperative and opportunistic behaviour.

However, these problem types assume that users are able to express their needs, which is normally not the case. Systems have to "become active" and to provide advice, adapting to different travel decision processes as well as navigation styles have identified, based on a study on 200 human - human and human - machine counselling sessions, 6 different traveller groups such as highly predefined, recommendation oriented or geography oriented ones. Two groups of factors are identified: personal, i.e., socioeconomic and psychological/cognitive factors, and travel features, i.e., travel purpose, travel party size, the length of travel or the distance to the destination.

An application example of such an approach is Tripf&dvice. Based on Case Based Reasoning (CBR), it adapts its dialogue as it learns more about the user, supports product aggregation for a given travel, provides personalised recommendations based on previous system experience, and it applies query refinement methods helping to adjust queries according to the data available in a given product catalogues. Thus, it integrates topical information and "good" examples of product bundling contained in previous travels built by a community of users.

Dietorecs, another example, extends this approach by integrating the iterative presentation and evaluation of alternative proposals. It assumes that by presenting specific images, which implicitly represent the most discriminating offers within a given product catalogue, the evaluation of the user provides indications about his/her references. At the beginning the systems performs a cluster analysis of the offers within a given catalogue. The user's choice is the starting point of an iterative process of refocused clustering and presentation. At the end, either the user directly takes the chosen product, or the obtained criteria serve as input for a CBR process.

These examples show, that different decisions styles as well as the seamless switching between them have to be supported. Due to the multisensory nature of tourism products, textual ways of describing vacations are very limited to convey a complete picture that can be used to formulate product expectations serving as a basis for decision.

A possible approach is to look at product trails these are sources of information for the formation of brand beliefs since they involve an experience of the product through multiple senses–describing leisure experiences and to draw conclusions on how to present tourism information and how to guide a user in a non rational navigation process. Gretzel and Fesenmaier looked at 3000 randomly selected persons who were asked to imagine a trip and to report the colors dominating their mental image, the scents they would like to smell, and the sounds they expect to hear. They identified a number of such sensory categories, which were clustered to experiences representing coherent bundles such as Autumn or Scenic / Nature.

Finally, travellers need access to information whenever and wherever they want, making tourism a perfect application field for mobile computing. Latest generations of mobile devices and wireless networks offer new opportunities, but mobile devices still suffer from restrictions compared to web based systems. Moreover, the mobile context imposes a very different interaction style and decision model. But, on the other side, mobile applications could take advantage when linked to existing web sites and refer to already existing personal profiles and selected travel products. The mobile Intelligent Travel Recommender (mITR) supports travellers to complement their product while travelling. The objective of mITR is to improve iteratively the "fitness" of recommended products.

System Features–Intelligent Networking

System designed to support such applications should

i) Allow users to access information whenever and wherever they want,

ii) Guide the user in the decision and travelling process, and

iii) Allow the user to create product bundles.

Business services for the traveller may use Web services to be more easily integrated and bundled into new, ad-hoc products. Web services provide an open, flexible, modular, layered architecture that can integrate multiple communication models. But these services do only facilitate the "manual" combination of components across different platforms. Another enabling technology might be Peer-to-Peer (P2P) services to directly exploit resources present at other nodes without intervention of any central server, where nodes may join and be integrated in an ad- hoc manner. Such services need to be described for the respective peer device and discovered in an ad-hoc manner in a decentralised scheme, without a centralised registry as this may be unavailable in a mobile environment; to be composed ad-hoc and to interact not only with servers, but also with other peers; and to be connectable to legacy systems.

However, when taking the supply side's point of view, the requirements become even more complicated: For instance, a middleman might search for 100 individual web services hosted by several individual, privately-owned hotels and with golf courses nearby in the Tyrol within a diameter of 100 kms in order to bundle them with flights into tourist packages. In this case functions are needed to

i) Enable middlemen to create sets of bundled products,

ii) Ease the participation of SMEs to larger networks, and

iii) Facilitate networking leading to virtual organisations.

In this context networked business operations could be defined as P2P enabled semantic Web services that integrate business networks allowing for an organisation and communication between participating enterprises. This transfers the level from composing individual instances of services to composing sets of services; and from ad-hoc integration between two participants to an arbitrary number of cooperating enterprises. The orchestration of a large set of web services requires possibilities for business planning with more refined means.

However, such a scenario is based on a non-existing assumption: there exists no agreed electronic standard to describe tourism services. Those existing such as the OTA (Open Travel Alliance) specifications are just adopted by few players. Given that the number of available tourism relevant information sites is huge. One approach to this problem is the European project Harmonise, creating an ontology based mediation and harmonisation tool. The project puts emphasis on the combination of a social consensus process with the application of new technologies. The goal is to allow participating tourism organisations to keep their proprietary data format while cooperating with each other. Specific tourism mediators are dedicated to the "translation" needs between these data sources. Such a mediator looks at information from a higher conceptual semantic level using this level of abstraction for the mapping purpose .

The data model of a source document, assuming XML, is first lifted to a local conceptual schema (C-Normalisation) and then semantically mapped to the terminology specified by the shared ontology, which is built by domain experts. The output of the mapping process is a set of reconciliation rules, which a reused in order to transform the local data and to code them according to the ontology content. Harmon is e is based on RDF(S) as "language" for representing local conceptual schemata as well as the mediating ontology. But Harmon has several limitations:

i) it does not solve the problem of ontology versioning, which is severe in a domain with constantly new products;

ii) and Harmonise, though mapping between different conceptual models, does not support ontology reasoning, or even more advanced concepts such as approximate reasoning, needed in a domain which is based not only on true axioms or facts.

The tourism business is changing. More specialised services, flexible network configurations and further consumer integration into internal business processes will lead to smart market places, integrating all stakeholders. But it also demonstrates that this industry poses hard challenges, which offer interesting research opportunities. This has also been acknowledged by the European Union, placing tourism as one of the preferred application fields of the Europe an IT research .

E-Tourism Planning

Tour planning is an essential part of a successful trip. Before the advent of Information & Communication Technologies (ICT), planning a holiday or a trip was a cumbersome process. A tourist was required to manually seek information from various tourism operators and travel agencies in order to make travel arrangements. Developments in ICT have revolutionised the way various businesses are conducted. Current websites facilitate users to access tourism related information, where they can research information about the places they want to visit by looking at different websites, on-line images, and even down loading video clips.

Current tourism websites also provide facilities for users to make hotel reservations, hire cars, and book flight tickets. However, this is still a complex procedure as the user has to visit a number of websites to gather information and make such bookings. There is a need for a tour planner that provides easy access to required information, and a streamlined process to plan and book the travel arrangements. We propose to develop an Ontology-Based e-Tourism Planner that provides a mechanism for planning trips using semantic web technologies. This system uses intuitive interfaces developed using rich internet application programming techniques. It enables users to specify their travel preferences, vendors to advertise their products, and the tool matches the user's travel preferences with the vendor offerings to develop an itinerary. The user can easily plan their trip from start to end.

Australian Sustainable Tourism Ontology (AuSTO)

An ontology is a data model that represents a domain; it can be used to reason about the objects in that domain and the relations between them. Ontologies represent knowledge about the world or some part of it, they consist of:

i) *classes:* collection of objects;

ii) *attributes*: properties an object can have and share;

iii) *relations:* represent the way the objects are related; and

iv) *individuals:* which are instances of the class.

To create a productive ontology a well defined methodology has to be followed. Methodology encompasses the tools, techniques and procedures followed to develop ontologies. There are a number of established methodologies such as Uschold & King Methodology,

Gruninger & Fox Methodology, Berneras et al Methodology, Methontology, Sensus Methodology. The methodology adopted to develop an Australian Sustainable Tourism Ontology (AuSTO) is similar to Uschold and King methodology and was previously applied to develop an ontology in the Multimedia Design and Planning Pyramid project.

This methodology involves *identifying the purpose behind ontology development* which involves analysing why the ontology is being built, what is its intended use, and who would be the end users. The next step is to capture knowledge into the ontology which involves *determining the scope of the ontology* and selecting an approach for ontology development, and transforming the concepts into the ontology. This is then followed by *coding the ontology* which requires representing the ontology in a formal language. Numerous ontology editors are available to create ontologies. *Refinement* follows coding and during this stage the ontology is further rectified. Refinement consists of two stages: intra coding refinement and extra coding refinement. *Intra coding refinement* involves perfecting the ontology and eliminating errors during the programming phase. *Extra coding refinement* is conducted at the post coding phase; the implementation is tested and debugged for any defects. *Testing* takes place once the implementation is complete; and final debugging is performed to eliminate deficiencies.

The AuSTO ontology is a knowledge store for the tourism domain information. It consists of classes, which describe various activities in the tourism domain. Some of the important classes in AuSTO are *Involved Party* which represents a traveller, vendor or operator. *Traveller Requirements* class is used to store the requirements of a traveller for a trip, the *Offering* class stores information regarding the vendor offerings, *Resource* class stores information regarding tourism resources, *Traveller Preference* class stores information regarding traveller preferences, *Tourism Related Event* class stores information regarding tourism related events such as conference event, entertainment event etc.

AuSTO System Design

The underlying system design of the AuSTO consists of three layers:

the Ontology Layer (OL), the Business Logic Layer (BLL) and the Graphical User Interface layer (GUIL). The OL contains the tourism ontology; the BLL includes two common components, which are the Inference Engine (IE) and the Custom Logic (CL) and part of the tour planner. The GUIL layer includes the Graphical User Interface (GUI) components of the tour planner application.

Ontology Layer

The Ontology Layer consists of the ontology which embodies knowledge about the domain and some additional specifications. This layer is the core of all semantic web systems. The three important approaches to develop class hierarchies are top-down, bottom-up and a combination approach. In the top-down approach the development process starts with the definition of the most general concepts in the domain, followed by specialised concepts. In the bottom-up approach the development process starts with the definition of the most specific classes, which form the leaves of the class hierarchy tree, with subsequent grouping of these classes into more general concepts. The combined approach uses a combination of top-down and bottom-up processes. The approach used to develop AuSTO is the bottom-up approach. This approach is usually driven by the need for having a workable vocabulary. AuSTO is an OWL ontology. The Ontology Layer (OL) acts as a knowledge store for the AuSTO system as it contains data regarding the tourism domain and the Business Logic Layer (BLL) acts upon this layer to generate itineraries.

Business Logic Layer

The Business Logic Layer (BLL) is the layer responsible for generating outcomes, it takes the user queries from the GUIL and matches them with the domain knowledge residing in the Ontology Layer and returns the results to the user via the GUIL. The BLL consists of a reasoner and custom logic, since the knowledge base is very large, inferencing mechanisms are needed to search through the knowledge base and deduce results in an organised manner. The BLL, which contains the reasoner, fulfils this need. The reasoner software applies axiomatic knowledge in the knowledge base to the task-specific data embodied for arriving at some conclusions . The Custom Logic is a mechanism which acts as a mediator between the reasoner, user interface and the ontology.

Graphical User Interface layer

The Graphical User Interface Layer (GUIL) comprises intuitive interfaces that allow the user to interact with the AuSTO tour planner tool. These interfaces allow users to enter travel requirements for a tour, including accommodation, transport facility, and venue booking. Other interfaces also available in this layer enable vendors to enter their offerings and services, such as hotels advertising their products. Once users have finalised their travel arrangement, their itinerary is produced by the system and then displayed to the user.

System Development and Interfaces

The user interface design for a system plays a crucial role in its success. Users want an easy to use and efficacious interface that takes them no more than ten minutes to learn. A user interface with these properties enhances the chances that users will return to use the system in the future. The first step in user interface design is to use task-modelling techniques to create a task model of the user interaction.

Task modelling technique is used to model the behaviour of a system from the user's perspective, thus enabling the requirements and actions of the system to be defined as a set of tasks. This allows the designers to improve the Human Computer Interaction (HCI) aspects when designing a systems operation. Task models play an important role because they represent the logical activities that should support users in reaching their goals, thus knowing the tasks necessary for attaining their goal is fundamental to the design process.

CTTE (Concur Task Tree Environment) is a Java applet based tool developed by Human Computer Interaction Group-ISTI (Pisa) (*CTTE: Concur Task Trees Environment*, n.d.); it provides the ability to build task models from a visual perspective. These task models have guided the development of AuSTO user interfaces.

AUSTO System Implementation

The AUSTO system is deployed using the Semantic Web Application

Model. The system model employs the commonly used client-server model. The user interfaces that reside on the client-side are developed as Rich Interface Applications, using the Ajax development technique. The server includes a combination of applications that form the structure of the AuSTO semantic web. This includes an Apache Web-Server that hosts the website; Jena Semantic Web Toolkit; and a Database Server using MySQL used for the Ontology repository. Further details of the different technologies used to implement the AuSTO system are presented in the following.

Semantic Web Application Model

The Semantic Web was thought up by Tim Berners-Lee as a mesh of information linked up in such a way so as to be easily processable by machines. Currently, the World Wide Web enables searching, sharing, and exchange of information, which identifies it as being the world's largest library. As the accessibility of information grows at an exponential rate, sourcing the 'right' information makes it cumbersome.

The semantic web helps overcome this problem by describing relationships between software such that machines can interpret. Semantic web also provides a platform for the creation of so called intelligent applications; these intelligent applications are based on a bundle of semantic web technologies, and Ontologies lie at the core. The AuSTO tour planner application is an intelligent application developed based on semantic web technologies.

The AuSTO system is based on various semantic web technologies. It can be viewed as a two tier architecture, comprising a browser client, and a server side system. The server side system contains the ontology which is the knowledge base, Jena middle ware and the XML server. The client side operations formulate the user queries which are compiled by the user interfaces; these queries are converted into Java Script and sent to the Ajax Engine. The Ajax Engine sends an HTTP request to the server, this request is received by an XML server, which forwards the request to the Jena middleware, the Jena middleware in-turn queries the ontology, the results are sent back from the server to the client and then displayed via the user interfaces. Details of these technologies are given in the following.

Ajax (Asynchronous Java Script and XML)

Ajax is a combination of technologies which allows the development of interactive web applications. The present shortcoming of standard web applications is that each time the user places a request, an HTTP request is sent to the server, and when the server responds, the entire page is reloaded. Ajax overcomes this by adding an Ajax engine between the user and the server. The Ajax engine sends small parts of the data to the server rather than the entire content of the page. The technologies that comprise Ajax are XHTML and CSS for marking up information, Java Script to dynamically display information and the XML.Http Request object to exchange data asynchronously with the web server.

Web and XML Server

An XML server is used to dynamically receive, interpret and generate XML documents. The XML documents generated will be used for the purpose of data interchange between applications. The XML server is a server-side component which can receive data via HTTP and generate output in XML format. In the AuSTO application model the XML server receives the HTTP request in the form of a query from the browser, the query is processed and the result is forwarded back to the browser in the form of an XML document.

Jena Middleware

Middleware is the software that connects the *reasoner*, the ontology and the user interface. Custom made middleware can be created for an application, but it is much easier to use existing middleware software such as Jena. Jena is a Java framework for building semantic web applications; it is open source and has been developed by HP Labs. Jena started as an RDF (Resource Description Framework) API (Application Programming Interface), and has extensive support for XML. It has been extended with an OWL-aware API and database connectivity and two forms of query languages, namely RDQL (RDF Query Language) and SPARQL (Simple Protocol and RDF Query Language). In Jena, all operations are completed by manipulating the Jena model.

Jena has four subsystems: the query engine, database interface, reasoning engine and ontology management. Jena's architecture allows external reasoners to be plugged into the Jena models. The user queries are sent via a user interface to the Jena model, Java code converts these queries into SPARQL format, which can be read by Jena; and the result is sent back to the user. This query retrieves Business Name and URL of all Apartment-Holiday Units in St Kilda with Five Star rating that have Swimming Pool and Air-conditioning facilities.

Database Server for Ontology

The AuSTO ontology is the knowledge base repository for storing information regarding the tourism domain, and is loaded into a database. MySQL is an open source RDBMS (Relational Database Management System) for processing data in the database. MySQL is commonly used in web applications. MySQL provides support to Jena libraries, which allows Jena to manipulate the ontology when loaded in the database.

Future

The AuSTO tour planner acts as an itinerary planning tool, it relies on the AuSTO ontology as the source of tourism domain knowledge. Currently the tour planner is restricted to generating travel plans or itineraries; we intend to extend the functionality of the tour planner so that it can suggest places to visit based on the user preferences stored in the AuSTO ontology. Investigations are being conducted into deployment of AuSTO and the development of tools that will enable it to interoperate with the Harmonise ontology. We also are conducting research into using AuSTO for creating Visual Travel Recommender Systems. Usability studies of the AuSTO tour planner are being conducted at all phases of research and development to ensure that the system satisfies the requirements of a common traveller. Usability studies will be conducted at three levels: 1. Interface level, 2. System level, and 3. Service level.

At the interface level, this will require conducting heuristic as well as empirical usability tests with real users, where they will be required to perform tour planning functions using the developed interfaces. Performance factors, such as error count and task completion times will be monitored to determine whether the user can complete given tasks within a certain error and completion time limit. At the system level, such investigations will involve determining whether the system provides sufficient response times, and feedback to the user that enhances their experience rather than making the system cumbersome to use. At the Service level, factors such as available bandwidth, delays, response times, and errors will be observed to ensure that the network can deliver the required traffic.

References

Theobald, William F. (1998). *Global Tourism* (2nd ed.). Oxford [England]: Butterworth–Heinemann.

UNWTO World Tourism Barometer June 2009". *UNWTO World Tourism Barometer* (World Tourism Organisation) 7 (2). June 2009.

Wurzburger, Rebecca; et al (2009). *Creative Tourism: A Global Conversation: How to Provide Unique Creative Experiences for Travelers Worldwide:* As Presented at the 2008 Santa Fe & UNESCO International Conference on Creative Tourism in Santa Fe, New Mexico, USA. Santa Fe: Sunstone Press.

4

Economic Impacts of Travel and Tourism

Economic impact studies in travel and tourism are undertaken to determine the effects of specific activities in a given geographic area on the income, wealth and employment of that area's residents. They are conducted for cities, counties, towns, states, provinces, nations, and for individual facilities and events. They often relate to an annual period, although seasonal and event impact studies are not unknown. The results indicate the contribution or cost of tourism activity to the economic well-being of residents of an area, usually in monetary terms. In the broadest sense, economic impact studies can indicate the gross increase in resident wealth resulting from the activity, the reduction in wealth resulting as well, and the net of the two influences.

While implicit in economic impact studies, explicit consideration of the wealth effects of tourism is seldom found. Rather, measurement is limited to the impact on income. Since wealth is created primarily through income, it is clear that concentrating on the latter is consistent with the objectives of economic science.

Economic impact studies are understood to include objective analyses of travel activity's impact on resident wealth or income in a defined area. On the benefit side, this normally means the study provides estimates of travel spending and the impact of this spending on employment, personal income, business receipts and profits, and government revenue.

A great number of studies have been limited to estimating travel spending in an area, often through direct surveys of travellers. No attempt is made in these studies to track the effects of this spending on area employment, income or other economic variables.

Such travel expenditure studies are specifically excluded from this discussion. However, the broader impact studies which are considered here include the essential elements of the limited expenditure studies, so the reader will gain an understanding of them in what follows here.

The reason for this exclusion is that travel expenditures tend to obscure the impact on resident wealth and income. Although such expenditures may be substantial in an area, they often have little to do with resident earnings and employment. Travellers may spend millions of dollars in the hotel each year, but the contribution to the wealth or income of the residents is virtually non-existent.

A similar case can be found in the developed economy. Consider a popular self-service gasoline service station in a resort area. Visitors purchase gasoline and oil provided by non-resident suppliers. The station itself is owned by an oil company headquartered elsewhere. The employees may be residents, but it takes only one to oversee the sale of several hundred thousand dollars of petroleum products a year. The dollars spent are a poor guide to the impact on resident wealth or income.

The point is that travel expenditures can be quite misleading in evaluating the economic benefits or the economic costs of travel and tourism in an area. They are best viewed as merely the initial monetary activity that stimulates the production process and initiates realistic measurement of economic impact.

Direct and Other Impacts

Economic impact should be understood to include both direct or primary costs and benefits, and secondary costs and benefits. The former occur as a *direct* consequence of travel activity in the area. Travel expenditures become business receipts which in turn are used to pay wages and salaries and taxes, the direct benefits of tourism Visitor use of recreation areas requires expenditures on services for the visitors as well as on redressing any environmental damage: these are direct costs. These benefits and costs are directly related to the travel activity.

In addition to these primary impacts, there are secondary effects of travel activity. On the benefit side, entrepreneurs spend part of their receipts on goods and services they require to serve customers, including investment in new equipment and structures.

The other type of secondary benefit is *induced*. Here we track the consumption spending of the wage and salary income directly generated by the travel expenditures in the area.

We can also speak of secondary costs of travel. These arc related to the public goods and services required to serve those businesses and employees that are impacted at the secondary level.

Economic Models

The world of tourism is quite complex. Economists develop theories that abstract the most powerful relationships in order to deal with such complexities. An economic model is a "representation of a theory or a part of a theory, often for the purpose of illuminating cause-and-effect relationships." Economic models come in all shapes an sizes, each reflecting a particular theory to be tested or applied.

Definitions and Data

At first glance, travel economic impact estimation appears quite arcane. This is due to the heterogeneous nature of what we call "travel demand" and the "travel industry." The travel industry cannot be defined the way industries normally are for example, U.S. industries are generally understood as collections of business firms or establishments with the same "primary activity, which is determined by its principal product or group of products produced or distributed, or services rendered".

This "type of product" classification system is not consistent with the definition of travel and tourism as "end-use" activities, that is, defined by the purpose of the purchase. We view travel expenditures as those made by people travelling away from home. More often, travellers purchase a minority portion of a type-of-product industry's output.

It is difficult to square the end-use definition of travel with the type-of-product statistics available from government. Government data indicate total restaurant sales, for example, but not those attributable to travellers. That this is not easy is readily indicated by the number and complexity of current approaches to measuring the economic impact of travel.

TRAVELLERS AND VISITORS

It is important to clarify whether the study objective is to measure the economic impact of travellers or of visitors. At the national level, the comprehensive measurement of tourism's economic impact is based on *travellers*, that is, all people travelling away from home and the industry that serves them.

However, studies conducted on smaller geographic areas usually concentrate solely on visitors: that is, non-residents entering the area on a trip away from home. Because researchers are interested solely in the economic contribution of outsiders to the community, they are not concerned with travel expenditures by residents, such as purchase of common carrier tickets and other items preparatory to taking a trip.

This distinction is vital because it determines the expenditure categories and travel industry components to be included in an impact model. If we are concerned with the impact of visitors to an area, we should exclude air tickets purchased by that area's residents travelling to outside destinations. The employment and payroll of travel agencies in the area are generally not included in a *visitor* impact study, for example, since they primarily service *resident* consumers and businesses.

IMPACT ESTIMATION APPROACHES

There are four major techniques we can apply in attempting to measure tourism's economic impact:

i) Observation;

ii) Experiments, where the researcher controls the conditions under which two or More groups of people make economic decisions;

iii) Analysis, based on prior assumptions about how individuals and firms act and Relate to one another;

iv) Statistical analyses, through sample surveys and secondary data.

Observation

Observation has major drawbacks as a method of economic impact analysis in tourism. It is difficult to determine whether an individual spending money is a tourist or not by watching him.

Direct observation approaches are apt to be partial in scope. That is, they virtually always focus on one measure of impact, usually travel expenditures, rather than consistently following the impact of this activity on income and employment down through the primary and secondary links in the impact chain.

It is conceivable that someone could observe employees in travel-related establishments, account for how much work time they spend serving travellers, and then apportion their compensation accordingly. However, it is obvious that this is a cumbersome and costly approach. Moreover, it tends to break down in estimating secondary impact on suppliers and the effects of travel-related employees spending their income in the area under study.

Attempts have been made to survey business operators to obtain their estimates of travel-generated receipts as a proportion of total receipts. However, this has not proved a viable method in examples available to date. The businesses and agencies involved cannot distinguish between activity attributable to travellers, and that produced by local residents unless they conduct valid sample surveys of their customers.

Controlled Experiments

Controlled Experiments appear not to have been attempted for estimation of tourism's economic impact. The difficulty comes in isolating two or more groups or geographic areas so that they are not affected by any force except those under the researcher's control.

Analysis

Analysis has been employed in economic impact studies through the construction of economic models. The usual approach is to build a model incorporating the major relationships at work among consumers and businesses and governments. The model is necessarily a simplification embodying only the most important relationships. What is deemed most important varies among those building the models, depending upon their perceptions of the world and their analyses of existing data available to them describing travel activity and impact.

These models vary between being simple and complex, explicit and implicit, partial and integrated. Explicit models are comprised of clearly-stated relationships, usually in the form of equations. Partial models estimate only one element of economic impact, usually traveller expenditures. Integrated models, on the other hand, use expenditures to drive estimates of employment, income, tax revenue and other economic variables.

Statistical Analysis

By far, the most popular method of estimating traveller spending has been through *statistical analysis*. The favoured method is to draw a sample of travellers and administer a survey to it asking for expenditure data. Then means are computed for the various expenditure items and these are multiplied by estimates of the traveller population.

Criteria For Evaluating Economic Impact Methods

Methods of estimating travel's economic impact are numerous and vary widely in their approaches and output. It is important to judge the approaches by some formal criteria that permit us to objectively evaluate the quality of a model, because there are so few independent measures of travel's impact we can use to assess an estimation effort.

It is vital to judge an approach used for travel economic impact estimates as objectively as possible. We should be especially interested in the relevance, coverage, efficiency, accuracy, and transferability of the approach suggested for use.

Relevance

The approach should measure tourism's economic impact and not that of some other activity. For example, a study of the economic effects of restaurants in a community would not accurately represent travel's impact because most of the business could be derived from local residents.

Specific attention should be directed to ensuring an impact estimation method and the data used in it represent the community, city, state, region, or other area under study. We should be particularly interested in three aspects of the approach in terms of relevancy: does it relate to travel alone?, does it fairly represent the area under study and only that area?, and does it cover the time period under study?

Coverage

The approach should also cover *all* of travel away from home and related activities. On the economic benefit side, the impact of purchases in anticipation of a trip as well as those during the trip should be included in a tourism impact study. Anticipatory purchases include major consumer durables such as recreational vehicles and vacation homes, and minor items, such as tennis rackets and camping equipment. But again, the distinction between visitors and travellers should be observed, and the expenditures measured should truly occur in the area under study.

Efficiency

Since funds available for economic impact estimation are generally limited, the approach should make maximum use of existing data commensurate with satisfying the other criteria. Primary data collection is costly and difficult to do well. It should be avoided whenever possible in favour of relevant, comprehensive and accurate secondary data.

Accuracy

We should also judge the approach on the basis of its accuracy. Are the input or survey data accurate measures of travel activity? Does the approach accurately reflect real relationships? Are the results reasonable? This involves investigating the techniques used to generate primary or secondary data. Since these other measures generally do not pass these five evaluation criteria themselves, a good deal of judgment is often required to assess the accuracy of an approach and its output.

Transfer Ability

The approach should be applicable to different geographic areas and different time periods, rather than requiring data unique to one particular case. It should also be sensitive to differences in travel patterns, industry structure and prices in different places and times. This permits valid comparisons across time and space and provides a broader track record on which to assess the model.

These five criteria should be applied to the structure of the estimation procedure, the input data, and the results. They should also be applied to sample design, questionnaires, interview models, expansion factors and weighting in surveys. The user can weight the criteria based on his own requirements as to relative importance if he chooses.

Economic Benefits of Travel and Tourism

An "economic benefit" is best understood as a gross increase in the wealth or income, measured in monetary terms, of people located in an area over and above the levels that would prevail in the absence of the activity under study, *ceteris paribus*.

We are interested in "gross" increases because we will estimate the costs of the activity separately. Subtracting the gross costs from the gross benefits produces a measure of net economic benefit, either positive or negative.

We concentrate here on the economic benefits (or costs) for the sake of convenience, not because other, non-monetary, benefits are insignificant. Most economic benefits are measured in terms of money , and are amply documented in data available. It is far more difficult to measure the psychic benefits of travel, such as a relaxed feeling, lower blood pressure, or enjoyment of beautiful surroundings.

It is important to understand that economic benefits should actually accrue to the people located in the area under study. If we want to estimate the economic benefits of tourism to the people who live or work in Missouri, we should be sure the economic benefits actually redound to these people.

Our analysis assumes the absence of these benefits if travel did not occur in the area, *ceteris paribus*. One could argue that with the cessation of tourism in an area, other industries would spring up to provide the same amounts of employment and income. However, this is by no means assured. We want to know what travel is contributing to the economy of an area under certain conditions. Analysis of alternative industries that could replace tourism should tourism disappear is beyond the scope of the study of travel's economic benefits.

Finally, a word about terms used to represent economic benefits. The one most often found in economic discussions of travel is "travel expenditures". However, a little thought reveals expenditures imply little in themselves to the income and wealth of a community.

If travellers purchase all their goods and services from residents who employ labour and supplies originating solely in the area, then travel expenditures represent income to the community. However, it is far more common for travel-related businesses to purchase most of the supplies they need, and often labour as well, from sources outside the community. Expenditures on an airline ticket do not remain in the community for long, but rather are remitted to some central office to pay for salaries, depreciation, fuel and other items not found in the community where the ticket was bought.

Many of the goods purchased by travellers are likely to have high import content, that is, consist primarily of intermediate goods produced outside the community. Consequently, to focus on travel expenditures as the measure of economic benefits to an area's residents is to grossly misstate the actual benefits generated in the area in many cases.

For a more accurate view, we must calculate the labour income, corporate profits, and rents generated by travel spending. We can also look at employment as an important economic policy objective.

Travel expenditures are an initial cause of economic benefits, but should not be confused with these effects.

Economic Costs of Travel and Tourism

We normally think of the "costs of travel" as the explicit prices the traveller pays for his trip, his "private costs". He purchases transportation, lodging, food, entertainment, and numerous other goods and services, all at explicit prices in the marketplace.

However, it is important to recognise that all of the costs associated with a trip are not paid explicitly by the traveller or the traveller's employer in the case of a business-related trip. Some are paid explicitly and implicitly by others. These costs borne by others but related to the traveller's activities fall in the general class economists call "spillover costs" or "detrimental externalities" . The distinction is between the "private costs" of the trip, those paid explicitly by the traveller for goods and services in the marketplace. and "incidental costs," which represent other resources that are sacrificed in the process: all the disutility generated by the production process that is not recompensed by traveller purchases.

To the extent that we can make all incidental costs explicit and include them in the costs the traveller pays, we will maximise welfare. The higher costs are also a signal to industry that competitive advantage can be gained by producing at lower than the prevailing costs, through greater efficiency either in directly serving the traveller or mitigating the detrimental externalities generated by the traveller. However, in practice, there will always be uncompensated incidental costs resulting from tourism.

Frequently, other distinctions are made in discussing the overall costs of tourism: economic costs, social costs, environmental costs, fiscal costs, and life quality costs. These distinctions are valid if we are interested in who initially bears the burden, or what is initially sacrificed. They are also useful for actually measuring the costs associated with tourism. However, it should be recognised that these distinctions are not very useful for determining who *finally* bears the burden of visitation to a community.

The term "economic costs" covers all costs, both private and incidental, explicit and implicit, and refers to the value that must be sacrificed in order to provide the visitor experience. It is important to remember that we are interested in the sacrifice of *scarce* goods and services to provide the experience. The fact that a visitor breathes air or absorbs the sun is not a cost to the community, because the residents are not giving up anything scarce that they own and value.

Like economic costs, the term "social costs" is used to cover all costs of the visitor experience. It is the sum of private costs and incidental costs, emphasising the total cost to the society.

"Environmental costs" are reductions in the quality of air, water, land, flora and fauna in our area. These are initially imposed upon residents of the host area. "Fiscal costs" are those imposed by government on residents or visitors through taxes, user fees, license fees, fines and admission charges. "Life quality costs" are those that reduce our standard of living in some non-monetary way.

Environmental costs, fiscal costs and reduction in resident standards of living or quality of life are all incidental costs, and denote which group or entity is initially bearing the cost at the current time. They do not designate who finally sacrifices value.

However, as residents we have several options. For one, we can persuade the government to impose admission fees for the park. This will not only limit visitor demand somewhat and reduce crowding, but will also provide funds for cleaning up the stream and hiring park attendants to prevent pollution. If the admission fees now reduce crowding to its pre-visitor level and provide funds for returning the environment to its pre-visitor state, then the environmental life quality costs have become private costs and have been shifted to the visitors and residents who use the park.

There is another option. The residents can vote to spend public funds on enlarging the park and fencing in the stream. If successful in returning the park to its pre-visitor level of congestion and environmental quality, this tactic has turned one type of incidental cost into another (fiscal). However, in the absence of higher admission fees, the citizens run the danger of attracting even more visitors than before, and there is no guarantee that the taxes required to pay for the park enlargement will be generated by the visitors or local users. The fact that the costs are now fiscal instead of life quality does not tell us who finally pays them. It may be that the residents have just transformed these costs into higher property taxes and still bear them on behalf of the visitors. Residents can also attempt to reduce congestion and other ill effects of tourism by treating visitors in a repellent manner. In this way, travellers may be dissuaded from returning.

Uses of Economic Impact Studies

Measurement of the economic benefits and costs of travel and tourism can help meet a variety of objectives for both marketers and planners.

These studies can inform public officials and business managers of the net benefits of investing in travel promotion or tourism and recreation facilities.

Economic impact studies can help tourism marketers evaluate the effectiveness of marketing efforts and the effects of additional facilities on demand for current ones.

Estimates of tourism's economic impact can educate travel-related employees about their role in economic and business development, and how their services contribute to the economic health of their communities.

By displaying the net returns to promotional and facility investment, these studies can encourage both business and government to seek out cooperative ventures with other organisations for mutual benefit.

By demonstrating the effects of travel development to the general public, economic impact studies can help citizens rationally choose whether to encourage or resist additional tourism marketing or development efforts.

Economic impact studies also aid public officials in developing laws and policies that best promote the economic, social and cultural health of their citizens, and avoid decisions that would threaten this health.

In short, the estimation of the economic benefits and costs of travel and tourism activities permit consumers, business and government to make efficient and effective marketing and development decisions.

Economic Impacts Assessment

Businesses and public organisations are increasingly interested in the economic impacts of tourism at national, state, and local levels. One regularly hears claims that tourism supports X jobs in an area or that a festival or special event generated Y million dollars in sales or income in a community. "Multiplier effects" are often cited to capture secondary effects of tourism spending and show the wide range of sectors in a community that may benefit from tourism.

Tourism's economic benefits are touted by the industry for a variety of reasons. Claims of tourism's economic significance give the industry greater respect among the business community, public officials, and the public in general. This often translates into decisions or public policies that are favourable to tourism. Community support is important for tourism, as it is an activity that affects the entire community. Economic benefits and costs of tourism reach virtually everyone in the region in one way or another. Economic impact analyses provide tangible estimates of these economic interdependencies and a better understanding of the role and importance of tourism in a region's economy.

Tourism activity also involves economic costs, including the direct costs incurred by tourism businesses, government costs for infrastructure to better serve tourists, as well as congestion and related costs borne by individuals in the community. Sound decisions rest on a balanced and objective assessment of both benefits and costs and an understanding of who benefits from tourism and who pays for it.

Tourism's economic impacts are therefore an important consideration in state, regional and community planning and economic development. Economic impacts are also important factors in marketing and management decisions.

A variety of methods, ranging from pure guesswork to complex mathematical models, are used to estimate tourism's economic impacts. Studies vary extensively in quality and accuracy, as well as which aspects of tourism are included. On the other hand, media coverage of these studies tend to oversimplify and frequently misinterpret the results, leaving decision makers and the general public with a sometimes distorted and incomplete understanding of tourism's economic effects.How can the average person understand these studies sufficiently to separate good studies from bad ones and make informed choices? The purpose of this bulletin is to present a systematic introduction to economic impact concepts and methods. The bulletin is organised around ten basic questions that either are asked or should be asked about the economic impacts of tourism.

Economic Impact Analysis

A variety of economic analyses are carried out to support tourism decisions. As these different kinds of economic analysis are frequently confused, let's begin by positioning economic impact studies within the broader set of economic problems and techniques relevant to tourism. Each type of analysis is identified by the basic question(s) it answers and the types of methods and models that are appropriate.

Benefit cost analysis and economic impact analysis are frequently confused as both discuss economic "benefits". There are two clear distinctions between the two techniques. B/C analysis addresses the benefits from economic efficiency while economic impact analysis focuses on the regional distribution of economic activity. B/C analysis includes both market and non-market values, while economic impact analysis is restricted to actual flows of money from market transactions.

While each type of economic analysis is somewhat distinct, a given problem often calls for several different kinds of economic analysis. An economic impact study will frequently involve a demand analysis to project levels of tourism activity. A comprehensive impact assessment will also examine fiscal impacts, as well as social and environmental impacts.

Be aware that an economic impact analysis, by itself, provides a rather narrow and often one-sided perspective on the impacts of tourism. Studies of the economic impacts of tourism tend to emphasise the positive benefits of tourism. On the other hand environmental, social, cultural and fiscal impact studies tend to focus more on negative impacts of tourism. This is in spite of the fact that there are negative economic impacts of tourism and in many cases positive environmental and social impacts.

An economic impact assessment (EIA) traces changes in economic activity resulting from some action. An EIA will identify which economic sectors benefit from tourism and estimate resulting changes in income and employment in the region. For many problems economic impact analysis will be part of a broader analysis. Environmental, social, and fiscal impacts are often equally important concerns in a balanced assessment of impacts.

An economic impact analysis will assess the contribution of tourism activity to a region's economy. The basic questions an economic impact study usually addresses are:

i) How much do tourists spend in the area?

ii) What portion of sales by local businesses is due to tourism?

iii) How much income does tourism generate for households and businesses in the area?

iv) How many jobs in the area does tourism support?

v) How much tax revenue is generated from tourism?

An economic impact analysis also reveals the interrelationships among economic sectors and provides estimates of the changes that take place in an economy due to some existing or proposed action. The most common applications of economic impact analysis to tourism are:

i) To evaluate the economic impacts of changes in the supply of recreation and tourism opportunities. Supply changes may involve a change in quantity, such as the opening of new facilities, closing of existing ones, or expansions and contraction in capacity. Supply changes may also involve changes in quality, including changes in,

  a) the quality of the environment,

  b) the local infrastructure and public services to support tourism, or

  c) the nature of the tourism products and services that are provided in an area.

ii) To evaluate the economic impacts of changes in tourism demand. Population changes, changes in the competitive position of the region, marketing activity or changing consumer tastes and preferences can alter levels of tourism activity, spending, and associated economic activity.

iii) To evaluate the effects of policies and actions which affect tourism activity either directly or indirectly. Tourism depends on many factors at both origins and destinations that are frequently outside the direct control of the tourism industry itself. Economic impact studies provide information to help decision makers better understand the consequences of various actions on the tourism industry as well as on other sectors of the economy.

iv) To understand the economic structure and interdependencies of different sectors of the economy. Economic studies help us better understand the size and structure of the tourism industry in a given region and its linkages to other sectors of the economy.

v) To argue for favourable treatment in allocation of resources or local tax, zoning or other policy decisions. By showing that tourism has significant economic impacts, tourism interests can often convince decision-makers to allocate more resources for tourism or to establish policies that encourage tourism.

vi) To compare the economic impacts of alternative resource allocation, policy, management or development proposals. Economic impact analyses are commonly used to assess the relative merits of distinct alternatives. The economic contribution of expanded tourism offerings may be compared for example with alternatives such as resource extraction activities or manufacturing.

Tourism has a variety of economic impacts. Tourists contribute to sales, profits, jobs, tax revenues, and income in an area. The most direct effects occur within the primary tourism sectors —lodging, restaurants, transportation, amusements, and retail trade . Through secondary effects, tourism affects most sectors of the economy. An economic impact analysis of tourism activity normally focuses on changes in sales, income, and employment in a region resulting from tourism activity.

A simple tourism impact scenario illustrates. Let's say a region attracts an additional 100 tourists, each spending $100 per day. That's $10,000 in new spending per day in the area. The million dollars in spending would be distributed to lodging, restaurant, amusement and retail trade sectors in proportion to how the visitor spends the $100. Perhaps 30% of the million dollars would leak out of the region immediately to cover the costs of goods purchased by tourists that are not made in the local area. The remaining $700,000 in direct sales might yield $350,000 in income within tourism industries and support 20 direct tourism jobs. Tourism industries are labour and income intensive, translating a high proportion of sales into income and corresponding jobs.

The tourism industry, in turn, buys goods and services from other businesses in the area, and pays out most of the $350,000 in income as wages and salaries to its employees. This creates secondary economic effects in the region. The study might use a sales multiplier of 2.0 to indicate that each dollar of direct sales generates another dollar in secondary sales in this region. Through multiplier effects, the $700,000 in direct sales produces $1.4 million in total sales. These secondary sales create additional income and employment, resulting in a total impact on the region of $1.4 million in sales, $650,000 in income and 35 jobs. While hypothetical, the numbers used here are fairly typical of what one might find in a tourism economic impact study. One can also estimate the tax effects of this spending by applying local tax rates to the appropriate changes in sales or income. Instead of focusing on visitor spending, one could also estimate impacts of construction or government activity associated with tourism.

There are several other categories of economic impacts that are not typically covered in economic impact assessments, at least not directly. For example:

i) Changes in prices: tourism can sometimes inflate the cost of housing and retail prices in the area, frequently on a seasonal basis.

ii) Changes in the quality and quantity of goods and services: tourism may lead to a wider array of goods and services available in an area.

iii) Changes in property and other taxes: taxes to cover the cost of local services may be higher or lower in the presence of tourism activity. In some cases, taxes collected directly or indirectly from tourists may yield reduced local taxes for schools, roads, etc.

iv) Economic dimensions of "social" and "environmental" impacts: There are also economic consequences of most social and environmental impacts that are not usually addressed in an economic impact analysis. These can be positive or negative.

Direct, Indirect and Induced Effects

A standard economic impact analysis traces flows of money from tourism spending, first to businesses and government agencies where tourists spend their money and then to :

i) *Other businesses:* supplying goods and services to tourist businesses,

ii) *Households:* earning income by working in tourism or supporting industries, and

iii) *Government:* through various taxes and charges on tourists, businesses and households

Formally, regional economists distinguish direct, indirect, and induced economic effects. Indirect and induced effects are sometimes collectively called secondary effects. Any of these impacts may be measured as gross output or sales, income, employment, or value added.

i) *Direct effects:* are production changes associated with the immediate effects of changes in tourism expenditures. For example, an increase in the number of tourists staying overnight in hotels would directly yield increased sales in the hotel sector.

ii) *Indirect effects:* are the production changes resulting from various rounds of respending of the hotel industry's receipts in other backward-linked industries. Changes in sales, jobs, and income in the linen supply industry, for example, represent indirect effects of changes in hotel sales. Businesses supplying products and services to the linen supply industry represent another round of indirect effects, eventually linking hotels to varying degrees to many other economic sectors in the region.

iii) *Induced effects:* are the changes in economic activity resulting from household spending of income earned directly or indirectly as a result of tourism spending.

By means of indirect and induced effects, changes in tourist spending can impact virtually every sector of the economy in one way or another. The magnitude of secondary effects depends on the propensity of businesses and households in the region to purchase goods and services from local suppliers. Induced effects are particularly noticed when a large employer in a region closes a plant. Not only are supporting industries hurt, but the entire local economy suffers due to the reduction in household income within the region. Similar effects in the opposite direction are observed when there is a significant increase in jobs and household income.

Final demand is the term used by economists for sales to the final consumers of goods and services. In almost all cases, the final consumers of tourism goods and services are households. Government spending is also considered as final demand. The same methods for estimating impacts of visitor spending can be applied to estimate the economic impacts of government spending, for example, to operate and maintain a park or visitor centre.

Regional Economic Models

An input-output model (I-O model) is a mathematical model that describes the flows of money between sectors within a region's economy. Flows are predicted by knowing what each industry must buy from every other industry to produce a dollar's worth of output. Using each industry's production function, I-O models also determine the proportions of sales that go to wage and salary income, proprietor's income, and taxes. Multipliers can be estimated from input-output models based on the estimated re-circulation of spending within the region. Exports and imports are determined based upon estimates of the propensity of households and firms within the region to purchase goods and services from local sources. The more a region is self-sufficient and purchases goods and services from within the region, the higher the multipliers for the region.

Input-output models make a number of assumptions. The basic ones are that:

i) All firms in a given industry employ the same production technology, and produce identical products.

ii) There are no economies or diseconomies of scale in production or factor substitution.

iv) The model doesn't explicitly keep track of time, but analysts generally report the impact estimates as if they represent activity within a single year.

v) One must assume that the various model parameters are accurate and represent the current year. I-O models are firmly grounded in the national system of accounts, which relies on a standard industrial classification system (SIC codes) and various federal government economic censuses, in which individual firms report sales, wage and salary payments and employment.

vi) Multiplier computations for induced effects generally assume that jobs created by additional spending are new jobs, involving new households in the area. Induced effects are computed assuming linear changes in household spending with changes in income.

Multiplier Effects of Tourism

Multipliers capture the secondary economic effects (indirect and induced) of tourism activity. Multipliers have been frequently misused and misinterpreted in tourism studies and are a considerable source of confusion among non-economists. Multipliers represent the economic interdependencies between sectors within a particular region's economy. There are many different kinds of multipliers reflecting which secondary effects are included and which measure of economic activity is used (sales, income, or employment).

Multiplying a Type I sales multiplier times the direct sales gives direct plus indirect sales. Multiplying a Type II or III sales multiplier times the direct sales gives total sales impacts including direct, indirect and induced effects. The multipliers defined above are called ratio type multipliers as they measure the ratio of a total impact measure to the corresponding direct impact. Ratio multipliers should be used with caution.

A common error is to multiply a sales multiplier times tourist spending to get total sales effects. This will generate an inflated estimate of tourism impacts. The problem is that tourism spending or sales is not exactly the same as the "direct effects", appearing in the multiplier formula. Tourist purchases of goods are the primary source of the problem.

To properly apply tourist purchases of goods to an input-output model (or corresponding multipliers), various margins must be deducted from the "purchaser price" of the good to separate out the "producer price". In an I-O model, retail margins accrue to the retail trade sector, wholesale margins to wholesale trade, transportation margins to transportation sectors and the producer prices of goods are assigned to the sector that produces the good.

In most cases the factory that produces the good bought by a tourist lies outside of the local region, creating an immediate "leakage" in the first round of spending and therefore no local impact from production of the good. Before applying a multiplier to tourist spending, one must first deduct the producer prices of all imported goods that tourists buy Generally, only 60 to 70% of tourist spending appears as final demand in a local region. While all tourist purchases of services will accrue to the local region as final demand , only the margins on goods purchased at retail stores should be counted as local final demand. The ratio of local final demand to tourist spending is called the capture rate.

Capture rates, like multipliers, will vary with the size and nature of the region as well as the kind of tourist spending included. One must therefore be cautious in taking a multiplier or capture rate cited in one study and using it in another.

Another way of calculating a multiplier is as a ratio of income or employment to sales. This kind of multiplier is sometimes called a Keynesian multiplier or response coefficient.

This income (employment) multiplier produces total income (employment) impacts when multiplied by the direct sales. One must still be careful in distinguishing between tourism spending/sales and direct sales effects.

Measuring Economic Impacts of Tourism

The economic impacts of tourism are typically estimated by some variation of the following simple formula:

Economic Impact of Tourism = Number of Tourists * Average Spending per Visitor * Multiplier

The formula suggests three distinct steps and corresponding measurements or models:

Estimating the Change in the Number and Types of Tourists

Estimates or projections of tourist activity generally come from a demand model or some system for measuring levels of tourism activity in an area. These must come from carefully designed measurements of tourist activity, a good demand model, or good judgement. This step is usually the weakest link in most tourism impact studies, as few regions have accurate counts of tourists, let alone good models for predicting changes in tourism activity or separating local visitors from visitors from outside the region.

Estimate Average Levels of Spending

Spending averages come from sample surveys or are sometimes borrowed or adapted from other studies. Spending estimates must be based on a representative sample of the population of tourists taking into account variations across seasons, types of tourists, and locations within the study area. As spending can vary widely across different kinds of tourists, we recommend estimating average spending for a set of key tourist segments based on samples of at least 50-100 visitors within each tourism segment. Segments should be defined to capture differences in spending between local residents vs. tourists, day users vs. overnight visitors, type of accommodation and type of transportation. In broadly based tourism impact studies, it is useful to identify unique spending patterns of important activity segments such as downhill skiers, boaters, convention & business travellers.

Multiplying the number of tourists by the average spending per visitor gives an estimate of total tourist spending in the area. Estimates of tourist spending will generally be more accurate if distinct spending profiles and use estimates are made for key tourism segments. The use and spending estimates are the two most important parts of an economic impact assessment. When combined, they capture the amount of money brought into the region by tourists. Multipliers are needed only if one is interested in the secondary effects of tourism spending.

Apply the Change in Spending to a Regional Economic Model or set of Multipliers to Determine Secondary Effects

Secondary effects of tourism are estimated using multipliers or a model of the region's economy. Multipliers generally come from an economic base or input-output model of the region's economy. In many cases multipliers are borrowed or adjusted from published multipliers or other studies. Generally, multipliers are higher for larger regions with more diversified economies and lower for smaller regions with more limited economic development. A common error is to apply a statewide multiplier to a local region. This will yield inflated estimates of local multiplier effects.

Multipliers can also be used to convert estimates of spending or sales to income and employment. Simple ratios can be used to capture how much income or jobs are generated per dollar of sales. These ratios will vary from region to region and across individual economic sectors due to the relative importance of labour inputs in each industry and different wage and salary rates in different regions of the country. Be aware that job estimates are generally not full time equivalents, making them difficult to compare across industries with different proportions of seasonal and part time jobs. Income or value added are generally the preferred measures of the contribution of tourism to a region's economy.

Typical Approaches for an Economic Impact Assessment

At the simple, "quick and dirty" end of the spectrum are highly aggregate approaches that rely mostly on judgement to determine tourism activity, spending and multipliers. Such estimates can be completed in a couple hours at little cost and rest largely on the expertise and judgement of the analyst. In between are a wide range of options that employ varying degrees of judgement, secondary data, primary data, and formal models.

Different levels of detail and corresponding expense and accuracy are possible for each of the three steps—estimating tourist volume, spending, and multiplier effects. Four typical approaches illustrate the levels of detail that are possible and the associated methods .

i) Subjective estimates that rely mostly on expert opinion
ii) Secondary data in aggregate form, adapting existing estimates to suit the problem
iii) Secondary data in disaggregate form, permitting finer adjustment of data to fit the situation
iv) Primary data and/or formal models, usually involving visitor surveys and regional economic models.

One can employ different levels of aggregation in visitor segments, spending categories, multipliers, and economic sectors to finely tune the data and models to a particular application and also yield more detailed information about the economic impacts. For example, spending data from previous surveys may be adjusted over time using consumer price indices (CPI). Data for distinct tourism market segments is also valuable in tailoring secondary data to a particular application. For example, separate estimates of the average spending for day users and overnight visitors allows one to adjust the spending estimate to reflect a given mix of day users and overnight visitors.

Examples of Economic Impact Studies in Tourism

Some examples serve to illustrate the range of possibilities for estimating the economic impacts of tourism. The following three examples are presented in greater detail in a companion bulletin.

i) *The National Park Service's "Money Generation Model:* " is a simple fill-in-form for generating economic impacts. While an extremely simple approach, it captures the essential elements, of an economic impact analysis. The number of visits, average spending per visitor and an aggregate sales multiplier are entered on a simple worksheet to generate estimates of the direct and total sales effects of visitor spending. Tax effects of visitor spending can also be estimated by applying local tax rates to sales estimates. With sound judgement in choosing the parameters, the MGM model can yield reasonable ballpark estimates of economic impacts at minimal cost.

ii) *The Bureau of Economic Analysis's (BEA) RIMS II user handbook:* illustrates how to apply published multipliers to estimate economic impacts. This approach starts with visitor spending divided into a number of spending categories and makes use of sector-specific multipliers to estimate the direct and total sales, income and employment effects. Multipliers from the BEA's RIMS II models are used to estimate secondary effects. Multipliers are reported for 39 sectors for each state in the second edition of their report.

iii) *The MI-REC/IMPLAN System:* Stynes and Propst have developed a fairly complete micro–computer based system for estimating economic impacts of recreation and tourism. The system combines spreadsheets for estimating spending with the

IMPLAN input-output modelling system. IMPLAN uses county level data to estimate 528 sector input-output models for regions down to a county level. IMPLAN generates a complete set of economic accounts for the region including multipliers and trade flows. Spending is then bridged to the IMPLAN model sectors to estimate direct, indirect and induced effects in terms of sales, income and employment. Users may estimate spending via visitor surveys or use the MI-REC database of spending profiles, compiled from previous studies. The system also includes price indices to easily update spending data to a current year.

Two other systems for estimating economic impacts of tourism should be noted. The TEIM or Travel Economic Impact Model developed by the U.S. Travel Data Center has been widely used to estimate tourism and travel impacts at state and national levels. A more recent development is the satellite accounting approach developed by the World Travel and Tourism Council. They are not readily applied to estimate the impacts of particular policies and actions at the local level.

The TEIM relies on national travel surveys to estimate trip volume and spending on a state-by-state basis. Local estimates of impacts are obtained using simple allocation formulas to distribute statewide impacts to counties and cities within the state. These local estimates do not account very well for the distinct types of tourism activity or spending patterns in different sub-regions of a state.

The WTTC effort also focuses on national and statewide accounting of tourism's economic significance. Their satellite tourism account identifies the contribution of travel and tourism to gross national product (GNP) or gross state product (GSP). Using the standard national system of accounts, they identify the portion of sales, taxes and investment attributable directly to travel and tourism. The WTTC system captures a great deal of travel-related economic activity, not covered by visitor trip spending, such as durable goods purchases (boats and RV's), construction and investment in tourism, and government expenditures.

Steps for Conducting a Tourism Economic Impact Study

An economic impact study involves four basic steps:

i) *Step 1:* Define the problem
ii) *Step 2:* Estimate the change in final demand (tourism spending).
iii) *Step 3:* Estimate the regional economic effects of this change
iv) *Step 4:* Interpret, apply, and communicate the results

Procedures for carrying out steps 2 and 3 are outlined under question 6 (above) and illustrated in more detail in the companion report. We therefore focus on the key elements to consider in defining problems for an economic impact analysis.

The most important part of any study is the first step—clarifying the nature of the problem being addressed and intended uses of the results. Before launching an economic impact study, be sure this is the kind of study that is needed rather than one or more of the other kinds of economic analyses summarised in question 1. Stynes and Propst identify seven factors that should be specified as part of defining a problem for an economic impact assessment:

1) *Define the Action:* to be evaluated. Begin by clarifying the action or actions involved in the problem. Actions may include construction, government investment, changes in marketing, management, or policies, or changes in the quality or quantity of tourist facilities.

2) *Identify the Change in the Amount and Kinds of Recreation/ Tourism Activity Resulting from the Action:* The action must be defined precisely enough in step one to be able to estimate the changes in the number and types of visitors to the area and/or their spending patterns. As a general rule, the analysis should be with vs. without the action rather than simply before vs. after. Thus, if tourism has been growing by 5% per year and a new promotional program increases this to 10% this year, only half of the 10% growth can likely be attributed to the promotional program. Identifying the net changes in activity that are attributable to an action can be a complex and difficult task. Assessments of economic impact, however, rest firmly on such estimates, so attention to these details is very important. Evaluating a range of alternatives also helps to evaluate the sensitivity of the results to your initial estimates of changes in activity levels.

3) *Identify the Kinds of Spending to be Included:* Tourism may impact the local economy through visitor trip spending, durable goods purchases, government spending, or investment and construction. Which to include in a given analysis depends on how the problem is defined, and again, on attributing given spending changes to the proposed action.

4) *Identify the Study Region:* Perhaps the most important, yet often neglected part of a recreation and tourism impact assessment is the definition of a study region. The region defines the area for which impacts are desired, as well as the portions of visitor spending that are relevant. An impact assessment evaluates the impacts on households, businesses, and organisations within the given region. Since little economic data exists below the county level, the county is generally the smallest region one should consider for a tourism impact assessment.

5) *Identify Key Economic Sectors and Desired Sectoral Detail:* The proposed action and anticipated uses/users of the results should suggest the key sectors that will be impacted. Recreation and tourism activity typically impact the lodging, restaurant, amusements, retail, transportation and government sectors most directly. In the problem definition stage consideration of impacted sectors helps to identify relevant categories of spending. The desired sectoral detail plays an important role in structuring the presentation of results.

6) *Identify the most Important Measures of Economic Activity:* Tourism impacts may be reported in terms of visitor spending, business receipts/sales/production, wage and salary income, proprietors income and profits, value added, and employment. Simple ratios can be used to convert direct spending or sales to the associated income and jobs. Input-output models and multipliers are needed only if one is interested in secondary effects.

7) *Identify the Tolerable Levels of Error in the Results:* Although confidence intervals and estimates of error are rare in economic impact studies, this doesn't mean they are not important. You should have at least a ballpark idea of how much error you can tolerate in the analysis, as this will dictate how much effort and expense you must put into it. The more accuracy you demand, the

greater the requirements to gather up-to-date local data on visitation, spending and economic activity.

Evaluating or Interpreting a Tourism Economic Impact

Evaluating, interpreting and applying an economic impact study requires a clear understanding of the findings and at least some knowledge of the underlying concepts and methods. Here's some questions to ask when reading or evaluating a tourism economic impact study.

i) *Impact of what?: The* report should identify the action being evaluated. An economic impact assessment is most useful when evaluating the effects of a particular action or policy. If so, the action and assumptions about alternatives should be spelled out in presenting a with vs. without scenario. If the study reports impacts of existing tourism activity, identify how tourism is defined (if at all). What kinds of tourism activity and spending are included? Which trip expenses are included? Does the study include all visitor spending or only spending of tourists who live outside the local region?

ii) *On What Region?:* The study region should be defined. It should be viable both economically and as a distinct tourism destination area. Spending that is included should be restricted to spending in this region and multipliers should represent the given region of interest. A short profile of tourism & economic activity in the region provides useful background for an economic impact study.

iii) *Sources and Quality of the Data:* The report should identify the sources of the data for estimating visits, spending, and regional economic multipliers/models. The methods that were used to estimate impacts should be clear. Judgements of the quality of the estimates must be based largely on an understanding of the data and methods that were used. A more disaggregate analysis reporting spending within at least six categories, visitors for two or more distinct segments, and multipliers and results broken down by sector will generally be more accurate and meaningful than a study that only uses aggregate data. The fundamental question is whether the visit estimates, spending profiles and multipliers adequately represent the intended population and study area.

iv) *Quality of methods:* There are a number of issues to watch for in evaluating methods.

a) *Visits:* Has the study clearly defined which visits/visitors will be affected by the proposed action, separated local visitors from tourists, and identified which visitors would be lost or gained due to the action (with vs. without the action)? Are secondary sources of visitation reliable?

b) *Spending:* How accurate are the spending estimates? Do the spending averages or totals seem reasonable? If spending averages are taken from a secondary source, evaluate the source, as well as how well these averages may apply to the intended application. What year does the spending represent? Has the data been price adjusted to the current year? If spending data come from a visitor survey, evaluate the survey methods – how was spending measured, what was the sample size, the response rate, soundness of the analysis? Are variances and confidence intervals reported for the spending estimates? Are visitors divided into distinct segments to reduce variances?

c) *Multipliers: If* "off-the-shelf" or borrowed multipliers are used, investigate the source. Does the study clearly define what type of multiplier is being used and use the multiplier appropriately? In particular, watch for studies that multiply tourism spending by a multiplier taken from an input-output model. They should adjust for the capture rate either by reducing spending, only using retail margins on goods purchased by tourists, or using a "tourist spending" multiplier that takes the capture rate into account.

iv) *Communication and Reporting of Results:* The study should communicate the study results in terms that are understandable to the intended audience. For most audiences, a summary and glossary of economic terms is helpful. Most readers will not fully understand terms like indirect and induced effects, Type I and Type III multipliers, and input-output models. Formal definitions of the measures of sales, income, and jobs that are reported are also needed to clarify what each of these terms include and the measurement units. For example, is income only wage and salary income or does it also include proprietors income, rents and profits? Study limitations and errors should be indicated.

Cost of an Economic Impact Study

The costs of a tourism economic impact study can range from $500 to $50,000 and more. Costs will depend largely on the size and scope of tourism activity to be covered, the size and complexity of the study region, how much primary data are to be gathered and the level of accuracy and detail desired. The greatest and perhaps most significant cost will be the technical expertise of the analysts involved. Tourism economic impact studies require considerable technical judgement of specialists and a mix of corresponding skills:

i) Knowledge of tourism
ii) Expertise in conducting tourism surveys, particularly spending studies
iii) Regional economic modelling skills, including knowledge and access to economic data bases, multipliers and input-output modelling systems
iv) Communication skills

The cost of conducting economic impact studies has dropped substantially in the past ten years due to improvements in microcomputer programs for estimating spending and regional economic models. The three principal components of an economic impact estimate each involve different costs and somewhat different skills.

If levels and types of tourism activity are known and spending averages and multipliers may be taken from secondary sources, a complete economic impact assessment can be conducted in less than a month and in many cases for under $5,000. You are paying primarily for the time, judgement and skills of the analyst. A small visitor spending survey may add another $5,000. For a more complete analysis of secondary effects using a formal input-output model, figure another $2,000- $5,000. Increase the cost estimate if several distinct alternatives are to be evaluated or multiple regions are involved. Costs will increase significantly if the number and types of visitors must be estimated using a general visitor survey or a demand model. Large scale spending surveys and custom input-output models based on primary data will also increase costs considerably.

In many cases, the tourism activity and visitor spending data needed for an economic impact analysis can be gathered in a general visitor survey or market study. Spending averages for particular tourist segments can be estimated by having a portion of the general survey respondents complete an extra page of spending questions.

References

Archer, B. H.(1973). *The impact of domestic tourism*. Bangor: University of Wales Press.

Frechtling, Douglas C. (994). Assessing the economic impacts of travel and tourism – Measuring economic benefits. In. *Travel, Tourism and Hospitality Research*, second edition. J.R. Brent Ritchie and Charles R. Goeldner (eds). New York: John Wiley and Sons Inc.

Johnson, Peter and Thomas, Barry (eds). (1992). *Choice and demand in tourism*. London: Mansell.

Propst, D. B. (Compiler). (1985). Assessing the economic impacts of recreation and tourism: conference and workshop (64 pp.). Asheville, NC: U.S. Department of Agriculture, Forest Service, Southeastern Forest Experiment Station.

5

Tourism and Business Travel

World Tourist Organisation (UNWTO), the worldwide monitoring agency on tourism, measures flows in terms of numbers and receipts. Its data define one category only: combined business and leisure travel.

In 2006, the Organisation for Economic Co-operation and Development (OECD) produced a paper entitled "Harmonised statistics on immigrant inflows preliminary results, sources and methods" by Lemaître et al.. Although the paper focuses on permanent movements only, it concludes with the stated intention of extending the work to shorter-term movements.

Business and leisure travel is, by some measures, one of the world's largest industries: tourism receipts in 2003 represented approximately six per cent of global exports of goods and services.

Worldwide, international tourism receipts were estimated at USD 680 billion (EUR 547 billion) in 2005, with all regions and sub regions sharing in the increase from 2004. Europe gained an additional USD 20 billion, raising receipts to over USD 348 billion (51% of the world total); the Americas added USD 13 billion to USD 145 billion (21%) and Asia and the Pacific increased their total by USD 11 billion to USD 139 billion (20%).

The majority of international tourist tourists still originate mainly from industrialised arrivals concerned leisure, recreation and holidays European countries (55.7%), the Americas (17%) and (50% of the total, or 402 million), while business Asia and the Pacific (19.1%). However, over the last travel accounted for some 16 per cent or 125 million, decades and with rising levels of disposable incomes, and visiting friends and relatives (VFR), religious many emerging economies have shown rapid growth purposes/pilgrimages, health treatment and the like as sources of tourism, in particular in Northeast for 26 per cent or 212 million. By region, Africa was not specified recorded the largest increase in relative terms (+ 8.2%), followed by Asia and the Pacific (+ 6.9%) and the Between 1950 and 1990, Europe and the Americas Middle East (+ 6.9%).

Many countries now see tourism, especially international tourism, as a large potential source of revenue and are diversifying their production and marketing strategies to attract increasing numbers of tourists. There are clear economic and social benefits of tourism, but there are also social as well as environmental costs. The two countries experiencing the fastest growth in international tourist receipts between 2004 and 2005 were China and Turkey. In terms of numbers of arrivals, three out of the top ten countries are developing countries: China (ranking 4th), Mexico (7) and Turkey (9). Some countries experienced remarkable growth in 2005: Laos (65.1%), Cambodia (34.7%), Papua New Guinea (17%), Fiji (10%), Honduras (25.9%), Venezuela (45.2%), Swaziland (82.8%) and Senegal (15.3%). However, the figures are volatile and often start from a low base.

A "Northern bias" often "pervades much national tourism planning across the developing world". According to Ghimire, "the dominant official concept of tourism in developing countries focuses on wealthy foreign visitors from the industrialised North" and neglects "the potentials - as well as the problems - related to mass tourism involving domestic and regional tourists."

In that regard, South Africa is unique in the developing world in paying attention to its own and the rising global level of "South-South" tourism. Regional tourists are identified separately and their massive contribution to the South African economy is measured and acknowledged. In 2003, they accounted for approximately 4.5 million out of a total of 6.5 million tourists. There is a concerted strategy to encourage regional tourism not only for economic reasons, but also as a means of driving transformation and black economic empowerment. The strong desire to travel among urban populations, growing national economies, rapid developments in transport and increased workers' benefits are some of the most important. Motivations include pilgrimages, VFR, business and leisure travel. Upper-income travellers are joined by middle–income and lower–income persons.

The discussion below considers a number of different forms of tourist movement, including medical tourism. It then addresses the interrelationship between tourism and migration, the challenges involved in managing the entry and stay of tourists, and the place of Working Holiday schemes in tourist management policies.

Medical Tourism

Medical tourism accounts for a growing share in regional tourist flows, but it is seldom identified as such and, if data are collected, they are not necessarily retained and therefore scarce. Australia is an exception and the data collected on various forms of short-term movements show that 3,982 visas for medical treatment were issued at its consular offices overseas and 911 onshore in 2001-02.

Long waiting lists, high costs, lack of or inadequate insurance coverage are some of the reasons. Governments and/or hospitals with in bound medical tourists have deliberately marketed their services.

Leng explains that Malaysia, Singapore and Thailand developed this strategy in response to the 1997 Asian financial crisis. Private hospitals were struggling to survive in the face of lower numbers of private patients and the high costs of drugs, and they "turned to foreign countries to attract patients, a move that had the full support, if not the active leadership, of the government". Hospitals and hotels have since teamed up to offer packages, while some preliminary diagnostic tests are conducted and the cost of the treatment is assessed in the country of origin before the patient travels abroad. In future, there may be an increased focus in Malaysia on healthcare for the elderly, linked to retirement tourism.

Medical tourism also accounts for a significant share of international tourist travel, for example to China for traditional Chinese herbal treatment and acupuncture; India for various western, ayurvedic and yogic treatments; Thailand for treatment in world-class hospitals; Cuba for advanced medical care and Singapore for heart, eye and cancer treatment. Singapore's aim is to increase the number of international patients from 200,000 in 2006 to one million by 2012.

The economic gains are obvious, but there will also be additional demand for nurses, nursing aides, doctors, ancillary workers and others to staff the growing number of private medical facilities. This demand could, in turn, lead to further international labour mobility. Many of these private medical service suppliers are not only regionally but also internationally integrated. As a result, they can refer patients and transfer staff from a hospital in one country to a medical facility in another.

At the same time, home country governments may be promoting or organising patient outflows or "medical tourists" as a means of cutting their own costs, or to alleviate pressure on their own systems when necessary health services are not immediately or locally available, or to reduce long waiting periods. The U.K. is at the forefront of this development and is sending patients overseas for treatment under the National Health Service (NHS). The Department of Health website states:

Treatment in the EEA (European Economic Area) is one of the options open to NHS Primary Care Trusts wishing to manage their waiting lists and reduce waiting times, and offer greater patient choice where this represents good value for money and increased convenience. Since January 2002, almost 600 patients have received treatment in the EEA in France, Belgium and Germany. The majority of these referrals have been for orthopaedic and some cardiac procedures. An independent evaluation of the overseas treatment pilot scheme found patients' reactions to be very positive. Feedback has remained positive in the "live" project and patient take-up rates have exceeded expectation.

This form of medical tourism from the U.K. is known as the E112 referral system, which covers maternity care and referral for specific medical treatment. Treatment is provided on the terms of the particular scheme in the country concerned, and the NHS pays the provider directly. Recent decisions handed down by the European Court of Justice and domestic courts have confirmed this right to "direct purchase".

Medical tourism, as tourism generally, falls under the designation of trade in services—the WTO's General Agreement of Trade in Services (GATS) Mode 2, namely, services that are supplied and consumed abroad. GATS Mode 3, commercial presence, covers the establishment of an affiliate, subsidiary or representation for the purpose of providing a particular service in a third country. Hence, the establishment of, for example, tour companies, hotels and hospitals and the corresponding placement of staff in a foreign country is classed as trade in services, though the distinction between this and labour mobility in general is clearly not always easy.

The importance of tourism for the purpose of religious pilgrimages, special events sporting events and many similar occasions needs to be acknowledged. While many of the flows are short-term, they may have long-term consequences if visitors subsequently decide to migrate to live or to do business in the country concerned.

Interrelationships between Tourism and Migration

The complex mutual interrelationships of tourism and migration have been explored since the early 1990s. Many flows for leisure and business are unrelated to earlier migration movements, but others spring from, or are related to, former migration patterns. However, many such movements do not arise spontaneously and are linked to earlier migration flows. In turn, tourist movements can generate new or additional forms of migration as people decide to move to what were originally their holiday destinations or to other parts of their own country.

Various researchers have examined the manner in which migration can generate tourist flows, in particular through the geographical expansion of friendship and kinship networks. Such tourist flows are significantly shaped by the particular characteristics of migrant populations, such as composition, duration and direction, with each round of migration generating new spatial patterns of friendship and kinship networks, which potentially represent VFR tourism flows. The study found that 92 per cent of outbound tourism, mostly to China, was for VFR and the remainder for business and holidays.

On the other hand, tourism may also generate other types of mobility, including labour migration flows. First, tourists often prefer guides, cooking and food from their homeland; thus, over time, tourism and the preferences of tourists contribute to labour migration from their home countries, including of entrepreneurs. Second, tourism may eventually lead to the acquisition of new or second homes by regular tourists, and their relocation there following retirement or even earlier. Many people visit a country several times as tourists before they eventually decide to move there permanently or on a long-term basis. These movements are particularly pronounced to the sunbelts of Europe, North America and Australia, and other attractive destinations. All of this has implications concerning the necessary resources in terms of workforce and qualified staff to construct and manage facilities. Third, as observed earlier, the growing phenomenon of medical tourism has specific implications for the number of health professionals needed at the destination, and the workforce required to build and manage hospitals and other facilities.

Migration Management Issues

As travel and communication costs decline, "visa requirements and border formalities have the potential to become the most significant impediments to the growth of travel and tourism" . However, a 1996 Asia-Pacific Economic Cooperation (APEC) Tourism Impact study emphasises that visa requirements per se are not obstructive; rather, the problems encountered concern the availability of information concerning visa requirements, the time involved in visa issuance and the processing of visas at entry points.

The realisation of the value of in bound tourism has often led to increased national and regional marketing and promotion strategies, and a relaxation of regulations and visa requirements to make travel and entry procedures relatively straightforward and not too costly.

Visa-Free Schemes

Visa–free schemes are clearly the most liberal arrangement and enable unrestricted travel between certain countries or within particular regions. In the ASEAN, an agreement providing for visa–free travel for nationals of member countries is also expected to be in place by 2010.

Visa Waiver Schemes

The U.S. and Canada have introduced visa waiver programmes to enable tourists and business travellers from particular countries to travel without a visa, subject to certain conditions. Visa waiver schemes rely on relationships of trust between the countries to ensure that visitors return home.

Developing countries or countries in economic transition also unilaterally lift, or substantially ease, visitor visa requirements for tourists from developed countries with a view to facilitating tourism to the country and generating revenue. For example, some Commonwealth countries do not require visas for tourists from the U.K., even though the U.K. maintains visa restrictions on their nationals.

Issues of Facilitation and Control

The management of visitor movements requires a delicate balance between facilitation and control as, on the one hand, governments seek to streamline and speed up the issuance of visas for bona fide arrivals while, on the other, they need control mechanisms to prevent abuse.

Australia has an Electronic Travel Authority (ETA) scheme available to passport holders from 34 countries, locations and regions. Since its introduction in 1996, more than 21 million travellers have been granted ETAs to come to Australia. ETAs now account for almost 83 per cent of all Australian tourist and short-term business visas granted worldwide. The ETA system can be accessed by more than 300,000 travel agents worldwide, over 75 airlines and through the Internet. ETA arrangements offer significant benefits in terms of speed, convenience and security to travellers, as well as airlines and the Australian authorities.

More recently, the fear of terrorism has led many governments to tighten their visa requirements. For example, students have had to satisfy much more stringent language tests to ensure that they are legitimate students prior to obtaining a visa.

A further reason why some countries continue to maintain strict visa regulations is their concern over the potential cultural, social and environmental impact of large numbers of tourists. This is particularly important in some developing countries that do not have sufficient airline capacity or hotel or tour operating facilities and therefore only cater to a limited volume of tourists as, for instance, in Laos and Bhutan. Limiting access through visa restrictions sets a ceiling on in bound movements.

Problem of Overstay

The overstaying of tourist visas, or using tourist visas for purposes other than legitimate tourist activities, is very common. The relative ease of obtaining tourist visas relative to other visas has led to their being used as a means of entry for ulterior motives, such as overstaying the visa entitlement or to transit to other countries, and to live and work there without being authorised to do so. Many countries, including those with tight immigration controls face this situation, but few make public the actual numbers of tourists overstaying or irregularly present within their borders. The visa requirements for nationals of countries perceived to be at a higher risk of generating irregular migration, such as overstaying visa entitlements and transit to a third country, have been tightened. However, in the absence of relatively accessible and enforceable regular migration channels, such additional controls are also viewed by some as ineffective to dissuade and mostly failing to curtail further irregular migration from the countries concerned and thus to reduce irregular entries. Clearly, a viable solution to and the proper management of this issue calls for closer cooperation and coordination by the parties concerned regarding the control of such movements, and of the respective employment and immigration policies in effect.

Place of Working Holiday Schemes in Tourist Management Policies

Many countries and regions have introduced working holiday schemes over the last few decades. Such programmes are usually reciprocal and enable young people to travel and work in countries parties to bilateral arrangements, subject to certain conditions. The schemes vary as to the degree to which they are explicitly aimed at filling sectoral or seasonal gaps in the labour market concerned. A growing tendency to attract young and highly skilled people, who could potentially become permanent or long-term immigrants, can also be observed. The following three case studies illustrate the various schemes and trends.

United Kingdom

In the U.K., the Working Holidaymaker Scheme entitles young citizens of any Commonwealth country, aged 17 to 30, to work for any employer in any type of work for up to two years. According to Salt, annual numbers have risen from around 23,000 in 1990 to 45,800 in 1999, to fall again to 35,775 in 2001 before rising steeply to 62,400 in 2004. The dominant source countries are the "Old Commonwealth"—Australia, Canada, New Zealand and South Africa, which together accounted for the bulk of working holidaymakers (81.5%) in 2004.

Though "little is known about the characteristics of working holidaymakers in the U.K., it may reasonably be assumed that they are generally well educated and adaptable". It is not possible to know how many of them will be working at any one time, nor what their total contribution to the labour market is. However, given the numbers it is likely to be substantial. "There is no regional breakdown in the statistics for working holidaymakers, nor is it known what jobs they take". Nevertheless, they provide a supply of young, mobile, largely English-speaking workers who may eventually become permanent residents.

Australia

The Australian Working Holiday and Work and Holiday Programmes "provide opportunities for people aged between 18 and 30 to holiday in Australia and to supplement their travel funds through incidental employment".

For 2005-06, agreements were concluded with 20 countries, with the largest cohorts of Working Holidaymakers (WHMs) coming from the U.K. (28,821), followed by Republic of Korea (South Korea) (24,077), Ireland (12,554) and Germany (12,089). In recent years, there has been a notable diversification of source countries and regions with the addition of Belgium, Estonia and Taiwan Province of China. A 1997 survey conducted by Harding and Webster (2002), at a time when eight WHM agreements were in effect, found that 85 per cent of

WHMs were in paid employment during their visit, averaging 2.9 jobs each during that period.

Around three-quarters of WHM jobs were low-skilled, covering basic or intermediate office duties, production and transport and general manual activities, relative to 46 per cent across the whole workforce. The main occupations were as waiters, harvesting fruits, providing basic services, secretarial work, labourer and similar manual and construction work.

A positive effect of the Working Holiday and Work and Holiday Programmes was the creation of an additional 8,000 full-time jobs in Australia for every 80,000 WHMs through the employment generation effects of WHMs. Though WHMs were active in a range of low-skilled jobs, they were not shown to displace Australians who had not been interested in taking up these positions. The Migration Regulations 1994 were amended in July 2006 to increase the length of time holders of both Subclass 417 and Subclass 462 visas were permitted to work and study. The limitation on working for any one employer was extended from three to six months, and the study or training limitation from three to four months. These "changes were based on representations made by various stakeholders, including Australian tourism and education bodies, and provide greater flexibility for visa holders and their employers".

New Zealand

The N.Z. Working Holiday Schemes (WHS) allow persons of 18 to 30 years of age from partner countries to spend 12 months in New Zealand and accept work of a temporary nature, and foresee reciprocal arrangements for young New Zealanders to work abroad. New Zealand has concluded WHS with 23 countries, providing for a total of 31,000 WHS visas in 2004-05, though only 21,025 work permits were actually issued. There is an annual cap for each participating country. In general slightly more women (54%) than men were issued work permits. For the U.K. and most other European countries, the ratio of men to women was about equal. In contrast, among WHMs from Chile, Italy and Uruguay men outnumbered women, although total numbers in these schemes were also relatively low. A high proportion of WHMs were in their early twenties, with 40 per cent aged between 22 and 25.

A number of adjustments were introduced in mid 2005 to enhance the attractiveness of the N.Z. WHS and turn them more into an employment programme. For example, it is now possible to convert from a WHS permit to permanent residence status and, in 2004-05, 182 individuals present in the country under the WHS obtained permanent residence status. Although numbers are low, this is an indication of the use of these schemes to fill labour market gaps on a more ongoing basis.

These developments point to a general trend towards the provision of longer-term employment opportunities for WHMs. They concern a self-selected group of young, often well educated tourists who are now being "tapped" as possible workers or permanent residents. The delineation between tourism management and the management of migration for short and long-term employment and even permanent migration is becoming increasingly blurred for countries such as Australia, New Zealand and the U.K.

Short-term Movements for Business

As with tourism, short-term movements for business and entrepreneurial purposes have greatly increased in all parts of the world in recent years. The interrelationship between this type of mobility and migration is more readily apparent than that of migration and tourism, although its nature and scope escape precise definition and analysis. The growth of business travel and its diversity, particularly in the developing world, give rise to a number of economic and social benefit in developing countries, but also pose challenges that are not that dissimilar from migration management concerns.

Issues of Definition

The first issue is to consider the various terminologies and definitions used in some countries concerning the issuance of visas to control or manage entry. While permanent or long-term migration is characterised by the use of a large variety of terms and definitions, this is even more the case for short-term movements, though the concept is not well defined, recorded or researched by policymakers or others.

Globalisation has generated a large increase in the volume and type of temporary business movements as not only multinationals but also the international expansion of many small and medium-sized enterprises has led to the rapid increase in the mobility of business people.

International movements within transnational corporations (TNCs) are significant, but not always easy to identify as they concern a select group moving within specific channels and not subject to the same constraints as other business travellers.

This group does not include the "suitcase traders" or small, self-employed entrepreneurs, who repeatedly move between different parts of the world. Though their numbers and individual trajectories are difficult to quantify on account of their erratic, circular and self-determined movements, they represent a growing group of merchants who move to trade or to set up small businesses as and where opportunities arise.

The international mobility of service providers gives rise to another potentially large group of short-term business travellers, as defined under the WTO's GATS Mode 4. There is some overlap and confusion as to how to differentiate between labour movements and GATS Mode 4 movements for services, but business persons and intra-company transferees could potentially refer to GATS Mode 4 to provide services on a short-term basis in another country. They would, however, be subject to various conditions, such as quotas and restrictions, educational qualification requirements and economic needs tests, stipulated by countries of destination in their GATS Schedule of commitments. At the moment, there is no specific GATS Mode 4 visa and people are admitted under the existing visa regulations of destination countries.

Management of Short-term Business Visits

Countries are increasingly developing various types of short-term business visas to facilitate the entry of business people. However, there is significant diversity and attempts at harmonisation have been slow and difficult.

(i) Asia-Pacific Economic Cooperation (APEC)

The APEC Business Travel Card (BTC) was introduced to lower trade transaction costs. This is a national visa waiver or three-year multiple entry visa valid for all participating economies for persons who satisfy the requisite visa conditions. Other provisions may eventually be attached to the APEC Business Travel Card, namely, an agreed 30-day service standard for intra-company transferees and an agreement to consider the streamlining of access to employment for spouses of intra-company transferees.

The aim is to move towards common agreed standards for the short and long-term entry of business people; to date, however, most countries, including a number of APEC participating economies, impose additional visa requirements on business people wishing to visit. Some of these are outlined below.

(ii) Australia

Australia defines short-term business visits as covering

i) Attendance at a conference or training session;

ii) The conduct of business with an Australia-based company;

iii) The conduct of business negotiations, or

iv) An exploratory business visit. A choice of five business visitor visa options is available:

   a) *Short Stay Business Visitor (subclass 456):* 3 months— for business people to make a short business visit to attend a conference, conduct negotiations or make an exploratory business visit.

   b) *Sponsored Business Visitor (subclass 459):* 3 months—for business people who have an approved sponsor in Australia and may not be eligible to apply for an Electronic Travel Authority (ETA).

   c) *ETA (Snort Validity) (subclass 977):* 3 months—an electronically stored authority available to passport holders from a number of countries and regions. Applications must be made from outside Australia.

   d) *ETA (Long Validity) (subclass 956):* 3 months, repeat visits—for business people to make regular short business visits, granted for the length of the validity of the passport.

e) *APEC Business Travel Card:* 2 months, repeat trips—to streamline travel for business people from 16 participating economies in the APEC region.

The number of visas issued in four of these categories from 2001 to 2006. The short stay visas are by far the most numerous. The persons in the sponsored 459 subclass are most probably intra–company transfers.

It is interesting to note that a number of temporary entrants and visa categories, including the Class 457 Temporary Business (Long Stay) visa and the Working Holiday and Work and Holiday programmes, are linked to business migration. Class 457 entrants are actually sponsored employees.

According to Khoo et al, the majority of 457 visa holders had applied for long-term temporary residence in Australia after a previous stay there under the Working Holiday and Work and Holiday programmes or as students. Conversely, 457 visa holders from India are least likely to have visited the country prior to their present stay.

Drawing on the findings of Coleman and Rowthorn, Khoo et al. suggest that temporary skilled migration is the source of many economic benefits to Australia because it brings in young, well qualified and highly skilled people.

(iii) Canada

Canada receives a very large number of short-term visitors every year, with around 20 million annual crossings of the Canada/U.S. border alone. There is no statistical breakdown of the particular motives for a visitor's stay in Canada. A large majority of the many millions of business visitors entering Canada every year would not need visas as they are from visa-exempt countries, particularly the U.S. and Europe.

(iv) Japan and Republic of Korea

Both Japan and South Korea require short-term business visas for visits of up to three months for most business entrants. However, Japan and South Korea also waive visa requirements for nationals of certain APEC economies. South Korea offers multiple entry visas for nationals from Australia, Canada, China, Japan and the U.S., in accordance with relevant bilateral agreements.

(v) New Zealand

The possibilities for short–term business visits to New Zealand are limited. The Long-term Business Visa (permit) requires the prior submission of a business plan. N.Z. participates in the APEC BTC scheme and certain APEC economies benefit from the visa-waiver arrangements.

(vi) United Kingdom

The U.K. has a new business visa for entries of up to six months. It makes a distinction between a business visitor and an employee, and the conditions for admission are clearly stated, as are the eligible occupations, the nature of the direct or contractual working relationship with the sending company and the type of work that can be undertaken. The visa conditions provide for considerable flexibility concerning the corporate activities to be undertaken.

The same flexibility is foreseen under the generally long-term visas issued for the purpose of business creation, such as, for instance, the Sole Representative Visas for Employers, valid for two years for the establishment of a branch office of an overseas business in the U.K., or the U.K. Innovator Visa, also valid for two years for persons intending to realise a highly innovative business idea in the U.K.

(vii) United States

The U.S. Office of Immigration Statistics (OIS) produces an *Annual Flow Report* that includes data on temporary flows. It examines the temporary non-immigrant admissions to the U.S., mainly tourists and business travellers on short-term trips. The bulk of the 175.1 million non-immigrant admissions in 2006 were from Canada and Mexico, and the remaining 33.7 million from all other countries . Canadians and Mexicans who hold a non-resident Border Crossing Card, commonly known as a laser visa or a multiple-entry non-immigrant visa, are not required to complete an I-94 Form.

Of the 33.7 million I-94 admissions, 73.9 per cent were for tourist purposes and 15 per cent for business travel, granted to 25.8 million individuals of whom 4.4 million were entitled to multiple entries. The U.S. data provide a good breakdown. Temporary business visitors can be separated from intra-company transferees and their families and from exchange visitors and their families.

Almost half (45.8%) of non-immigrant (I-94) admissions concerned nationals from Mexico, U.K. and Japan, followed by Germany, France, Republic of Korea, India, Italy, Australia, Brazil and the Netherlands. Men accounted for 52.9 per cent of all I-94 admissions, and 56.3 per cent were aged 15 to 44.

The U.S. also has a visa category for "treaty traders and treaty investors". These E1, E2 or E3 visas are intended for nationals of countries with which the U.S. has concluded treaties of commerce and navigation, who wish to come to the United States to carry on substantial trade, including trade in services, or to develop and direct the operations of an enterprise in which they have invested or are in the process of investing, and who are not required to fill out an I-94 Form.

Although the U.S. does not participate in the APEC BTC, nationals of Australia, Brunei Darussalam, Japan, New Zealand and Singapore are granted a visa waiver for up to 90 days.

Intra–Company Transfers

Of all business travels, intra–company transfers are among the most difficult to document. Although no easily accessible data on such short-term business movements are available for Australia, a recent survey conducted by Khoo et al. showed that 30 per cent of 457 visa arrivals to Australia were intra-company transferees.

Business Travel in the Developing World

Globalisation and deregulation have opened up many developing countries where conditions are seen to be economically, socially and politically conducive to significant inflows of short-term business travellers or visiting nationals from more developed countries.

In recent years, temporary business visits from countries in Asia, Europe, North America and Oceania to many of the world's global cities and other major sites have become very prevalent. The expansion of multinationals and the establishment of offshore branches or client offices in mining, manufacturing and the services sector have given rise to countless and repeat visits by managers, technicians, engineers and supervisors.

Disparities in economic development between neighbouring countries frequently give rise to short-term and often irregular movements for the purpose of trade. For example, in 2003, over 300,000 individuals crossed the border from Mongolia into China, mostly for trading purposes. The building of a free-trade zone and a new Trading Hall in Erlianhaut in Inner Mongolia led to an increase in cross-border activities.

The dismantling of the apartheid regime in South Africa led to a more liberal migration regime and, since the early 1990s, many people from other parts of Africa have been able to enter on a 30-day visitor's permit issued at the border. The declining contract labour migration to the mines has led to the growth of informal migration for work or to conduct business.

For years, cross-border shoppers from Southern Africa have flocked to Johannesburg, South Africa's financial centre, to buy cheap goods that can be taken home and sold at a profit. The shoppers' spending bonanza includes cash-register sales and expenditure on overnight accommodation, meals and transportation. In 2004 the latest year for which data are available—the major points of attraction for more than half a million African visitors were South Africa's array of shops, mainly wholesalers. "These are typically low to middle-income people who come because there is a wide variety of goods and good quality. And these stores may just be popping up in their own country", says urban consultant Neil Fraser of the newly formed Joburg Cross-Border Shopping Association.

Many irregular migration flows from China and other parts of Asia, Latin America and Africa , as well as from eastern Europe to the more developed countries in Europe have been associated with the establishment and operation of small businesses. In recent years, southern Europe has attracted many new irregular migrants including Chinese nationals, to take up job opportunities in the informal sector.

New types of flows have often emerged in response to tighter regulatory systems in developed countries. Peraldi documents the rise of Algerian suitcase traders throughout the Mediterranean region, replacing traditional labour migration to France. "Often serving tourist markets, their moves take place within family networks which allow them to seize trading opportunities in whichever city they are present".

Such business movements are generally unrecorded or included in tourist figures.

Benefits of Short-term Business Movements

The circulation of people as part of international business activities, aid programmes and projects and for other reasons is significant, but difficult to quantify. However, both countries of origin and of destination stand to gain from short-term business migrants. Host countries can sell more goods and provide accommodation and other services for business clients, and are themselves introduced to new products, technologies and business and management practices. The private sector is considering to contribute to the effort through the construction of basic lodgings with cheap overnight rates.

At an early stage of its industrial development, Taiwan Province of China realised the value of the contribution its citizens abroad, particularly in the U.S., could make to its economy and society. Beginning in the 1950s, it implemented a series of policies and programmes to encourage the return of highly educated expatriates. Such return was to be preferably permanent, but short-term exchange and business trips were also promoted.

The contribution of short trips to economic growth is evident, but the means to measure such contributions are mostly lacking. One exception is research by Tani, who surveyed business travellers at Sydney Airport and found that most Australian business persons going abroad were male, aged 35 to 54, highly skilled, had a university degree (83%) and were born abroad (64%). His survey reported that 38 per cent of these business travellers go to attend a conference or trade fair or to look for international alliances (37%), that is, to seek out information or to share knowledge. Only 31 per cent travelled for reasons related to production and administration. Incoming business travellers were more likely to be intra-company movers (44%) followed by 32 per cent attending conferences. The combination of inflows and outflows, or gross flows, is a better measure of the importance of such mobility per se in the "formation and diffusion of knowledge". He makes a distinction between "embodied" and "disembodied" knowledge, and argues that business movements generate "disembodied" knowledge. The more trips, the more knowledge is generated that benefits both the source and destination countries.

Challenges Posed by these Different Types of Movements

The rapid growth of large trading and business locations and the difficulties in providing them with adequate housing, health, education and other facilities can be a major issue. For example, a study on the spread of HIV/AIDS in Northeast Asia found that the growth of major trading posts/towns on the borders between China and the neighbouring countries of Mongolia, Russia and North Korea, posed major infrastructure problems. At the same time, the emergence of an underground sex industry added another, very volatile factor. Together they have the potential to create a major health issue.

Zheng and Ren emphasise that, in order to stop the spread of HIV/AIDS in the general population, relevant services or projects should not only focus on the high-risk populations, but also the "bridge populations", i.e. those who may have sexual contact with the high-risk population. Urgent programmes and research are needed to focus on two broad areas:

i) Groups vulnerable to HIV infection and their "bridge populations", such as overseas contract workers and their partners, commercial sex workers and their clients, transport workers/ traders and their partners/families.

ii) "Hot spots" where there is a volatile mix of highly mobile people or temporary workers and commercial sex workers.

On the other hand, the tendency for short-term business migrants to seek to become permanent residents is met with different responses. It is encouraged in some developed countries, viz. Australia, New Zealand and the U.K., while others have provisions that enable some "desirable" short-stay business migrants to apply for permanent residence status. They frequently meet with a different response. Their situation is often regarded as being identical to that of many other irregular migrant workers who stay on after their working visas have expired and who are subject to mandatory return provisions.

Countries are endeavouring to find the best ways to handle these mushrooming flows that, on balance, are perceived to be beneficial to their economies and societies. Short-term business travel is productive for source and destination countries, as well as for the individuals themselves, and therefore warrants good management rather than limitation.

Innovative ways of encouraging skilled migrants, in particular, to invest in or manage businesses at home are being found and such information needs to be disseminated so that developing and not only developed countries, can benefit from their skilled diasporas. Mahroum et al. stress the important role for governments in source countries in connecting with their diasporas, establishing networks, recognising the potential contribution diasporas can make and creating opportunities that would allow them to contribute to local development through short-term visits to their home countries.

6

Strategic Marketing of Tourist Destination

Global competitiveness and tourism concentration create numerous challenges and problems in the creation of consumer loyalty and sustainable competitive advantage in the tourism product market. Involvement of a great number of different organisations in creation and marketing of tourism products of a tourist destination makes it difficult to align their different interests and aims. On the other side, these organisations enter different kinds of partnerships for the purpose of achieving individual and mutual effects. Balancing the strategic aims of stakeholders and increasing total economic benefits are the most important objectives of the strategic marketing of a destination.

Tourism, as an economic activity, has a growing importance for the development of not only a particular region, but also national economy as a whole. This is an area of increasing development. According to UNWTO data in the last 50 years tourism revenue increased with the average annual growth rate of 11%. The data according to which tourism has a ¼ share in the total service export indicates the importance of tourism for economic development. The data regarding the EU is also illustrated. Approximately 4% of the total number of employees in the EU work in the tourism sector. In the countries belonging to the group of 20 most developed, the percentage is higher and totals 5%. The share of tourism in GDP is 4%. Tourism is the generator of economic development.

The development and implementation of innovative marketing strategies of a tourist destination demand a change in its definition and understanding. Marketing and management literature is constantly enriched by new approaches to tourist destination as an integrated tourist product. The bases of this product comprise:

i) *Destination attraction:* the range of original factors that represent the basis for the image creation of a particular destination.

ii) *Destination accessibility:* measured by economic distance expressed in travel expanses,

iii) *Conditions of visiting a destination:* availability of objects for accommodation and other important contents of stay.

The traditional view of a tourist destination as a geographic area is replaced by a new one that starts with consumer perception depending on a cultural environment, travel purpose, education level and past experience. For some tourists a cruise is a destination, for others the ports visited during the travel. On the other side, there are destinations that are artificially divided by geographic and political barriers. However, tourists perceive them and consume as a part of the same product. In that sense, a tourist destination represents the product mix consummated by tourists under the destination name. The key characteristics of a destination are:

i) Attractions.

ii) Accessibility.

iii) Amenities.

iv) Available packages.

v) Activities.

vi) Ancillary services.

Holistic marketing of a tourist destination is viewed as a strategic approach. The development of holistic marketing of a tourist destination enables tourism workers efficient utilisation of resources and capability for undertaking rational actions that contribute to the realisation of strategic aims.

Tourist Destination Management

Destinations are some of the most difficult entities to manage and market, due to the complexity of the relationships of local stakeholders. Managing and marketing destinations is also challenging because of the variety of stakeholders involved in the development ad production of tourism products.

Their strategic interests and aims can be different and often conflicting. Consumers, however, experience a particular destination as a total experience comprising, in essence, resources of a region, services and products that represent the collection of professional and personal interests of all the people living and working in that destination. Marketing strategy should under these conditions ensure strategic alignment of aims of a tourist destination, its long term attraction and competitiveness. Conflicts among stakeholders increase when they are oriented towards achieving short term benefits. Managing a marketing destination, also, must integrate the principles of sustainable tourism and of ensuring rational utilisation of public assets. A compromise encompassing all these interests is extremely difficult if not impossible, but is the key to long-term success.

Managing a tourist destination, under contemporary conditions, is based on a strategic approach according to which providing innovative and well co-ordinated tourism products is therefore exceedingly important for tourism regions. Producing innovative and specialised tourism products will enable destinations to attract intentional demand and to differentiate their products. Destination product differentiation is based on the research and recognition of unique tourist needs for a tourist destination as a specific geographic and socio-cultural region. The key marketing aim is generating satisfaction of tourists and satisfactions among interacting tourists and hosts, and not the increase of the number of tourists and consumption of tourism as a commodity. It must adopt societal marketing strategies.

Therefore, the strategic aims of a destination must incorporate the aims of all stakeholders involved in the creation of value for tourists as well as long-term interests of the environment. The development and implementation of strategic objectives at destinations depends on relationships between stakeholders and thus the implementation of the key generic strategic objectives:

i) Enhance the long–term prosperity of local people;
ii) Delight visitors by maximising their satisfaction;
iii) Maximise profitability of local enterprises and maximise multiplier effects;

iv) Optimise tourism impacts by sustainable balance between economic benefits and socio-cultural and environmental costs.

Understanding of the image of a tourist destination is of essential importance for strategic management. Tourists perceive a destination as a brand composed of numerous products and services. Their initial perception of a destination is formed on the basis of past experience, mouth propaganda, commercial sources of an enterprise.

The image of a destination comprises two connected components: perceptive assessment related to knowledge and personal beliefs and emotional assessment related to the emotions of individuals regarding a particular destination. These components together create the image in the eyes of tourists, which is the basis for next choices and passing on to others. Tourist overall experience is composed of numerous small encounters with a variety of tourism principals (such as taxi drivers, hoteliers, waiters), as well as with elements of the local attractions . Their overall impression develops their image of a destination after their visit. As a consequence there is overlapping between strategic marketing of a destination and each individual supplier in the region. Their competitiveness is, on one side, interrelated, but very different on the other.

The image of a destination represents the essence of its value that management has managed to use for the creation of a favourable market position. In order to be a source of competitive advantage, the image must be unique for the creation of a stable and strong impact on consumers in the process of decision making about buying. The whole image is the result of the combination of tangible and non-tangible elements used for the creation of a wanted image on the market: attractive, functional, tangible and organisational. Attractive elements are the objects and space parts that have utility value since they satisfy the needs of tourists. These motives can be natural and anthropogenic. Functional elements are development forms of tourist circulation that reflect socio-economic and space characteristics of tourism . Tangible elements comprise different types of services in tourist circulation, which form the material basis of circulation which form the basis of tourism in the destination. Planning of tangible elements is in direct connection with the functional elements of a destination. Organisational elements represent a system of measures for optimal development and alignment of heterogeneous aims of tourism in the destination.

If consumer perception of a destination creates delight, consumers are ready to pay premium price. Therefore, local resources and their sustainability become a central asset for destinations and tourism suppliers. On the other side, destinations may involve de-marketing.

Competitiveness Advancement of a Tourist Destination

The most important objectives of strategic marketing of a destination are: identification of the type and characteristics of the destination, identification of the life cycle phase of the destination, selection and choice of the target market. Understanding and appreciating the type of destination enables marketers to develop suitable destination marketing mixes and deliver them to the appropriate target markets. Nevertheles, most destinations can be classified into several categories which represent their principle attractiveness: urban destination, seaside destinations and resorts, alpine destinations, rural tourism, authentic countries, unique–exotic exclusive. Some of these destinations satisfy combinated needs of tourists: business trips, vacation, relaxation, shopping, cultural needs. Certain destinations, however, are oriented towards demand during vacations. Recently, there has been a growing demand for authentic places, countries and destinations offering unique experience to consumers as preferences for non–conventional destinations. These are, as a rule, destinations that do not represent the right choice for tourists. One of the main reasons for choosing a non-conventional destination is adequate relation of delivered value and paid price, which is valuable information to be used in developing marketing strategy. It is also important to know the needs and requests of not only existing but also potential demand. Information like this is the basis for the development of product portfolio and programming other instruments of marketing mix of different holders of tourist offer at a destination for a target market.

Consumer behaviour studies indicate that a wide range of criteria is used to select tourism products. These criteria are altered according to the purpose and features of the trip, elements of the external environment, the characteristics of the customer and the particularities and attributes of destinations.

Competitiveness of a tourist destination depends on its distinctive capabilities. Image represents an important distinctive capability of a destination. It supposes a set of attributes stemming from past actions. Respectable image and reputation ensure the creation of satisfaction and loyalty of tourists, broadening of positive attitudes and attracting new ones, the possibility of reaching premium price, creation of satisfaction and loyalty of employees, favourable assessment by financial institutions, etc.

Creation of good and recognisable reputation is a result of investing in numerous activities, the aim of which is the creation of a wanted image in the consciousness of all key constituents of an enterprise. Sustainability of local resources becomes one of the most important elements of the image of a destination. The conception of sustainable development needs marketing approach oriented towards environment and socially responsible development. In programming marketing instrument, it is necessary to start with the protection of consumer interests, environmental protection and control of available resources.

The development of marketing strategy of a tourist destination demands identification of a stage in its life cycle. The main utility of the destination life cycle is to facilitate the understanding of the evolution of tourist products and destinations and to provide guidance for strategic decision making. The life cycle of a tourist destination comprises the following stages: introduction, growth, maturity, saturation, decline. This also illustrates that different stages of the life cycle require different marketing strategies and planning actions. In the early stages demand exceeds supply whilst this relationship is reversed in the maturity and consolidation stages. Marketing strategies should focus on building awareness and promoting the destination product in the early stages of the cycle while they probably have to deal with image alteration and redesigning and re-launching the product in the later stages. The marketing mix therefore will need to be differentiated to accommodate the needs of destinations at each stage of their life cycle.

In the creation of a respectable image of a destination, tourist perception is the key factor for establishing the set of attributes that they value: attraction, accessibility, amenities, available, ancillary services, etc. Research and meeting tourists demand their segmentation and the choice of target factors. Consumers, under contemporary conditions, in order to save time and reduce expanses, often combine business trips with leisure, and leisure trips often include elements of business trips.

Business trips are not flexible, given that business meetings are determined by business possibilities and other reasons. Business trips are also seasonal with small demand intensity in certain periods of the year. The choice of a destination for business trips is determined by meeting partners, host organisations, as well as company policy. Pursue of consumer loyalty of a certain destination as an additional criterion for market segmentation sets forth the rate of loyalty, becomes the rate of loyalty and membership in the club of loyal consumers. On the other side, the choice of destination by consumers that travel for leisure is the result of the use of a complex set of criteria. This group of consumers has higher price elasticity from the previous group and therefore the price is a key element in the assessment of decision making.

Demand has a seasonal character and social status to a great extent determines the choice of a destination. In that sense, marketing channels have a great role in promoting the destination and influencing the end consumer.

Affinity groups can be operationalised as an efficient concept of market segmentation, because they are based on self-selection of individuals. An affinity group can be understood as a collection of people sharing an interest, place, concern, or ideal. Traditionally, marketing literature distinguishes four types of segmentation variables: geographic, demographic, psychographics and behavioural variables. Multi-attribute segmentation uses several variables in order to identify a smaller, well defined target group. Affinity group segmentation has to be considered as such a multi–attribute segmentation as it combines interpersonal and intrapersonal aspects to form a homogenous behavioural segment. Tourism service providers strive to attract subjects to travel to an object which may be a hotel, a museum, an amusement park to name but a few.

Challenge for Marketing of a Tourist Destination

Under the impact of the world financial crisis, important changes in the economies of all countries have been created. The impact of these changes is evident in banking sector, in decreased capital inflow, decrease of demand for products and services.

The financial and economic crises influence the business activity of all the participants in the tourism market, and impose the need for proper strategic response. Whether the holders of tourist demand will transform dangers into opportunity for success or will the threat endanger their strategic position, depends on the manner of response. Experience on the ways of the response of enterprises and organisations under the crisis conditions in the past periods is the starting but not sufficient foundation for risk reduction.

Contemporary conditions of business activity have been changed in relation to past periods and demand new ways of response. Changes are necessary in the whole value chain and demand managers to continually re-examine their business portfolio, to align strategies with the changes in the environment. Acquiring and maintaining the competitive advantage demands a response to several key issues: what is the structure and dynamics of the industry and competition like, how many competitors can survive in the long term and compete in the dynamic market, what current and potential competitors can survive, who are the vulnerable ones who are the drivers of new changes and movements within certain industries, whether an enterprise can affect the direction and intensity of the changes within the existing structures of industry and market and use all this for superior value creation.

Competitive advantage of a certain tourist destination based on comparative advantage is increasingly less sustainable. Under the contemporary conditions, competitiveness is sustainable if it is acquired and based on connecting different participants in the value chain. Networking and development of partner relations has become the key capability used for competitive advancement of certain destinations. Interdependence in the networks is a dynamic category, changeable over time and conditioned by resource engagement and capability of each involved subject in the development of optimal relationships is possible to identify different levels of relatedness between certain participants in the market. Each level of relatedness demands proper relationship management. Relations can be different: between tourist enterprises, tourist organisation at different levels, public sector, different connected organisations, civil society, state, etc. Networking is a special business connection in which partners share risks and benefits.

Relationship management in the networks is more successful if the key business processes are shaped in order to:

i) Contribute to the development of new solutions in addressing problems in the system of consumption, i.e. to the advancement of the existing ones,

ii) Increase continually the capability for acquiring and creating new inputs and their transformation into the results wanted by consumers,

iii) Create and increase leverage of connections between participants, internal as well as external involved in relationships.

By examining relevant literature it is possible to conclude that there are different network classifications. The classification used by Achrol is often used to identify the following network types: internal market networks, vertical market networks, concentric networks and possibility networks. From the perspective of competitiveness advancement of a certain destination, it is possible for each holder of tourism offer to choose the type of networks to be used for the value creation.

Certification as a Tourism Marketing Tool

The tourism industry is a marketplace. However, sustainable tourism certification programs, tourism businesses, funders, and policy makers who assume that certification will automatically attract tourists and intermediaries and generate revenues are underestimating the challenges of the marketplace. Having a marketing plan and strategy ensures success and long-term sustainability of the certification program and tourism business a win-win situation.

There are numerous definitions of marketing and what constitutes a marketing strategy. Often marketing is thought of only as the promotion of products, especially advertising and branding. A marketing strategy is the business' approach to promoting its products and services expressed in broad terms.

Marketing strategies are dynamic and interactive. They are partially planned and partially unplanned. A flexible marketing strategy allows the program to react to changes in the marketplace.

A marketing strategy, in turn, forms the basis of the marketing plan. The marketing plan contains the set of specific activities required to successfully implement a marketing strategy. Thus the marketing strategy serves as the fundamental underpinning of a marketing plan which is designed to reach marketing objectives. It is important that these objectives have measurable results.

Certification is a market-based tool. It links players in the value chain by guaranteeing, or certifying, to users that the suppliers adhere to a specific set of standards and indicators of sustainable practices. In this day of globalisation and increasing tourism to remote destinations, the certification label provides the trust and confidence bridging the various market players.

Most certification programs have insufficient funds for effective, broad-scale consumer marketing which can be notoriously expensive. In addition, they often lack expertise in marketing to tourism intermediaries the media, travel shows, or elsewhere.. Beyond these audiences, certification programs must be promoted to governments, potential funders, and relevant non-governmental organisations. Business planning should include marketing as an important line item. Effective marketing of certification programs takes time and money.

Developing a Marketing Strategy and Plan

The United Nations Environmental Program (UNEP) report "Marketing Sustainable Tourism Products" provides valuable guidance on marketing sustainable tourism products. The full report is free and available on their website.

The model used in the UNEP report is simple and applicable for certification programs. It begins with a review of the key stages of a marketing plan: Analysis, Marketing Strategy and Marketing Mix. Below are excerpts from the UNEP report:

The first stage in developing a market plan is a thorough analysis of the market, including resources, competitors, and the business environment.

The second stage is to decide on the strategic choices of how to segment markets, to determine the sectors to be targeted, and to plan an appropriate product positioning.

The last stage is to determine the marketing mix, which in its most basic sense means how the product will be offered to consumers – the price that will be charged, how the product will be communicated, and how it will be placed or distributed.

Market Analysis

The first stage in developing a market plan is a thorough analysis of the market, including resources, competitors, and the business environment.

Again, remember that certification is a market-based tool. It is critical to understand the market, the demand for the certified services and product, the competitors, and the other tourism stakeholders. This analysis provides the foundation for developing a strategy to address the threats, challenges, barriers, opportunities, and competitors. This can be done via a SWOT analysis that lists in a grid the Strengths, Weaknesses, Opportunities and Threats faced in marketing certification programs.

The marketing reports produced by CESD and TIES are based on analysis of existing marketing studies, interviews with key players in U.S., Europe, Asia-Pacific, Africa, and Latin America, and studies of successes and failures in the marketing of certification within tourism and other industries. Then finding highlighted challenges;

Creating Sufficient Supply and Demand

In order for markets to be interested in certified products (demand), there must be sufficient number of alternatives and options (supply). There must be a critical mass of certified products. This is not yet the case:

i) By 2007, total certified products in Europe were estimated to be between 6000 and 10,000; in Latin America's four programs there were 168 certified accommodations and tour operators.

ii) With certification programs spread unevenly around the world, there are limited opportunities for consumers to learn about certification.

iii) Tour operators and other marketers cannot give preference in their catalogues if there are not enough quality certified products in their market.

iv) Most 'green' tourism labels have several dozen or at the most a few hundred of certified businesses or products. One of the most successful programs, Nature's Best in Sweden, began in 2002 and by 2007 had certified 75 companies and about 300 activities.

Second we move onto Addressing Consumer and Industry Confusion. Most sustainable tourism certification programs are nationally based, operate only regionally, and have limited consumer recognition. The two main exceptions are Blue Flag and Green Globe 21, both of which operate in many countries and have gained considerable market recognition.

Blue Flag, one of the oldest and most successful tourism certification programs has certified over 3200 beaches and marinas in 39 countries across Europe, South Africa, Morocco, New Zealand, Canada and the Caribbean.

Green Globe 21 (GG21), which was first developed in the mid-1990s by the World Travel & Tourism Council (WTTC), has undergone numerous revisions which have strengthened and expanded its criteria and procedures. Now based in Australia, Green Globe 21 has "benchmarked" or "certified" over 200 accommodations and other tourism facilities in 75 countries.

While it is widely recognised that nationally or regionally based sustainable certification programs allow criteria to be tailored to local realities, there is a need for universally accepted procedures and basic criteria against which all programs can be measured and harmonised.

Building a Global Standard and Brand

At present there is no global criteria or standard for the 80-odd sustainable tourism certification programs. There are, however, two important documents that are serving informally as a template for helping to harmonise certification programs.

The second is the Baseline Criteria drawn up from existing programs by the Sustainable Tourism Certification Network of the Americas.

In Europe, surveys find that consumers support creation of a single eco-label. There are two initiatives to harmonise criteria and collectively market 'green' certification programs for accommodations: the European Union's Flower ecolabel which is awarded to tourism businesses and many other product groups that meet agreed upon core ecological and performance criteria and the VISIT (Voluntary Initiatives for Sustainability in Tourism) initiative, an NGO effort to create a network of sustainable tourism eco-labels in Europe that meet a common set of criteria certificate.

The creation of a global accreditation body, the proposed Sustainable Tourism Stewardship Council (STSC) which is being spearheaded by the Rainforest Alliance, seeks to create a framework of criteria and procedures and an easily-recognised logo that would assure all users that member certification programs meet internationally accepted standards of sustainable tourism. A worldwide accreditation logo can foment brand recognition.

The "Green Gap" and Consumer Preference

While surveys show consumer support for environmentally and socially responsible tourism, there is also evidence of a "green gap" between what consumers say they would do and actual behavior.

i) In the U.S., 80% of tourists say preserving environment is important, but only 14% say they ask if a hotel has an environmental policy.

ii) In Germany, over 70% of domestic travelers say an environmental label for tourism is important, but only 53% say they would use an eco-label, if available, to chose a vacation.

This pyramid illustrates that most fundamental to consumer decisions are health, safety, accessibility, and price issues. However, once price, quality, and safety are assured, a growing number of consumers say they prefer companies that are environmentally and socially responsible.

i) More than two-thirds of U.S. and Australian travelers, and 90% of British tourists, consider active protection of the environment, including support of local communities, to be part of a hotel's responsibility.

Lack of Marketing Staff

Few certification programs have staff or budgets dedicated to marketing. Not only do constrained resources limit an organisation's ability to promote its program, but more importantly, the organisation is often unable to monitor trends to take advantage of new market opportunities. The *Economist, Newsweek, Travel & Leisure, Plenty,* and *The New York Times* have all recently published articles about ecotourism, sustainability and certification labels.

Key Opportunities

Certification programs with limited geographical scope, small staffs, and tight budgets, can take advantage of marketing opportunities by focusing on:

i) Working with key intermediaries in the supply chain, including tour operators, the media, and guidebooks.
ii) Establishing alliances with other organisations - public or private, local or international - to reach more people.
iii) Uniting logos or brands within a region and marketing under one umbrella.

Market Strategy

The second stage is to decide on the strategic choices of how to segment markets, to determine the markets to be targeted, and to plan an appropriate product positioning.

Below is a list of steps to consider in developing a marketing strategy:

Steps to Developing a Marketing Strate

i) Build a Critical Mass:
   a) Increase consumer demand over time
   b) Leverage the supply chain
   c) Motivate businesses to become certified

ii) Incorporate health, safety, and quality standards into 'green' certification programs.

iii) Define tangible incentives to help industry buy-in to certification

iv) Understand international trade agreements to avoid conflicts

v) Promote a global accreditation body

Build a Critical Mass

There is currently insufficient awareness among consumers and the tourism industry about the value of sustainable tourism certification. On the supply side, most sustainable tourism certification programs have relatively few certified products. It is estimated that most programs have less than 50 businesses on board and that only between 1-5% of the potential pool of sustainable businesses are certified. In contrast, the best-recognised labels, such as Blue Flag for beaches for the five star quality and service labels, have thousands of certified businesses or products. A critical mass is essential for 'green' tourism certification programs to be credible, for consumer recognition to increase, and for the marketplace to have options. When developing a marketing strategy, it is important to consider several factors related to building a critical mass of certified businesses.

Consumer Demand takes Time to Build

A number of vocal critics maintain that 'green' tourism certification cannot be successful because there is little existing consumer demand. However, one of the principal conclusions of the CESD/TIES marketing studies is that successful certification programs in many industries are built over time and most start out without pre-existing consumer demand.Instead, demand develops over many years, long after industry decision-makers and intermediaries have begun to use certification as part of their due-diligence and purchasing criteria.

Certification program efforts to market directly to consumers frequently fail, at least in the first decade of a program's existence, because (a) there are initially not enough certified products; (b) the cost of direct consumer marketing is extremely high, and most certification programs have minimal income because they are striving to keep the cost of certification low and accessible to smaller businesses; (c) certification programs would have to pay the entire cost of a promotional program unlike retailers who market to consumers on a daily basis and can therefore add certification into their existing promotional packages at little additional cost; and (d) again, unlike retailers, certification programs are generally unskilled in primary consumer marketing.

Leverage the Supply Chain

Analysing the tourism commercialisation chain will help certification programs identify the most effective partners for marketing. Certification programs should ask where certification can best be marketed —"where is the most leverage?"

It is generally not effective for certification programs to target tourists directly: it is too costly and requires considerable skill. Instead, certification programs should use intermediaries. Marketing of certified products to consumers is usually most successful when done by the final intermediary, who retails products directly to the consumer. For instance, retail stores in the United States such as Lenox, Carrier, Sears, and Lowes all co-market EnergyStar certified appliances directly to the consumer, with substantial success. Similarly, consumer demand for Forest Stewardship Council (FSC) products greatly increased after retail chains such as Home Depot and Ikea adopted a purchasing policy for certified timber and after Kinko's began purchasing certified paper. Similarly, the Marine Stewardship Council (MSC) does little marketing to consumers, and instead concentrates on selling to retailers such as Legal Seafood and Whole Foods who, in turn, promote the label to consumers.

In the travel industry, tour operators are viewed as an important intermediary for marketing certified businesses and products. Many tour operators Europe, as well as a few in North America, are implementing "sustainability policies." These tour operators can help influence hotels and other businesses to become certified, just as Home Depot has exerted pressure to help motivate timber certification.

Motivate Businesses to become Certified

Unless a certification program is long established and has excellent brand recognition, simply adding a certification logo to a business's advertising is not going to increase occupancy. There are, however, two other important early gains that tourism businesses can receive from certification: 1) improved standards through compliance with recognised norms of best practices, whether for quality, environmental protection, or social responsibility, and 2) cost savings. Several studies have demonstrated important cost savings in energy and water that more than compensate for the cost of implementing certification in medium to large hotels.

The Green Tourism Business Scheme (GTBS), in Scotland, England and Europe, calculates that operating costs of its 1100 certified accommodations, attractions, and other businesses have been reduced by 10-30% and that over 30% of its members in Scotland can demonstrate an increase in profits as a result of participation in the certification program.

In addition, certification often requires substantial restructuring of poorly-run businesses and is likely to improve the quality of service of a business to meet the certification criteria. Reports from certified businesses also indicate dramatically improved staff morale and commitment, when they are involved in implementing a sustainability policy.

Certification programs should work with successful certified tourism businesses to promote the benefits of certification. For example, Green Globe 21 (GG21) encourages peer relationships among businesses interested in certification and companies that have already been certified.

Incorporate Health, Safety, and Quality Standards

Research suggests that environmental and social responsibility is important to consumers, but only once their demand for safety, quality, and price have been satisfied. In other words, a consumer who is offered a choice between a certified and a non-certified business might well choose the certified business, if all other factors are the same. Coffee and organic food certification programs only began to gain popularity when they incorporated quality along with environmental and social criteria. Stressing quality, price, and value would seem to be an essential ingredient of any 'green' tourism certification program's promotional campaign.

For certification programs there are two ways to address these important issues:

i) Businesses should already meet minimum quality and safety standards before being eligible for applying for sustainability certification, or

ii) The quality and safety criteria should be included as part of the sustainability standard.

This does not mean tourism businesses must adopt the five star system which is often inappropriate both for small businesses and for sustainability principles, but rather that it is vital that 'green' businesses also provide good service, and high standards of hygiene and safety.

For instance, Nature's Best, described as the "quality label" for Swedish ecotourism, includes "quality and safety" as one of its six basic criteria.

Define Tangible Incentives to help Build Industry buy-in to Certification

Analysis of existing certification programs reveals that there are a growing number of concrete incentives, many offered by government agencies, parks boards, guidebooks, and the media that are helping to increase business interest in becoming certified. Certification programs should work with all these public and private intermediaries to help publicise their program and certified businesses and products.

Government Incentives

Governments are increasingly recognising that certification helps ensure high standards for tourism businesses and protects a country's reputation with the public.

i) Barbados gives 150% tax deduction to businesses acquiring Green Globe 21 or other recognised certifications.

ii) The EU Commission directed that its member countries should try when possible to make its public purchases from certified and environmentally-friendly businesses, products, and services.

iii) The Canadian government's Green Travel Program encourages employees and business travelers to stay in hotels certified by Audubon Green Leaf Eco-Rating.

iv) In U.S., several states, including California, Florida, and Wisconsin, request state employees use environmentally-sound hotels whenever possible.

Tourism Boards

A number of government tourism boards are helping to publicise certified businesses.

i) The Queensland Tourism Board produced an attractive map for tourists of certified businesses. o Ecuador's Fundo de Promocion Turistica del Ecuador was established by the Ecuadorian government in 2002 in order to assist the Ministry of Tourism with its goal of promoting tourism growth.

Parks and Protected Areas

Protected area managers are increasingly looking to certification programs to help ensure that businesses operating within their parks conform to high social, environmental, quality and service standards. Some are actively providingcentives to certified businesses and products.

i) Australia's Great Barrier Reef Marine Park Authority gives longer operating license (15 years) to operators with EcoCertification.

ii) Western Australia's Conservation Department reduces fees and extends licenses for certified businesses on public lands from 1 to 3-5 years.

Guidebooks

A growing number of guidebook series are including information about certification programs and recognising certified businesses. These include Hunter Travel Guides for Ecuador & The Galapagos which has an insert on Smart Voyager, Lonely Planet for Guatemala which includes Green Deal, and Fodors guide for Costa Rica which includes information on the Certification for Sustainable Tourism (CST) program.

Understand International Trade Agreements to Avoid Conflicts

There has been concern that the large number of binding trade agreements in force, or likely to be ratified, will affect voluntary certification and the incentives that can be offered to certified businesses. However, a study of trade agreements and certification by Stanford University law professor Barton Thompson concluded that voluntary certification is not likely to violate trade agreements. Thompson's study examines the implications of General Agreement on Tariffs and Trade (GATT), Technical Barriers to Trade (TBT), General Agreement on Trade in Services (GATS), North American Free Trade Agreement (NAFTA), and Central American Free Trade Agreement (CAFTA) for the voluntary certification of sustainable tourism.

Where there is government involvement or incentives, programs must be equally applicable to all eligible businesses or products, irrespective of nationality. Tourism certification programs might have difficulty where there are government incentives that give preference to nationals over foreigners in purchasing, hiring, or ownership. Certification programs' marketing activities must ensure that there is no discrimination against any qualified businesses and that international and national businesses are treated equally.

Promote a Global Accreditation Body

It is unrealistic to achieve a single international certification program in the near future. Instead, an international baseline standard and a global accreditation body such as the Sustainable Tourism Stewardship Council (STSC) could establish credibility by establishing a mechanism to ensure that 'green' tourism certification programs meet a set of agreed upon criteria. A worldwide accreditation logo can foment brand recognition. A growing number of certification programs and networks have endorsed the STSC. These include EcoCertification in Australia, Green Deal in Guatemala, Green Globe 21, Green Seal USA, Smart Voyager in Ecuador, Sustainable Tourism International in the US.

Push and Pull Strategies for Certification Programs

Marketing resources in many certification programs are minimal or non-existent. However, as described above, there are a range of cost effective opportunities for certification programs to market smarter. While marketing benefits are only one of the reasons business get certified, the long term sustainability of certification programs will depend on building a critical mass of certified businesses and increasing the demand for certified products and services.

This involves a combination of PUSH and PULL strategies. The PUSH strategy maximises all the available channels of distribution to "push" certified product into the marketplace. This strategy includes government and business incentives, use of intermediaries and alliances. One of the most commonly touted benefits of tourism certification is that it will increase occupancy and sales to consumers. However, as discussed above, for most 'green' tourism certification programs, this has not yet been proven.

The PULL strategy is aimed at getting users of certified products and services such as travelers and tourism intermediaries – tour operators, guidebooks, websites, trade shows, parks, government agencies, tourism bureaus, socially and environmentally minded companies and institutions for instance – to DEMAND certified products and services. In doing so, these intermediaries can also help to market the certified businesses, products, and services.

The marketing plan is the recipe for certification programs to market smarter, despite limited resources and staff.

Marketing Plan or Mix

The last stage is to determine the general set of activities of the marketing plan. This includes determining the Marketing Mix or the 4Ps: Product, Pricing, Promotion, and Placement. There are many marketing models.

Product

Product management and marketing deals with the specifications of the certification program and how it relates to end-user's needs and wants.

i) Understand the market needs:

a) Consumers purchase first based first on price, quality, and safety. Therefore, 'green' certification labels must fulfill these needs, as well as ensuring environmental and social responsibility.

b) Quality and sustainability assurances should be integrated into the marketing plan.

ii) Include input from a diverse variety of stakeholders. When certification programs are designed with input and participation from a diverse variety of stakeholders.

iii) Seek alliances and support from governmental and international bodies, trade associations, and leading NGOs which can bring recognition, respect, and financing.

a) A number of certification programs are managed by ecotourism societies, including in Kenya, Sweden, and Australia.

b) Others, such as FTTSA in South Africa, Pan Parks in Europe, and Green Deal in Guatemala have been supported and promoted by leading environmental NGOs.

c) Rainforest Alliance has played a pivotal role in strengthening and promoting certification programs in the Americas, building a regional network, and raising funds, especially from the Inter-American Development Bank, to create and market new certification programs.

d) The EnergyStar program has been successfully run and marketed by the US' Environmental Protection Agency (EPA). More mixed is the experience of CST in Costa Rica.

Support the creation of an accreditation body to strengthen the marketing, particularly of nationally and regionally-based certification labels, and to promote international recognition.

Price

Pricing involves setting and marketing the cost for the certification process, including discounts, financial incentives, savings, in kind benefits, and services. Promote reduced costs energy, water, and operational that offset certification implementation costs.

Utilise financial incentives to reduce costs of certification such as tax incentives,credits, and grant programs.

Tax mechanisms dedicated to sustainable tourism programs include. airport departure taxes, tourism sales taxes, hotel taxes, land transfer taxes, and cruise passenger taxes.

Gaining access to funding from international donors, especially in developing countries. (In the Americas, the IDB has helped fund a number of programs.) Tax and license concessions for certified businesses and programs.

Document and promote positive impacts. This will serve to attract other businesses who want to become certified, as well as to encourage intermediaries and consumers to use certified businesses and products.

Promotion

This includes advertising, sales promotion, publicity, and word of mouth selling, and refers to the various methods of promoting both the certification program and certified businesses and products.

i) Provide a clear simple name or acronym and logo that captures the program's central message. Once a clear message is developed, it should be used in all communications and promotions. Work with all stakeholders – media, certified businesses, government, NGOs, etc – to get them to use the message, and provide them with materials and resources to do so.

   a) The ROC program created and run by Aboriginal Tourism Australia conveys a clear message of its core mission: "Respecting Our Culture".

   b) Also effective logos and names are Smart Voyager begun to certify boats in the Galapagos and Travel Green Wisconsin, one of the first state-wide programs in the U.S.

   c) The Blue Flag and Green Globe also logos (and names) successfully capture the spirit of each program and are now quite widely recognised.

   d) In contrast, both the CST, GTBS in Scotland, PCTS (Programa de Certificação em Turismo Sustentável) in Brazil. all suffer from awkward names and acronyms.

Gain recognition and credibility through eco-awards and endorsements.

i) For instance, Nature's Best was awarded the Swedish government's Grand Tourism Prize" in 2006 for "creating a strong label for Sweden. abroad" and awarded the Publisher's Prize in 2005, for the best Swedish webpage.

Enlist certified businesses, especially the best "success stories" to promote certification and its benefits.

1) In Costa Rica, for instance, Lapa Rios Eco-lodge, Finca Rosa Blanca Country Inn, and Horizontes Nature Tours have all earned the highest 5 Green Leaf rating under the Costa Rica's Certification for Sustainable Tourism (CST) program.

2) Many certified businesses do not take advantage of the opportunities certification offers to differentiate their business. Certified businesses should:

   a) Use the certification logo on all printed materials.

   b) Create a link from their website to the certification program.

   c) Educate travelers and intermediaries of their sustainable practices.

Identify the most appropriate and cost effective promotional channels and develop a media outreach plan.

i) Travel Media

   a) Contact airlines to explore possibilities to publish articles on sustainable tourism in their magazines and include a list of responsible tourism operations located in key destinations where the airlines travel to.

   b) Use negative news to promote standards and certification.

ii) Internet/Webpage

   a) Internet presence is critical in today's tourism commercialisation chain. In the US, over 80% of traveler's research and plan vacations on the internet.

   b) Websites as well as search engines, online guidebooks, and portals are important marketing venues for certification programs and businesses.

c) Website should include short articles or comments about tourism operators' efforts to become certified and implement best management practices.

d) Websites should including travelers' stories of their visits to certified hotels and with certified tour operators to reinforce word of mouth marketing.

e) Catalogues, brochures, and other print materials of certified companies and tourism products should be posted online for easy access and promotion.

iii) Guidebooks

a) Generally independent and rely on quality, objectivity, and trust.

b) While their influence has declined, still an estimated 10-15% of US travelers book vacations using guidebooks. Many more take guidebooks when they travel.

c) Sustainability is increasingly promoted, including certification.

iv) Familiarisation ("Fam") Trips

a) Use "fam" trips to showcase newly certified businesses or promote vacation packages using only certified businesses and products.

b) Tie familiarisation and press trips to existing or new events such as conferences and festivals.

c) Invite guidebook writers to participate in fam trips.

v) Trade Shows

a) While trade shows may not directly generate sales, they help certification programs and businesses gain exposure, make business to business, media and consumer contacts. and learn about markets.

b) Partnerships will reduce costs. The Sustainable Tourism Certification Network of the Americas and VISIT networks, for instance, market regional certification programs at various travel shows.

Placement

Placement or distribution refers to the channels by which a certification program and its businesses and projects are marketed within the commercialisation chain. By examining the commercialisation chain for tourism, 'green' certification programs can identify several important entry points to target.

i) *Marketing via Partnerships:* The formation of partnerships with a wide spectrum of interested parties for collaborative marketing can be very effective, especially when the partners exert significant or broad influence. Marketing partnerships may involve any of the following:

   a) Intermediaries such as wholesalers, distributors, tour operators, travel agents, educational travel organisers, etc., who buy tourism services and have direct contact with travelers.

   b) Non-governmental advocacy organisations that address environmental, social, indigenous and consumer issues.

      — *Green Holiday Guide Europe* by the European Center for Eco Agro Tourism.

      — *Campsite & Caravanning Guide* highlights certified sites (ADAC, Europe's leading touring club).

      — Rainforest Alliance's directory of *Certified Products in the Americas.*

   c) Other 'green' businesses and 'green' certification programs in other industries that address the same or similar markets as sustainable tourism certification, and producers and suppliers of environmentally and socially responsible products and services.

ii) *Travel agents:* used by half of US outbound travelers:

   a) Handle mainly mass tourism and therefore are less likely interested in certification o But can't afford to do due diligence and so could over time, interest could be built.

iii) *Educational Travel Programs/Affinity Groups:* such as museums, universities, zoos, etc. interested in quality & social/

environmental standards are a logical market because they need to ensure high standards.

iv) *Media Outlets:* including guidebooks, travel magazines, websites, etc., who are in the business of disseminating information and influencing their audiences.

v) *Online Travel Providers:* Large and small internet providers (such as Expedia, Responsibletourism.com) are marketing and selling sustainable tourism and increasingly recognising certified businesses.

vi) *Outbound and Inbound Operators:* while handling only a small fraction of the tourism market, they are highly motivated to use certified businesses as a tool to help ensure high environmental, social and quality/service standards.

   a) A recent global survey found more than 70% of tour operators consider "sustainable" tourism important to the quality of experience they are able to offer their customers.

   b) In Costa Rica, a group of inbound tour operators will require all accommodations they use to be certified by 2008.

vii) *Governments:* Governments benefit from sustainable tourism certification in a variety of ways: increased economies, employment opportunities, protection of sensitive areas, reduced water usage and improved waste management. Government agencies can assist certification programs through:

   a) Cooperative advertising and promotion for certified businesses at trade shows and in government-issued tourism booklets, websites and other materials. o Promotion through Ministries of Tourism and other government-sponsored tourism programs, many of which have strong tourism marketing capabilities. Protected area managers who have good reason to want to promote eco-labeling because certified businesses benefit the resources they manage.In addition to marketing, government agencies can provide a range of incentives for certified businesses. Examples include:

— Reducing interest rates on government loans and improved credit ratings.

— Offering tax credits or deductions to certified businesses.

— Providing longer term permissions preferential access to protected or sensitive areas, or discounts on concessions.

— Reducing fees for use of public resources, such as national parks.

— Providing endorsements for exemptions from certain policies or limited access regulations.

— Developing programs to help hotels and other industry sectors adopt sustainable practices.

— Offering training programs on environmental technologies, environmental management, human resources, socio-cultural practices, community relations, strategic planning, marketing, etc.

— Establishing purchasing policies requiring staff and contractors to opt for certified businesses.

— Officially endorsing certification programs, sometimes as a response for implementing environmental legislation.

The endorsement of existing certification programs by governments and multilateral agencies will enable tourism certification to move from niche to mainstream. Governmental tourism departments and institutes should include certification as part of the marketing efforts of their country. Thus the resources will be used in an environmentally responsible, socially equitable and economically viable way so that the users of the tourism products and services can meet the current needs without compromising future generations from using these same resources.

The Certification is useful to tour operators, because it:

i) Allows operator preliminary due-diligence screening, especially for new destinations and new companies. o Projects a positive image of the tour operator. Certified businesses tend to have overall high quality and service standards.

ii) Reduces costs of carrying out site inspections.

iii) (Re)insures companies require social and environmental sustainability criteria for large companies.

iv) Substitutes in-house guidelines for criteria reached through multistakeholder process and carried out through third party audits.

Finally, we question How can Certification Organisations work with Inbound and Outbound Tour Operators?

i) Educate the tour operator owners, managers and staff about your certification program and certified businesses.

ii) Provide materials to be sent to their clients (travelers) before they take their vacation.

iii) Talk to their suppliers about certification. Make sure they educate and inform their guests on what they are doing in sustainable tourism, and how it is making a difference on the natural and social surroundings.

iv) Send out to the traveler, once they have returned home, a communication that says "Your travel choice makes a difference". This communication can tell them more about sustainable tourism and certification, point them to places where they can get additional information, and encourage them to incorporate sustainability in their next trip.

REFERENCES

Crandall, Louise. (1994). The social impact of tourism on developing regions and its measurement. In. *Travel, Tourism and Hospitality Research*, second edition. J.R. Brent Ritchie and Charles R. Goeldner (eds). New York: John Wiley and Sons Inc.

Sheldon, Pauline J. (1990). *A review of tourism expenditure research. In Progress in Tourism, recreation and* hospitality management. C.P. Cooper (ed). New York: Belhaven Press.

World Travel and Tourism Council. (1993). *Measuring the size of the global travel and tourism industry*. London: WTTC.

7

Global Trends in Coastal Tourism

Tourism is the largest business sector of the world economy, accounting for 10% of global GDP, one in twelve jobs globally, and 35% of the world's export services. Since 1985, tourism has been growing an average of 9% per year. In 2005, receipts from international tourism reached US$ 6.82 trillion, an increase of $49 billion over 2004. If tourism were a country, it would have one of the world's largest GDP's, and would consume resources at the scale of a northern developed country.

Tourism has become increasingly important for developing countries, accounting for 70% of exports from the Least Developed Countries (LDCs). It is the principle foreign exchange earner for 83% of developing countries and in the 40 poorest countries, tourism and oil are the two top foreign exchange earners.

Environmental Impacts

Of particular concern for WWF are the environmental impacts of coastal and marine tourism. Tourism, probably more than any other industry, is dependent on a healthy environment. Yet because tourists naturally seek out beautiful places to spend their holidays, many of the world's most precious landscapes have been or are being targeted for tourism development and use. This can be especially damaging for coastal tourism because visitors come in search of the same conditions which tend to support high levels of biodiversity warm weather, sunshine, pristine nature, clear air, and clean water. When large numbers of tourists come to high–biodiversity areas, and the associated development is not well managed, there can be extremely negative effects on habitat integrity and drastically increased threat to vulnerable species.

In addition, the tradition patterns for constructing mass tourism infrastructure, including cutting down mangroves, can increase a destination's vulnerability. Without mangroves as a buffer, coastal resorts and other tourism facilities are at the mercy of the more intense and erratic storms which are growing in the wake of climate change. And all too frequently coastal tourism development erodes or destroys the very attractions that brought visitors there in the first place. In the Adriatic Sea, algae blooms have made the water unappealing to swimmers. Beaches have been closed in Haiti and Costa Rica because of raw sewage from hotels, while the lagoon that separates Cancun's hotel strip from the mainland, once part of the attraction, has suffered from pollution and much of the wildlife there is gone. Damage from tourism and related development has gotten so bad that Diego Masera, UNEP's director for Latin America and the Caribbean, declared that pollution and exploitation for tourism threaten or have already destroyed 90% of the coral reefs in the Caribbean.

Using consumption averages from various countries, statistics from the United Nations World Tourism Organisation (UNWTO), and projections of national tourism in relation of international arrivals, the UNEP proposed some estimates of the order of magnitude of resource consumption from tourism. The UNEP calculated that if the global tourism industry were represented as a country, it would consume resources at the scale of a northern developed country.

The most pronounced threat to biodiversity posed by tourism is land clearance and degradation resulting from tourism development. Developers in the hotspots and high-biodiversity wilderness areas are clearing out littoral forest, ripping up mangrove stands, dredging through seagrass beds, and filling in wetlands for tourism infrastructure and developments.

In this case, the picture on the left comes from a website selling land for development near Playa del Carmen, and the image on the right is an aerial shot of Playa del Carmen's increasingly dense tourism development. What isn't shown here is that inland from Playa del Carmen's beachfront is a bustling urban area where tourism industry workers and their families live.

The negative effects of physically altering the landscape can be exacerbated by the daily operating practices of tourism accommodations and attractions. The biggest concerns here are centered around water pollution which tends to result from poor wastewater treatment, solid waste disposal, and toxic chemical management. Poor run-off control during construction and afterwards can also lead to high sediment concentrations and nitrification in fresh waterways, seagrass beds, and eventually on coral reefs.

High levels of natural resource consumption can also be problematic. As tourists and new residents consume local resources, the water table can be drawn down and this can have negative effects on nearby communications, agriculture, protected areas, and other ecosystems. Water use by resorts for swimming pools, laundry, golf courses, showers, gardens, toilets and kitchens can be staggering. Additionally, visitors from diverse parts of the globe can also mean the introduction of invasive species – frequently posing a serious threat to endemic flora and fauna, particularly to fragile ecosystems like the Galapagos Islands.

Finally, as tourists flock to coastal areas for their holidays, they tend to demand that local seafood be present on the menu, and this is leading to over fishing of already strained fisheries in Zanzibar and other resort destinations. There is also a loss of by catch species that are not usually consumed, and reduced numbers of coral grazers can result in algal invasion and lowered coral productivity, as well as increased vulnerability to disease. Local governments are often poorly equipped to monitor and enforce fishing guidelines especially when demand by tourists for prized varieties of fin fish and shellfish can generate relatively high amounts of foreign currency. Persistent demand makes regulator's jobs even more challenging – and seasonal bans even harder to enforce.

Another way to catalogue the impacts of tourism on coastal ecosystems is the following table in a book by the German Federal Agency for Nature Conservation. This chart details the different ways tourism impacts as follows:

A great deal of the tourism activities and associated impacts outlined above occur in the world's most fragile ecosystems. Clearly, tourism development and related daily activity are having severe, negative impacts at a massive scale on areas of high biodiversity and existing threat.

Market Trends

After the tourism boom decade of the 1990s, with average annual global growth of 9%, the new millennium opened to what appeared to be a "perfect storm" of natural and manmade events. In quick succession, these included an economic recession. SARS virus, the 9/11 terrorist attacks and subsequent U.S. led war on terrorism in Afghanistan and Iraq, other terrorist attacks, the Indian Ocean tsunami, Hurricane Katrina and other extreme weathers, and emerging fears of a bird flu epidemic. In 2001 and again in 2003, there was a slump in tourism in many countries, and globally, international arrivals dropped by 1.2%, to 694 million in 2003.

Hardest hit were regions in eye of the war on terrorism – the Middle East and South Asia and destinations which experienced terrorist attacks, including the U.S., Kenya, Bali, Morocco, Egypt, and Spain. The 9/11 terrorist attacks caused a decline in the U.S. vacation and leisure travel market, and by the end of 2005, North America was the only sub-region in the world to have recorded a decline in arrivals since 2000. However, by in 2006, international arrivals to the U.S. had regained their pre-9/11 level and travel industry spending in the United States was valued at $700 billion – largely because of the strength of the domestic tourism market.

Tourism's strong recovery from a 'perfect storm' of unfavorable conditions between 2000 and 2004 demonstrates the industry's strength. As can be seen in the graph below, the convergence of these travel-discouraging factors resulted in a mere blip on the steep upward trajectory of global international arrivals.

The UNWTO forecasts that international arrivals are expected to reach nearly 1.6 billion by the year 2020. Of the worldwide arrivals in 2020, 1.2 billion are projected to be intraregional and 378 million to be long-haul travelers. The total tourist arrivals by region show that in 2020 the top three receiving regions will be Europe (717 million tourist arrivals), East Asia and the Pacific (397 million) and the Americas (282 million), followed by Africa, the Middle East and South Asia.

Although Europe and North America remain the top destinations in international travel, representing about 65% of all international tourist arrivals, these more mature regions are anticipated to show lower than average growth rates. Europe will maintain the highest share of world arrivals, although there will be a decline from 60% in 1995 to 46% in 2020. In addition, the more resource-intensive type of travel, long-haul, is predicted to grow even faster worldwide, at 5.4% per year over the period 1995-2020, while intra-regional travel is projected to grow at 3.8%.

Within this picture, two other tourism trends are particularly important: the role of 'baby boomers' in the U.S. and other developed countries, and the emergence of China as a major actor in tourism. More than ever before, the baby boomer generation is traveling, investing, and living overseas. According to the AARP, two times more baby boomers are traveling than 20 years ago. Some four million (non-military) Americans are living overseas, and 442,000 of these are receiving their social security checks abroad. Several countries in Central America, including Costa Rica, Panama and Belize, have special laws given tax and import duty breaks to attract foreign retirees who chose to live there. Baby boomers will be a particularly potent factor as second home sales continue to increase in parallel with the number of retirees from America and Europe. The ecological and cultural footprint of vacation homes and expatriate communities can overwhelm local resources and populations.

Meanwhile, on the other side of the globe, China is on the cusp of becoming the world's powerhouse in tourism, as more foreigners vacation in China and more Chinese travel at home and abroad. Today both international and domestic tourism in China is experiencing exceptional growth, with over 20 million international arrivals in 2005 and over 950 million domestic tourists. The rapid development of China's domestic tourism can be attributed to an increase in four major factors:

i) Disposable income,

ii) Public holidays,

iii) Motivations for travel and

iv) Travel products and services to facilitate domestic travel.

Meanwhile, China's growing middle class is no longer staying within its national borders: outbound travelers from China reached an estimated 35 million in 2006, a 13% increase over 2005, and by 2020, it is estimated that Chinese traveling outside the country will reach 100 million.

Concern, even alarm, has also grown that without sufficient management and controls, the shear number of vacationers will overwhelm China's natural and cultural attractions, from the Wolong Giant Panda Nature Reserve to the Great Wall of China. In response, a number of ecotourism projects have begun in China, particularly in and around protected areas and culturally rich areas such as Tibet. In 2006, China's first "planned ecotourism destination" was completed by an international team of architects and builders, in consultation with a rural community. Today, a growing number of tour operators are promoting ecotourism holidays in China. Given China's significant concentrations of biodiversity and cultural heritage, and in consideration of the serious threat posed by massive numbers of domestic travelers withi the country, as well as those going from China to sensitive destinations in the region, this country should be considered a high priority for tourism-related interventions.

The numbers behind tourism today can already be staggering like the $700 billion contribution tourism makes to the U.S. economy, the 650 million in international arrivals in 2006, or the 950 million domestic tourists in China in 2004 but these and similar figures are expected to continue to grow rapidly over the next dozen years.

Types of Coastal Tourism

There are a wide variety of terms describing different sectors of the tourism industry. Some describe the type of activity nature, cultural, historic, adventure, wildlife, agro–tourism. Others describe the location beach, urban, rural while still others describe the type of accommodation cruise, resort. And there are also a category of terms that seek to describe the impacts of the tourism on host communities and conservation ecotourism, geotourism, responsible tourism, pro-poor tourism, and sustainable tourism.

In terms of analysing the trends and proposing alternatives for coastal and marine tourism, it seems most important to understand the definitions of four types of tourism: beach resort tourism, cruise tourism, ecotourism, and sustainable tourism. These four types are most relevant in assessing current trends and alternative options for both coastal and marine tourism. Beach resort and cruise tourism are described below at length. Both are types of mass tourism that involve providing leisure activities to large numbers of people. In the 1950s and early 1960s, for instance, a combination of faster, long-range aircraft and U.S. statehood, helped to transform tourism in Hawaii from a scattering of lodges and hotels catering to wealthy world travelers into a mass tourism market, characterised by an expanding number of lower-priced, high-density hotels and resorts, plus retail and entertainment clusters, tours, and attractions. Both ecotourism and sustainable tourism are linked to the concept of sustainable development, as articulated in the 1987 Bruntland Report, *Our Common Future*, which says sustainable development is that which "meets the needs of the present without compromising the ability of the future generations to meet their own needs."

Importance of Ecotourism

Before turning to a fuller analysis of both coastal and cruise tourism, it is useful to describe in a bit more detail the history and significance of ecotourism and sustainable tourism because they contain the principles and good practices that, ideally, should be used for coastal and marine tourism. Ecotourism first entered the lexicon in the late 1970s and early 1980s. The concept evolved out of the new global environmental movement that took root in the 1970s, as a reaction to the environmental and social damage caused by mass tourism. Broadly stated, the roots of ecotourism can be traced to four sources:

i) scientific, conservation, and nongovernmental organisation (NGO) circles;
ii) multilateral aid institutions;
iii) developing countries; and
iv) the travel industry and traveling public.

Almost simultaneously but for different reasons, the principles and practices of ecotourism began taking shape within these four areas, and by the early 1990s, the concept had coalesced into a hot new genre of environmentally and socially responsible travel. Beginning in the early 1990s and growing into the new millennium, ecotourism became a hot new topic in the travel and environmental press and gradually even in the mainstream media.

The definition of ecotourism has, however, often been vague. The travel industry typically classifies ecotourism with nature, wildlife, or adventure tourism; it is frequently referred to as "responsible," "green," or "low-impact" tourism. By 2000, new terms such as "pro–poor tourism" and "geotourism" were complicating the picture and confusing the public. The most widely used definition was coined by The International Ecotourism Society (TIES) in 1990: "Responsible travel to natural areas that conserves the environment and improves the welfare of local people." While succinct, it omits some elements that are today considered important parts of ecotourism. A more comprehensive definition contains the following seven principles:

i) Involves travel to natural areas
ii) Minimises impacts
iii) Helps educate and facilitates interaction between the traveler and the host community
iv) Builds environmental awareness
v) Provides direct financial benefits for conservation
vi) Provides financial benefits and empowerment for local people
vii) Respects local culture, human rights, and democratic movements.

Within the tourism industry, it is difficult to calculate the size of the ecotourism sector. Unfortunately, there has been little systematic effort to gather data worldwide specifically on ecotourism as a category distinct from nature, wildlife, and adventure tourism. However, there are a range of estimates. During the 1990s, the annual growth in demand for ecotourism was said to be from 20% to 34%, while in 2004, the UNWTO estimated that ecotourism and nature tourism were growing three times faster than the tourism industry as a whole. In 2005, The Tourism Network also rated ecotourism as one of the fastest growing sectors in the tourism industry, with an annual growth rate of 5% worldwide, representing 6% of the world gross domestic product and, 11.4% of all consumer spending. Similarly, the LOHAS.

Today, ecotourism, or at least a revamped version of nature and wildlife tourism, is at the core of many Third World nations' economic development strategies and conservation efforts. Nearly every developing country is now promoting some brand of ecotourism. And the allure of pristine nature and exotic culture are major marketing tools for tourism departments in many developing countries, as the chart below illustrates.

In addition, over the last two decades, major international conservation organisations have initiated ecotourism-linked departments, programs, studies, and field projects, and many are conducting nature tours, adventure tours, or ecotours for their members. International lending and aid agencies, under the banner of sustainable rural development, local income generation, biodiversity, institutional capacity building, poverty alleviation, and infrastructure development, pump billions of dollars into projects with tourism components. According to a 2005 analysis, 12 international donors agencies, including the World Bank, U.S. In addition, the major travel industry organisations have set up programs, developed definitions and guidelines, and held dozens of conferences on ecotourism.

Over the last decade or so, the term "sustainable tourism" has emerged from within the field of ecotourism. Basically sustainable tourism involves applying the principles and good practices of ecotourism and sustainable development to sectors of the mass tourism market. As discussed later, there are growing number of certification programs designed to measure both ecotourism and sustainable tourism businesses, destinations, and activities. In distinguishing between the two concepts, ecotourism is more rigorous and has the goal of being a positive good, of enhancing and improving the environment and the host community where it operates. Sustainable tourism can be said to have a more modest goal; its aim is to do no harm, to be a net neutral on the environment and the community where it operates.

As detailed below, sustainable tourism is especially important along coasts where, largely because of the price of land, mass tourism development is typically the norm. In East Africa, for instance, growth prospects for coastal tourism in the region are strong, but environmentally sensitive and locally beneficial ecotourism products are relatively undeveloped in the coastal market. Instead, ecotourism is concentrated inland, around the national parks and private reserves, where East Africa's wildlife safari market is characterised by smaller scale ecotourism lodges, tented camps, private ranches, and small group tour operators. The same is true in Costa Rica where ecotourism is concentrated around the national parks and private reserves, most of which are not along the coasts. So the challenge is how to "green" these larger businesses so that they become sustainable over time.

All ecotourism is sustainable tourism. At present, sustainable tourism includes parts of the urban, coastal and cruise tourism sectors. Other parts of the nature-based, urban, coastal, and cruise tourism are not sustainable. Ideally, the entire tourism industry would eventually become sustainable.

Consumer Demand for Ecotourism

By the opening of the new millennium, ecotourism was no longer a 'specialty' industry with little global impact. It had become a significant economic activity, especially in developing countries, and was being used as a tool for conservation and community development. A 2005 analysis of dozens of recent surveys by the Center on Ecotourism and Sustainable Development found that more than two thirds of U.S. and Australian travelers, and 90% of British tourists, consider active protection of the environment, including the support of local communities, to be part of a hotel's responsibility. And, by 2001, half of all British tour operators said that their companies had developed some type of responsible tourism policy.

In addition, the principles and good practices of ecotourism were beginning to impact – and change – the broader, mainstream tourism industry. Green hotels, sustainable ski slopes, Blue Flag beaches and "committed to green" golf courses were signs that tourism as we had known it was beginning to change. By 2006, it seemed clear that ecotourism was being propelled forward by a rejuvenated and rapidly rising environmental consciousness. And travelers are increasingly looking for options that keep the earth and its occupants in mind: More than 75 percent of *Condé Nast Traveler* readers recently surveyed deemed it important for hotels near impoverished areas to help local people obtain education, clean water, food, and health care."

Indeed, many observers see a new green revolution in the making. While in the 1970s, the global environmental revolution led to the birth of scores of NGOs, most focused on influencing government policies, the green revolution at the opening of this millennium is driven once again by NGOs as well as by consumers, particularly the Baby Boomers. And while there is some focus on governments, a central theme is voluntary corporate social responsibility by the industry. One response has been a dramatic upswing in volunteer carbon offset programs for airline travel, as well as efforts to get the major airlines to offer such programs to their passengers.

The growth of the new green consumer movement that includes ecotourism was documented as early as 2002. According to the State Department report, "Trends in the U.S. ecotourism industry indicate growing numbers of educated ecotourists with average or above average annual family incomes, increases in the number of nature education and conservation programs, and increasing concern among the population about the degradation of resources due to poor management or overuse of ecotourism destination."

By 2007, ecotourism was indeed chic. Take, for instance, the *Knoxville News Sentinel*'s feature run on December 31, 2006. It begins, "Ecotourism – once a tiny niche in the travel industry – has grown into a worldwide multi-million dollar business."

The growth of the green hotels and green certification programs is just one of the signs of the rise and mainstreaming of environmentalism and of the growth of sustainable tourism that applies the good practices of ecotourism to larger and more mainstream sectors of the tourism industry. In 2007, for instance the American Hotel & Lodging Association, the hotel industry's leading trade organisation, announced that its next annual conference would focus on "educating the industry's leaders on best practices and the importance of environmentally-friendly green hotels."

Structure of the Tourism Industry

The tourism industry that funnels travelers to coastal and marine destinations around the world is a complex, multi-layered maze. In the country of departure, it includes travel agencies (retailers), tour operators (wholesalers), airlines, cruise lines, car rental agencies, credit card companies, public relations firms, advertising companies, tourism bureaus, and the media. In the destination or host country, it includes inbound tour operators, ground transporters, guides, accommodation facilities, national tourism bureaus, national and private parks and other recreational sites, cultural and craft centers, and special concessions such as providers of balloon, camel, and boat rides. Ecotourism and sustainable tourism receives support from conservation organisations and other NGOs, most of which are based in the United States and other developed countries but operate primarily in developing countries. One of the tenants of ecotourism and sustainable tourism is to strive to put a larger portion of the tourism dollars into host countries and communities through, for instance, hiring and buying locally and strengthening the capacity of locals to own tourism businesses.

Multinational institutions such as the World Bank, the International Monetary Fund (IMF), and the U.S. Agency for International Development (USAID) have facilitated the spread of tourism into new destinations. The American international travel industry, and especially the private airline companies, has always depended heavily on government subsidies and support. After World War II, the U.S. government used its surplus of military aircraft to subsidise the aerospace industry. It created financial institutions, such as the Export-Import Bank of the United States that gave low-interest loans to corporations for purchase of U.S.-made aircraft and equipment. U.S. assistance programs constructed and enlarged airports overseas, improved long-haul navigation, and financed development of long-range and wide body aircraft. More recently, federal funds and powerful financial institutions also have underwritten research, development, and application of computer technology for the booking of airline reservations, hotel rooms, and car rentals. This, coupled with airline deregulation policies, has enabled the integration and consolidation of the travel industry. Pan American World Airways was among the first to develop an integrated global reservation system. British Airways, working with Holiday Inn, and other airlines quickly followed the Pan Am model.

Since the 1980s, in particular, the tourism industry has been affected by economic globalisation and promotion of free trade. A proliferating number of U.S. backed international trade agreements are seeking removal of barriers, including investment regulations, labor standards, and environmental protection.

Non-tourism companies in industrialised countries have also assumed a significant role in the industry as it has globalised. Major banks, along with firms specialising in brewing, food processing, gambling, media, tele–communications, shipping and real estate, have bought shares in airlines and hotel chains. ITT Corporation, for instance, bought 100% of the Sheraton hotel chain in 1968. Midland Bank bought 78% of the Thomas Cook Group's shareholdings, and the Rothschild Group purchased a sizable slice of Club Mediterranee (Club Med).

This trend has continued. As Andrey Shlevkov, an official with the UNWTO, stated in a 2004 speech, "There is a clear trend for globalisation, concentration and consolidation in the world tourism industry competing hard for tourist euros and dollars. Just four global distribution systems dominate electronic reservations, while five global air alliances control 60% of international air traffic. In major European generating countries, a handful of tour operators dominate a lion's share of the market, and their clout may sometimes contribute to making or breaking a destination."

The five main economic agents in international tourism airlines, hotels, cruise lines, tour operators, and travel agents—have all become increasingly integrated in terms of their services, financing, management, research, and development. Take, for instance, the American Express Company, whose tourism-related activities were traditionally confined to banking, that is, the sale of traveler's checks. In the 1960s, American Express moved beyond traveler's checks, buying shares in tour operations, tourism financing companies, and computerised reservation systems. Today, American Express is the largest travel agency in the United States with offices in every important city around the globe and revenues of $29.1 billion in 2004. Worldwide spending on American Express cards in 2004 reached an all-time high of $416 billion, an 18% increase from the previous year.

American Express now handles many other travel related services, including hotel reservations and airline, cruise, and ground travel, traveler's checks and credit cards, financial and small business advice, computer services, guidebooks, passport-processing assistance, and real estate services. American Express has been an industry trendsetter in modernising, consolidating, and integrating various branches of the travel industry. The company renewed its support for conservation in 2006 with the launch of American Express Partners in Preservation, a $10 million, five-year commitment, through partnerships with the World Monument Fund and the National Trust for Historic Preservation, to ensure the preservation of cultural heritage sites around the world threatened by neglect, vandalism, armed conflict, or natural disaster. American Express is also partnered with the Caribbean Alliance for Sustainable Tourism (CAST) and the Caribbean Hotel Association (CHA), to annually recognise one large and one small hotel with the American Express Caribbean Environmental Awards.

The following are the major industry sectors in the international tourism industry that help shape coastal and marine tourism.

Airlines

The biggest–ticket item in an overseas holiday has traditionally gone to the airlines. Although the percentage varies with distance, size of group, carrier, and season, 61% of total U.S. travel agency sales went for airline tickets in 1995, with 14% going to cruise lines, 10% to hotels, 7% for car rentals, and 8% for other sales. However, by 2005, the percentage of travel agent sales going for airline tickets had fallen to about 25%, according to the American Society of Travel Agents (ASTA). The main reason has been the rapid growth of the Internet: Americans using the Internet to plan or book travel jumped 25% just between 2001 and 2002, and by 2002, airline tickets accounted for 77% of all online purchases.

With decolonisation beginning in the late 1950s, a national airline became an important symbol of political and economic independence. However, these new national airlines— sometimes with a fleet of only two or three planes—were involved in a David and Goliath contest. These deals were frequently financed by the U.S.

Export-Import Bank, which both made direct loans to foreign carriers and guaranteed loans made by commercial lenders. Other foreign airlines leased their planes and/or had management contracts with international commercial carriers such as Pan American, Compagnie Nationale Air France, and British Airways. As these nascent companies struggled to get a toehold in the international market, the big airlines from developed countries were acquiring wide-body aircraft with increased carrying capacity and decreased operating costs. They were also rapidly linking up with international hotel chains, travel agencies, tour operators, and car rental agencies for sales and promotional purposes and to offer discount tour packages. Inclusive tour packages offered by First World airline and air charter companies also undercut the market for the new national airlines.

In the 1990s, as economic liberalisation and deregulation took hold, international carriers, with hefty marketing budgets, name recognition, and hookups with other sectors of the tourism industry, entered the most lucrative foreign markets in developing countries. During this decade, Costa Rica's flagship airline, LASCA, a small but well-run operation, was gradually sold to foreign conglomerates. Without protective trade barriers to keep out competition and control fares, computer systems and other technological innovations, and integration with hotel chains, car rental agents, and tour operators, many small national airlines could not compete and were sold to foreign carriers.

In 1997, six of the top international carriers, led by USAir and United, formed the Star Alliance, which they called "the first truly global airline network in the world." The carriers agreed to meld their frequent flyer mileage programs, ground services, and airport lounge services and to simplify ticketing and link schedules "to provide seamless service on every continent." By 2006, Star Alliance included 18 airlines serving 842 destinations in 152 countries and offering travelers a choice of 15 different frequent flyer programs in which to earn mileage points. Meanwhile, American and United airlines have gained "an insurmountable edge over their Latin counterparts" because of their "vast international networks" and their "virtual lock on travel within North America," the destination of 75% of Latin Americans traveling outside the region. This, combined with high operating costs, forced more Latin American airlines to privatise, merge, or close. This phenomenon is not limited to U.S. and Latin American airlines; in Europe, the integration of Swiss International into the German-owned Lufthansa was announced in 2005, and the same year in Asia, China Eastern Airlines announced that it will consolidate with Yunnan Airlines and China Northwest Airlines.

With the rise of environmentalism and ecotourism, a number of the international carriers have given a nod to conservation by adopting some "green" practices, often in the form of fuel efficiency, which also saves on the corporate bottom line. One of the newer airline startups in the U.S., JetBlue, took steps to reduce consumption and decrease emissions by acquiring planes that burn up to 50% less fuel than older models. Japan Airlines established a set of Environmental Action Guidelines and by 2004, it had a recycling program; was purchasing more fuel-efficient airplanes, had reduced use of hazardous chemical, and had wastewater treatment systems.

Aircraft manufacturers, governments, and various agencies have also responded to rising fuel prices and environmental awareness by implementing new technologies, policies, and international agreements. General Electric has been developing a new aircraft engine, the GEnx, which is designed to deliver 15% better fuel consumption and reduce emissions to 94% below 2008 regulatory limits – while launching a huge advertising campaign hailing its 'green' practices. Manufacturers such as Boeing and Airbus continue to design newer and more fuel-efficient aircraft, such as the Boeing 787 Dreamliner and the Airbus A320. In order to reduce fuel consumption, which is the second largest cost item after employee wages, IATA has published a fuel and emissions checklist of industry "best practices", created training programs, and worked on initiatives to reduce flight time, improve airport traffic flows, and adopt more efficient operating procedures, designed to help airlines reduce fuel consumption on the scale that saved several billion dollars per year. In 2005, the Federal Aviation Administration (FAA) in the U.S. implemented a new procedure allowing more planes to fly preferred altitudes and routes, thereby saving an estimated $5.3 billion in fuel costs over the next decade.

Despite these environmental initiatives, there has been growing awareness of the impact of air transportation on climate change. Air transport is estimated to be the fastest growing source of greenhouse gases, contributing between four to ten% of carbon dioxide emissions by all types of transport. Although the world's aircraft fleet has improved its fuel efficiency by 70% in the past 40 years, global air traffic has quadrupled since 1970, from 350 billion passenger miles a year to 1,500 billion passenger miles a year. This led some to question whether long haul ecotourism is just too costly for the planet.

This is, however, hardly the solution, given that ecotourism is an increasingly important development tool for poor countries and communities as well as for biodiversity conservation. Global warming needs to be addressed on a wide range of levels, including traveling "smarter" —by, when possible, bus and train rather than car and planes, —and working in a variety of ways to reduce greenhouse gas emissions. British Airways began a program to encourage its customers to "neutralise" their travel emissions by contributing to Carbon Care which funds sustainable energy projects around the world. In 2006, Virgin Airlines CEO Sir Richard Branson captured headlines with his announcement to commit $3 billion over the next 10 years to combat global warming. Later that same year, Nature Air, a regional airline based in Costa Rica, announced that the company itself would contribute to carbon-offset programs for all its flights, thus becoming the "world's first and only emission-neutral airline." Other companies began to join the carbon-offset bandwagon. Online travel sites Expedia and Travelocity developed programs to encourage travelers to purchase carbon offsets as they bought their tickets. And shoe mogul Nike set out to reduce its offset its CO_2 footprint. Through its "Eco-Class Program," Nike teamed up with Delta Airlines and Hertz to offset airplane and auto emissions from business trips by Nike's employees.

Hotel Chains and Resorts

International hotel chains and resorts are significant components of coastal tourism in many countries. Growth is the cornerstone of any branded chain's strategy. The more flags can be planted around a country and around the world, the more a hotel chain can benefit from key customer agreements with large multinationals or tour operators to guarantee a steady flow of business.

Hotel chains typically use one of five different forms of investment in developing countries, most of which minimise their risks and maximise their ability to muscle aside small, locally owned hotels, lodges, and resorts. The types of investment used by multinationals are:

i) ownership or equity investment;

ii) management contracts;

iii) hotel leasing agreements, whereby the multinational pays the hotel owner a percentage of the profits;

iv) franchise agreements, whereby the owner uses the multinational's corporate name, services, and trademarks for a fee while maintaining certain operating standards; and

v) technical service agreements, whereby the multinational provides the local hotel with a consultant for management, marketing, and technology.

Most of the large chains no longer seek to own property, preferring "lighter" structures which require less financial commitment and reduce risk for the operator. The use of leases, management contracts, and franchises also allows for a more rapid rate of expansion. Developing countries have long paid a premium for such contracts. Whereas hotel management fees in industrialised countries range from 6 to 15% and average 12%, in developing countries they average 17% and can be as much as 23%. In addition, the international firm extracts additional fees for advertising and sales services, computerised reservation facilities, and routine inspections and consultations.

While affiliation with an international chain may be costly, it is frequently viewed as imperative in giving local investors a competitive edge over locally owned hotels — particularly in marketing, reservations, technology, training, and service standards, as well as bulk access to goods at lower marginal costs. Whereas only about 2% of the hotels in Western Europe are linked to multinational corporations through management contracts, in developing countries the proportion has approached, or well exceeded, 50%: 75% in the

Middle East, 72% in Africa, 60% in Asia, and 47% in Latin America.

Beginning in the 1990s, several prominent hotel chains — InterContinental Hotels and Resorts, Holiday Inn Worldwide, and Fairmont Hotels & Resorts — began taking steps to "green" parts of their operations. Typically, this involved reducing water and energy consumption, measures that were good for the environment while also saving money.

Along Costa Rica's Pacific coast, tourism and vacation home developments is concentrated in three zones: in Guanacaste (Papagayo, Playa Hermosa, Tamarindo), Central . Guanacaste is the main recipient of real estate investment, and is the home of the Guanacaste Conservation Area, which protects the last remnant of tropical dry forest in Mesoamerica. Guanacaste combines cattle ranches, extensive cantaloupe production, small cities and towns, protected areas areas. It is the centerpiece of Costa Rica's coastal development, where mass tourism began in early 1990s, and has been accelerating since then. Today this type of development is spreading down Costa Rica's Pacific coast. The Osa Peninsula in the South Pacific is considered as the new frontier for real estate development, with a paved road, new airport, and marina designed to attract a more mass tourism market.

In addition, the coastal regions of Costa Rica and Panama are also experiencing an increase in cruise tourism. However, as the CESD study demonstrates, cruise tourism is not as beneficial as stayovers tourism. In 2005, Costa Rica received 280,017 cruise passengers and 1,659,165 stayovers (six times more). While passenger spend an average of $55, stayovers spent $120 (two times more) per day and an average of $1260 (*23 times more*) on an average week-long stay.

References

Buckley, R. (1994). *Research Note, a framework for ecotourism*. Annals of Tourism Research. pp. 21(3):661–669.

Elper-Wood, M. (1998). *Ecotourism at a Crossroads: charting the way forward*. Nairobi, Kenya: The final report from the Conference of Ecotourism at the Crossroads.

Honey, Martha (2008). *Ecotourism and Sustainable Development: Who Owns Paradise?* (Second ed.). Washington, DC: Island Press.

8

Travelling and Health Risks

The number of people travelling internationally is increasing every year. According to statistics from the World Tourism Organisation (UNWTO), international tourist arrivals in the year 2008 reached 922 million. International tourism receipts rose to US$ 944 billion in 2008. International arrivals are expected to reach 1 billion by 2010 and 1.6 billion by 2020. In 2008, more than half of all international arrivals were motivated by leisure, recreation and holidays a total of 467 million. Business travel accounted for some 15% of arrivals and travel for other purposes for 27%. Slightly more than half of arrivals (52%) travelled by air transport in 2008 while the remainder arrived at their destinations by surface transport (48%) by road (39%), rail (3%) or over water (6%).

International travel can pose various risks to health, depending both on the characteristics of the traveller and on the type of travel Travellers may encounter sudden and significate changes in altitude, humidity, temperature and microbes, which can result in ill-health. In addition, serious health risks may arise in areas where accommodation is of poor quality, hygiene and sanitation are inadequate, medical services are not well developed and clean water is unavailable.

All individuals planning travel should receive advice on the potential hazards in their chosen destinations and understand how best to protect their health and minimise the risk of acquiring disease. Although the medical profession and the travel industry can provide a extensive help and advice, it is the traveller's responsibility to ask for information, to understand the risks involved and to take the necessary precautions for the journey.

Travel–Related Risks

Key factors in determining the risks to which a traveller may be exposed are:

i) Mode of transport;

ii) Destination(s);

iii) Duration and season of travel;

iv) Purpose of travel;

v) Standards of accommodation and food hygiene;

vi) Behaviour of the traveller; and

vii) Underlying health of the traveller.

Destinations where accommodation, hygiene and sanitation, medical care and water quality are of a high standard pose relatively few serious risks to the health of travellers, unless there is pre-existing illness. In contrast, destinations where accommodation is of poor quality, hygiene and sanitation are inadequate, medical services do not exist and clean water is unavailable may pose serious risks for the health of travellers.

The epidemiology of infectious diseases in the destination country is of importance to travellers. Travellers and travel medicine practitioners should be aware of the occurrence of any disease outbreaks in their destination countries. Unforeseen natural or man made disasters may occur; outbreaks of known or newly emerging infectious diseases are often unpredictable.

The mode of transportation, duration of visit(s) and the behaviour and lifestyle of the traveller are important in determining the likelihood of exposure to infectious agents and will influence decisions on the need for certain vaccinations or antimalarial medication. The duration of visit(s) may also determine whether the traveller is subjected to marked changes in temperature and humidity or to prolonged exposure to atmospheric pollution.

The purpose of the visit is critical in relation to the associated health risks. A business trip to a city, where the visit is spent in a hotel and/or conference centre of high standard, or a tourist trip to a well-organised resort involves fewer risks than a visit to a remote rural area, whether for work or pleasure. However, behaviour also plays an important role.

Whatever their destination or mode of travel, travellers should be aware of the risk of accidents, mainly in relation to road transport or the practice of sports.

Medical Consultation Before Travel

Any traveller intending to visit a destination in a developing country should consult a travel medicine clinic or medical practitioner before the journey. This consultation should take place at least 4–8 weeks before the journey and preferably earlier if long-term travel or overseas work is envisaged. However, last-minute travellers can also benefit from a medical consultation, even as late as the day before travel.

Dental and—for women— gynaecological check-ups are advisable before prolonged travel to developing countries or to remote areas. Travellers with underlying medical problems are strongly advised to consult a travel medicine clinic or medical practitioner to ensure that their potentially complex travel health needs are met.

Health Risks Associated with Travel

Medical advisers base their recommendations, including those for vaccinations and other medication, on an assessment of risk for the individual traveller, which takes into account the likelihood of acquiring a disease and how serious this might be for the traveller concerned. Key elements of this risk assessment are the destination(s), duration and purpose of the travel, the type of transport to be used, standards of accommodation and the health status of the traveller.

For each disease being considered, an assessment is also made of:

i) Availability of prophylaxis, emergency treatment packs, self-treatment kits possible side-effects and suitability for the traveller concerned;

ii) Any associated public health risks.

Collecting the information required to make a risk assessment involves detailed questioning of the traveller. A checklist or protocol is useful to ensure that all relevant information is obtained and recorded. The traveller should be provided with a personal record of the vaccinations given as vaccinations are often administered at different centres.

Medical Kit and Toilet Items

Sufficient medical supplies should be carried to meet all foreseeable needs for the duration of the trip.

A medical kit should be carried for all destinations where there may be significant health risks, particularly those in developing countries and/or where the local availability of specific medications is uncertain.

Certain categories of prescription medicine or special medical item should be carried together with a medical attestation on headed paper, signed by a physician, certifying that the traveller requires the medication or the items for medical condition. Some countries require not only a physician but also the national health administration to sign this attestation.

Toilet items should also be carried in sufficient quantity for the entire visit unless their availability at the travel destination is assured. These will include items for dental care, eye care skin care and personal hygiene.

Contents of a basic medical kit First-aid items:

1) Adhesive tape
2) Antiseptic wound cleanser
3) Bandages
4) Emollient eye drops
5) Insect repellent
6) Insect bite treatment
7) Antihistamine cream or tablets
8) Nasal decongestant
9) Oral rehydration salts
10) Scissors and safety pins
11) Simple analgesic

12) Sterile dressing
13) Clinical thermometer
14) Sunscreens
15) Earplugs

Additional items according to destination and individual needs:

1) antidiarrhoeal medication (to include an antibiotic, an antimotility drug and oral rehydration sachets with appropriate written instructions regarding their use)
2) Broad spectrum antibiotics (e.g. fucloxacillin, amoxicillin)
3) antifungal powder
4) antimalarial medication
5) bednet
6) Adequate supplies of condoms and the oral contraceptive
7) Medication for any pre-existing medical condition
8) Sedatives
9) Sterile syringes and needles
10) Water disinfectant
11) Sunscreen
12) Other items to meet foreseeable needs, according to the destination and duration of the visit

Travel by Air

The volume of air traffic has risen steeply in recent years and "frequent flyers" now make up a substantial proportion of the travelling public. The number of long-distance fights has increased. According to the International Civil Aviation Organisation, passenger traffic is projected to double between 2006 and 2020.

Air travel, particularly over long distances, exposes passengers to a number of factors that may have an effect on their health and well-being. Passengers with pre-existing health problems and those receiving medical care are more likely to be affected and should consult their doctor or a travel medicine clinic in good time before travelling. Health risks associated with air travel can be minimised if the traveller plans carefully and takes some simple precautions before, during and after the fight.

Then we have Cabin Air Pressure. Although aircraft cabins are pressurised, cabin air pressure at cruising altitude is lower than air pressure at sea level. At typical cruising altitudes in the range 11 000–12 200 m (36 000–40 000 feet), air pressure in the cabin is equivalent to the outside air pressure at 1800–2400 m (6000–8000 feet) above sea level.

Oxygen and Hypoxia

Cabin air contains ample oxygen for healthy passengers and crew. However, because cabin air pressure is relatively low, the amount of oxygen carried in the blood is reduced compared with sea level. Passengers with certain medical conditions, particularly heart and lung diseases and blood disorders such as anaemia may not tolerate this reduced oxygen level (hypoxia) very well. Some of these passengers are able to travel safely if arrangements are made with the airline for the provision of an additional oxygen supply during fight. An additional charge is often levied on passengers who require supplemental oxygen to be provided by the airline.

Gas Expansion

As the aircraft climbs, the decreasing cabin air pressure causes gases to expand. Similarly, as the aircraft descends, the increasing pressure in the cabin causes gases to contract. These changes may have effects where gas is trapped in the body.

Gas expansion during the climb causes air to escape from the middle ear and the sinuses, usually without causing problems. This airflow can sometimes be perceived as a "popping" sensation in the ears. As the aircraft descends, air must flow back into the middle ear and sinuses in order to equalise pressure differences. If this does not happen, the ears or sinuses may feel as if they are blocked and, if the pressure is not equalised, pain can result. Swallowing, chewing or yawning will usually relieve any discomfort. As soon as it is recognised that the problem will not resolve, a short forceful expiration against a pinched nose and closed mouth should be tried and will usually help.

For infants, feeding or giving a pacifier to stimulate swallowing may reduce the symptoms.

Individuals with ear, nose and sinus infections should avoid flying because pain and injury may result from the inability to equalise pressure differences.

As the aircraft climbs, expansion of gas in the abdomen can cause discomfort, although this is usually mild.

Some forms of surgery and other medical treatments or diagnostic tests may introduce air or other gas into a body cavity. Passengers who have recently undergone such a procedure should ask a travel medicine physician or their treating physician how long they should wait before undertaking air travel.

Cabin Humidity and Dehydration

The humidity in aircraft cabins is low, usually less than 20%. Low humidity may cause skin dryness and discomfort of the eyes, mouth, nose and exposed skin but presents no risk to health. Using a skin moisturising lotion, saline nasal spray to moisturise the nasal passages, and spectacles rather than contact lenses can relieve or prevent discomfort. The available evidence has not shown the low humidity to cause internal dehydration and there is no need to drink more than useful.

Ozone

Ozone is a form of oxygen that occurs in the upper atmosphere and may enter the aircraft cabin together with the fresh-air supply. In older aircraft, it was found that the levels of ozone in cabin air could sometimes lead to irritation of the lungs, eyes and nasal tissues. Ozone is broken down by heat and a significant amount of ozone is removed by the compressors that provide pressurised air for the cabin. In addition, most modern long–haul jet aircraft are fitted with equipment that breaks down any remaining ozone.

Cosmic Radiation

Cosmic radiation is made up of radiation that comes from the sun and from outer space. The Earth's atmosphere and magnetic field are natural shields and cosmic radiation levels are therefore lower at lower altitudes. Cosmic radiation is more intense over polar regions than over the equator because of the shape of the Earth's magnetic field and the "fattening" of the atmosphere over the poles.

Motion Sickness

Except in the case of severe turbulence, travellers by air rarely suffer from motion sickness. Those who do suffer should request a seat in the midsection of the cabin where movements are less pronounced, and keep the motion sickness bag, provided at each seat, readily accessible.

Immobility and Circulatory Problems

Contraction of muscles is an important factor in helping to keep blood flowing through the veins, particularly in the legs. Prolonged immobility, especially when seated, can lead to pooling of blood in the legs, which in turn may cause swelling, stiffness and discomfort.

It is known that immobility is one of the factors that may lead to the development of a blood clot in a deep vein so-called "deep vein thrombosis" or DVT. During long-distance travel, whether by car, bus, train or air. WHO set up a major research study, WHO Research Into Global Hazards of Travel (WRIGHT), in order to establish whether the risk of venous thromboembolism (VTE) is increased by air travel, to determine the magnitude of the risk and the effect of other factors on the risk, and to study the effect of preventive measures. The findings of the epidemiological studies indicate that the risk of venous thromboembolism is increased 2 to 3-fold after long–haul fights (>4 h) and also with other forms of travel involving prolonged seated immobility.

In most cases of DVT, the clots are small and do not cause any symptoms. The body is able to gradually break down the clots and there are no long-term effects. Larger clots may cause symptoms such as swelling of the leg, tenderness, soreness and pain. Occasionally a piece of a clot may break off and travel with the bloodstream, to become lodged in the lungs. This can occur many hours or even days after the formation of the clot in the leg.

The risk of developing DVT when travelling is increased in the presence of other risk factors, including:

1) Previous DVT or pulmonary embolism
2) History of DVT or pulmonary embolism in a close family member
3) Use of estrogen therapy – oral contraceptives ("the pill") or hormone-replacement therapy (HRT)
4) Pregnancy
5) Recent surgery or trauma, particularly to the abdomen, pelvic region or legs
6) Cancer
7) Obesity
8) Some inherited blood-clotting abnormalities.

DVT occurs more commonly in older people. Some researchers have suggested that there may be a risk from smoking and from varicose veins.

It is advisable for people with one or more of these risk factors to seek specific medical advice from their doctor or a travel medicine clinic in good time before embarking on a fight of four or more hours.

Precautions

The benefit of most precautionary measures in passengers at particular risk for DVT are unproven and some might even result in harm. Further studies to identify effective preventive measures are ongoing. However, some general advice for such passengers is given here.

i) Moving around the cabin during long fights will help to reduce any period of prolonged immobility, although this may not always be possible.
ii) Many airlines provide helpful advice on exercises that can be carried out in the seat during fight.
iii) Hand luggage should not be placed where it restricts movement of the legs and feet, and clothing should be loose and comfortable.
iv) In view of the clear risk of significant side–effects and absence of clear evidence of benefit, passengers are advised not to use aspirin specifically for the prevention of travel–related DVT.
v) Those travellers at greatest risk of developing DVT may be prescribed specific treatments and should consult their doctor for further advice.

Diving

Divers should avoid flying soon after diving because of the risk that the reduced cabin pressure may lead to decompression sickness . It is recommended that they do not fly until at least 12 h after the last dive; this period should be extended to 24 h after multiple dives or after diving that requires decompression stops during ascent to the surface. Passengers who undertake recreational diving before flying should seek specialist advice from diving schools.

Jet Lag

Jet lag is the term used for the symptoms caused by the disruption of the body's "internal clock" and the approximate 24-hour (circadian) rhythms it controls. Disruption occurs when crossing multiple time zones, i.e. when flying east to west or west to east. Jet lag may lead to indigestion and disturbance of bowel function, general malaise, daytime sleepiness, difficulty in sleeping at night, and reduced physical and mental performance.

Jet lag cannot be prevented but there are ways of reducing its effects. Travellers who take medication according to a strict timetable should seek medical advice from their doctor or a travel medicine clinic before their journey.

General measures to reduce the effects of jet lag:

i) Be as well rested as possible before departure, and rest during the fight. Short naps can be helpful.

ii) Eat light meals and limit consumption of alcohol. Alcohol increases urine output, with the result that sleep may be disturbed by the need to urinate.

iii) At the destination, try to create the right conditions when preparing for sleep and to get as much sleep in every 24 h as normal. A minimum block of 4 h' sleep during the local night known as "anchor sleep" is thought to be necessary to allow the body's internal clock to adapt to the new time zone.

iv) The cycle of light and dark is one of the most important factors in setting the body's internal clock. Exposure to daylight, preferably bright sunlight, at the destination will usually help adaptation.

v) Sleep patterns may also be helped by temperature control. When flying west, a warm shower in the evening helps with staying awake; when flying east, a cool shower in the evening is recommended to facilitate sleep.

vi) Short-acting sleeping pills may be helpful. They should be used only in accordance with medical advice and should not normally be taken during the fight, as they may increase immobility and therefore the risk of developing DVT.

vii) Melatonin is available in some countries. It is normally sold as a food supplement and therefore is not subject to the same strict control as medications. The timing and effective dosage of melatonin have not been fully evaluated and its side–effects, particularly in long–term use, are unknown.

viii) Trying to adjust to local time for short trips of up to 2–3 days may not be the best coping strategy, because the body clock may not have an opportunity to synchronise to the new time zone, and resynchronisation to the home time zone may be delayed after the return fight.

ix) Individuals react in different ways to time zone changes. Frequent flyers should learn how their own bodies respond and adopt habits accordingly.

Travellers with Special Needs

Airlines have the right to refuse to carry passengers with conditions that may worsen, or have serious consequences, during the fight. They may require medical clearance from their medical department/adviser if there is an indication that a passenger could be suffering from any disease or physical or mental condition that:

i) May be considered a potential hazard to the safety of the aircraft;

ii) Adversely affects the welfare and comfort of the other passengers and/or crew members;

iii) Requires medical attention and/or special equipment during the fight;

iv) May be aggravated by the fight.

If cabin crew suspect before departure that a passenger may be ill, the aircraft's captain will be informed and a decision taken as to whether the passenger is fit to travel, needs medical attention or presents a danger to other passengers and crew or to the safety of the aircraft.

Infants

A fit and healthy baby can travel by air 48 h after birth, but it is preferable to wait until the age of 7 days. Until their organs have developed properly and stabilised, premature babies should always undergo a medical clearance before travelling by air. Changes in cabin air pressure may upset infants; this can be helped by feeding or giving a pacifiers to stimulate swallowing.

Pregnant Women

Pregnant women can normally travel safely by air, but most airlines restrict travel in late pregnancy. Typical guidelines for a woman with an uncomplicated pregnancy are:

i) After the 28th week of pregnancy, a letter from a doctor or midwife should be carried, confirming the expected date of delivery and that the pregnancy is normal;

ii) For single pregnancies, flying is permitted up to the end of the 36th week;

iii) For multiple pregnancies, flying is permitted up to the end of the 32nd week.

Each case of complicated pregnancy requires medical clearance.

Pre–Existing Illness

Most people with medical conditions are able to travel safely by air, provided that necessary precautions, such as the need for additional oxygen supply, are considered in advance.

Those who have underlying health problems such as cancer, heart or lung disease, anaemia and diabetes, who are on any form of regular medication or treatment, who have recently had surgery or been in hospital, or who are concerned about their fitness to travel for any other reason should consult their doctor or a travel medicine clinic before deciding to travel by air.

Medication that may be required during the journey, or soon after arrival, should be carried in the hand luggage.

Frequent Travellers with Medical Conditions

A frequent traveller who has a permanent and stable underlying health problem may obtain a frequent traveller's medical card from the medical or reservation department of many airlines. This card is accepted, under specified conditions, as proof of medical clearance and for identification of the holder's medical condition.

Dental/Oral Surgery

Recent dental procedures such as fillings are not usually a contraindication to flying. However, unfinished root canal treatment and dental abscesses are reasons for caution, and it is recommended that each individual seek advice with regard to travel plans from the surgeon or dental practitioner most familiar with their case.

Security Issues

Security checks can cause concerns for travellers who have been fitted with metal devices such as artificial joints, pacemakers or internal automatic defibrillator. Some pacemakers may be affected by modern security screening equipment and any traveller with a pacemaker should carry a letter from their doctor.

Smokers

Almost all airlines now ban smoking on board. Some smokers may find this stressful, particularly during long fights, and should discuss the issue with a doctor before travelling.

Travellers with Disabilities

A physical disability is not usually a contraindication for travel. A passenger who is unable to look after his or her own needs during the fight will need to be accompanied by an escort able to provide all necessary assistance. Travellers confined to wheelchairs should be advised against deliberately restricting fuid intake before or during travel as a means of avoiding use of the toilet during fights, as this may be detrimental to overall health.

Airlines have regulations on conditions of travel for passengers with disabilities. Disabled passengers should contact airlines for guidance in advance of travel; the airlines' own web sites often give useful information.

Transmission of Communicable Diseases on Aircraft

Research has shown that there is very little risk of any communicable disease being transmitted on board an aircraft.

The quality of aircraft cabin air is carefully controlled. Ventilation rates provide a total change of air 20–30 times per hour. Most modern aircraft have recirculation systems, which recycle up to 50% of cabin air. The recirculated air is usually passed through HEPA filters, of the type used in hospital operating theatres and intensive care units, which trap dust particles, bacteria, fungi and viruses.

Transmission of infection may occur between passengers who are seated in the same area of an aircraft, usually as a result of the infected person coughing or sneezing or by touch. This is no different from any other situation in which people are close to each other, such as on a train or bus or in a theatre. Highly contagious conditions, such as influenza, are more likely to be spread to other passengers in situations where the aircraft ventilation system is not operating.

Transmission of tuberculosis (TB) on board commercial aircraft during long-distance fights was reported during the 1980s, but no case of active TB disease resulting from exposure on board has been identified subsequently. Nevertheless, increasing air travel and the emergence of drug-resistant TB require continuing vigilance to avoid the spread of infection during air travel.

During the outbreak of severe acute respiratory syndrome (SARS) in 2003, the risk of transmission of the disease in aircraft was very low.

To minimise the risk of passing on infections, passengers who are unwell, particularly if they have a fever, should delay their journey until they have recovered. Passengers with a known active communicable disease should not travel by air.

Aircraft Disinsection

Many countries require disinsection of aircraft (to kill insects) arriving from countries where diseases that are spread by insects, such as malaria and yellow fever, occur. There have been a number of cases of malaria affecting individuals who live or work in the vicinity of airports in countries where malaria is not present, thought to be due to the escape of malaria.

Disinsection is a public health measure that is mandated by the International Health Regulations. It involves treatment of the interior of the aircraft with insecticides specified by WHO. The different procedures currently in use are as follows:

i) Treatment of the interior of the aircraft using a quick-acting insecticide spray immediately before takeoff, with the passengers on board;

ii) Treatment of the interior of the aircraft on the ground before passengers come on board, using a residual-insecticide aerosol, plus additional in-fight treatment with a quick-acting spray shortly before landing;

iii) Regular application of a residual insecticide to all internal surfaces of the aircraft, except those in food preparation areas.

Travellers are sometimes concerned about their exposure to insecticide sprays during air travel, and some have reported feeling unwell after spraying of aircraft for disinsection.

Medical Assistance on Board

Airlines are required to provide minimum levels of medical equipment on aircraft and to train all cabin crew in first aid. The equipment carried varies, with many airlines carrying more than the minimum level of equipment required by the regulations. Equipment carried on a typical international fight would include:

i) One or more first-aid kits, to be used by the crew;

ii) A medical kit, normally to be used by a doctor or other qualified person, to treat in-fight medical emergencies.

An automated external defibrillator (AED), to be used by the crew in case of cardiac arrest, is also carried by several airlines.

Cabin crew are trained in the use of first-aid equipment and in carrying out first-aid and resuscitation procedures.

Contraindications to Air Travel.

Travel by air is normally contraindicated in the following cases:

i) Infants less than 48 h old.

ii) Women after the 36th week of pregnancy.

iii) Those suffering from:

   a) Angina pectoris or chest pain at rest;

   b) Any active communicable disease;

   c) Decompression sickness after diving;

   d) Increased intracranial pressure due to haemorrhage, trauma or infection;

   e) Infections of the sinuses or of the ear and nose, particularly if the Eustachian tube is blocked;

   f) Recent myocardial infarction and stroke ;

   g) Recent surgery or injury where trapped air or gas may be present, especially abdominal trauma and gastrointestinal surgery, craniofacial and ocular injuries, brain operations, and eye operations involving penetration of the eyeball;

   h) Severe chronic respiratory disease, breathlessness at rest, or unresolved pneumothorax;

   i) Sickle–cell anaemia;

   j) Psychotic illness, except when fully controlled.

The above list is not comprehensive, and fitness for travel should be decided on a case-by-case basis.

Travel by Sea

The passenger shipping industry has expanded considerably in recent decades. In 2008, 13 million passengers worldwide travelled on cruise ships. Cruise itineraries cover all continents, including areas that are not easily accessible by other means of travel. The average duration of a cruise is about seven days, but cruise voyages can last from several hours to several months.

The revised International Health Regulations address health requirements for ship operations and construction. There are global standards regarding ship and port sanitation and disease surveillance, as well as response to infectious diseases. Guidance is given on provision of safe water and food, on vector and rodent control, and on waste disposal. According to Article 8 of the International Labour Organisation Convention (No. 164) "Concerning Health Protection and Medical Care for Seafarers" (1987), vessels carrying more than 100 crew members on an international voyage of three days or longer must provide a physician for care of the crew. The contents of the ship's medical chest must be in accordance with the international recommendations and national laws for ocean-going trade vessels, but there are no special requirements for additional drugs for passenger ships.

The average traveller on a cruise line is 45–50 years of age. Senior citizens represent about one-third of passengers. Cruises of longer duration often attract older travellers, a group likely to have more chronic medical problems, such as heart and lung disease. More than half of all emergency visits to health clinics on board are made by passengers who are over 65 years of age; the most common health problems are respiratory tract infection, injuries, motion sickness and gastrointestinal illness. Extended periods away from home, especially days at sea, make it essential for passengers to stock up with sufficient medical supplies.

It is important to view a ship's medical facility as an infirmary and not as a hospital. Although most of the medical conditions that arise aboard ship can be treated as they would be at an ambulatory care centre at home, more severe problems may require the patient to be treated in a fully staffed and equipped land-based hospital after stabilisation on the ship. Most cruise vessels do not have assigned space for a dental office, and very few have a resident dentist.

The rapid movement of cruise ships from one port to another, with the likelihood of wide variations in sanitation standards and infectious disease exposure risks, often results in the introduction of communicable diseases by embarking passengers and crew members. In the relatively closed and crowded environment of a ship, disease may spread to other passengers and crew members; diseases may also be disseminated to the home communities of disembarking passengers and crew members. More than 100 disease outbreaks associated with ships have been identified in the past 30 years. This is probably an underestimate because many outbreaks are not reported and some may go undetected. Such outbreaks are of concern because of their potentially serious health consequences and high costs to the industry. In recent years, infuenza and norovirus outbreaks have been public health challenges for the cruise industry.

Communicable Diseases

Gastrointestinal Disease

Most of the detected gastrointestinal disease outbreaks associated with cruise ships have been linked to food or water consumed on board ship. Factors that have contributed to outbreaks include contaminated bunkered water, inadequate disinfection of water, potable water contaminated by sewage on ship, poor design and construction of storage tanks for potable water, deficiencies in food handling, preparation and cooking, and use of seawater in the galley.

Norovirus is the most common pathogen implicated in outbreaks. Between 1 January and 5 July 2006, 42 reported outbreaks of gastroenteritis on 13 different cruise ships sailing in European waters were confirmed or suspected to be caused by norovirus. Symptoms often start with sudden onset of vomiting and/or diarrhoea. There may be fever, abdominal cramps and malaise. The virus can spread in food or water or from person to person; it is highly infectious and in an outbreak on a cruise ship, more than 80% of the passengers can be affected. Some cruise companies ask that those who present with gastrointestinal symptoms at on-board medical centres are put into isolation until at least 24 h after their last symptoms, and some ships also isolate asymptomatic contacts for 24 h.

Infuenza and other Respiratory Tract Infections

Respiratory tract infections are frequent among cruiseship travellers. Travellers from areas of the world where infuenza viruses are in seasonal circulation may introduce such viruses to regions of the world where infuenza is not in seasonal circulation. Crew members who serve passengers may become reservoirs for influenza infection and may transmit disease to passengers on subsequent cruises.

Legionellosis

Legionellosis (legionnaires' disease) is a potentially fatal form of pneumonia, first recognised in 1976. The disease is normally contracted by inhaling *Legionella* bacteria deep into the lungs. *Legionella* species can be found in tiny droplets of water (aerosols) or in droplet nuclei. More than 50 incidents of legionellosis, involving over 200 cases, have been associated with ships during the past three decades.Prevention and control depend on proper disinfection, filtration and storage of source water, designing piping systems without dead ends. Regular cleaning and disinfection of spas are required to reduce the risk of legionellosis on ships.

Other Communicable Diseases

The outbreaks of varicella and rubella that have occurred underscore the need for passengers to make sure that they are up to date with routine vaccinations; major cruise ship companies are requesting that their crew be vaccinated against varicella and rubella.

Non–Communicable Diseases

Because of temperature and weather variations, changes in diet and physical activities, the cruise ship traveller may experience worsening of existing chronic health conditions. Cardiovascular events are the most common cause of mortality on cruise ships.Injuries and dental emergencies are also frequently reported.

Precautions

The risk of communicable and noncommunicable diseases among cruise ship passengers and crew members is difficulty to quantify because of the broad spectrum of cruise ship experiences, the variety of destinations and the limited available data. In general, cruise ship travellers should:

i) Consult their healthcare provider, a physician or travel health specialist before embarking. This may provide prevention guidelines and immunisations, specifically taking into account:

   a) The health status of the cruise ship traveller, the duration of travel, the countries to be visited and likely activities ashore;

b) All routinely recommended age and medical condition–specific immunisations;

c) infuenza vaccination as available regardless of season, particularly if the traveller belongs to one of the groups for whom annual vaccination against infuenza is routinely recommended.

d) Immunisation and other recommendations that apply to each country on the itinerary;

e) Medication against motion sickness, particularly if the traveller is prone to motion sickness.

ii) See a dentist to make sure they have good oral health and no active problems.

iii) Consider purchasing a special health insurance policy for trip cancellation, additional medical coverage and/or medical evacuation if necessary.

iv) Abstain to embark on their cruise if they are symptomatic with acute illness.

v) Carry all prescription medicines in the original packet or container, together with a physician's letter.

vi) Carry out frequent hand-washing, either with soap and water or using an alcohol-based hand sanitiser.

vii) Avoid self-medication in the case of diarrhoea or high fever while on board, but report immediately to the ship's medical service.

TRAVELLERS WITH PRE-EXISTING MEDICAL CONDITIONS

Health risks associated with travel are greater for certain groups of travellers, including infants and young children, pregnant women, the elderly, the disabled, and those who have preexisting health problems. Health risks may also vary depending on the purpose of travel, such as travel for the purpose of visiting friends and relatives or for religious purposes/pilgrimages, for relief work or for business. All of these travellers need general medical advice and specific travel health advice, including special precautions.

Air travel may cause discomfort to infants as a result of changes in cabin air pressure and is contraindicated for infants less than 48 h old. Infants and young children are particularly sensitive to sudden changes in altitude and to ultraviolet radiation. They have special needs with regard to vaccinations and antimalarial precautions. They become dehydrated more easily than adults in the event of inadequate fluid intake or loss of fuid as a result of diarrhoea and can be overcome by dehydration within a few hours.

Travel is not generally contraindicated during pregnancy until close to the expected date of delivery, provided that the pregnancy is uncomplicated and the woman's health is good. It is safest for pregnant women to travel during the second trimester. Airlines impose some travel restrictions in late pregnancy and in the neonatal period.

Pregnant women risk serious complications if they contract malaria or viral hepatitis E. Travel to areas endemic for these diseases should be avoided during pregnancy if at all possible.

Medication of any type during pregnancy should be taken only in accordance with medical advice.

Travel to high altitudes or to remote areas is not advisable during pregnancy.

Physical disability is not usually a contraindication for travel if the general health status of the traveller is good. Airlines have regulations on the conditions for travel for disabled passengers who need to be accompanied. Information should be obtained from the airline in advance.

People suffering from chronic illnesses should seek medical advice before planning a journey. Conditions that increase health risks during travel include:

1) Cardiovascular disorders
2) Chronic hepatitis
3) Chronic infammatory bowel disease
4) Chronic renal disease requiring dialysis
5) Chronic respiratory diseases
6) Diabetes mellitus
7) Epilepsy
8) immunosuppression due to medication or to HIV infection

9) Previous thromboembolic disease
10) Severe anaemia
11) Severe mental disorders
12) Any chronic condition requiring frequent medical intervention

Any traveller with a chronic illness should carry all necessary medication and medical items for the entire duration of the journey. All medications, especially prescription medications, should be stored in carry-on luggage, in their original containers with clear labels. A duplicate supply carried in the checked luggage is a safety precaution against loss or theft.

The traveller should carry the name and contact details of their physician on their person with other travel documents, together with information about the medical condition and treatment, and details of medication and prescribed doses. A physician's attestation certifying the necessity for any drugs or other medical items carried by the traveller that may be questioned by customs officials should also be carried.

Insurance for Travellers

All travellers should be strongly advised to travel with comprehensive travel insurance as a matter of routine. International travellers should be aware that medical care abroad is often available only at private medical facilities and may be costly. If death occurs abroad, repatriation of the body can be extremely expensive and may be difficult to arrange. Travellers should be advised (i) to seek information about possible reciprocal healthcare agreements between the country of residence and the destination country, and (ii) to obtain special travellers' health insurance for destinations where health risks are significant and medical care is expensive or not readily available.

Travel agents and tour operators usually provide information about travellers' health insurance. It should be noted that some countries now require proof of adequate health insurance as a condition for entry. Travellers should know the procedures to follow to obtain assistance and reimbursement. A copy of the insurance certificate and contact details should be carried with other travel documents in the hand luggage.

ROLE OF TRAVEL INDUSTRY PROFESSIONALS

Tour operators, travel agents, airline and shipping companies each have an important responsibility to safeguard the health of travellers. It is in the interests of the travel industry that travellers have the fewest possible problems when travelling to, and visiting, foreign countries. Contact with travellers before the journey provides a unique opportunity to inform them of the situation in each of the countries they are visiting. The travel agent or tour operator should provide travellers with the following health-related guidance:

i) Advise the traveller to consult a travel medicine clinic or medical practitioner as soon as possible after planning a trip to any destination where significant health risks may be foreseen.

ii) Advise last-minute travellers that a visit should be made to a travel medicine clinic or medical practitioner, even up to the day before departure.

iii) Inform travellers of any particular hazards to personal safety and security presented by the destination and suggest appropriate precautions.

iv) Encourage travellers to take out comprehensive travellers' health insurance and provide information on available policies.

v) Inform travellers of the procedures for obtaining assistance and reimbursement, particularly if the insurance policy is arranged by the travel agent or company.

vi) Provide information on:
   a) Mandatory vaccination requirements for yellow fever;
   b) The need for malaria precautions at the travel destination;
   c) The existence of other important health hazards at the travel destination;
   d) The presence or absence of good-quality medical facilities at the travel destination.

RESPONSIBILITY OF THE TRAVELLER

Travellers can obtain a great deal of information and advice from medical and travel industry professionals to help prevent health problems while abroad. However, travellers must accept that they are responsible for their health and well-being while travelling and on their return as well as for preventing the transmission of communicable diseases to others. The following are the main responsibilities to be accepted by the traveller:

1) The decision to travel;
2) Recognising and accepting any risks involved;
3) Seeking health advice in good time, preferably 4–8 weeks before travel;
4) Complying with recommended vaccinations and other prescribed medication and health measures;
5) Careful planning before departure;
6) Carrying a medical kit and understanding its use;
7) Obtaining adequate insurance cover;
8) Taking health precautions before, during and after the journey;
9) Obtaining a physician's lattestation pertaining to any prescription medicines, syringes, etc. being carried;
10) The health and well-being of accompanying children;
11) Taking precautions to avoid transmitting any infectious disease to others during and after travel;
12) Full reporting of any illness on return, including information about all recent travel;
13) Being respectful of the host country and its population;
14) Avoiding unprotected sexual contact and maintaining responsible sexual behaviour.

Medical Examination After Travel

Travellers should be advised to have a medical examination on their return if they:

i) Suffer from a chronic disease, such as cardiovascular disease, diabetes mellitus, chronic respiratory disease;
ii) Experience illness in the weeks following their return home, particularly if fever, persistent diarrhoea, vomiting, jaundice, urinary disorders, skin disease or genital infection occurs;

iii) They received treatment for malaria while travelling;

iv) Consider that they have been exposed to a serious infectious disease while travelling;

v) Have spent more than 3 months in a developing country.

Travellers should provide medical personnel with information on recent travel, including destination, and purpose and duration of visit.

References

Ap, J. and J.L. Compton. (1998). Developing and testing a tourism impact scale. *Journal of Travel Research* 37(2): 120-130.

Gunn, C.A. (1988). *Tourism Planning.* Taylor and Francis, New York.

Hampton, M.P. (1998). Backpacker tourism and economic development. *Annals of Tourism Research* 25(3): 639-660.

Hawkins, D.E. (Ed.). (1982). *Social and Economic Impact of Tourism on Asian Pacific Region.* Tokyo:Asian Productivity Organisation, p. iii.

Kahraman, N. (1994). Sustainable development and tourism. *Anatolia* V/4: 73-77.

9

Towards Sustainable Tourism

Tourism is an enormous and widespread industry. It is found all over the world, so its impacts, social, economic, and environmental, are also worldwide. These impacts can be positive, doing good, or negative, doing harm. Sustainable tourism usually aims to have minimal negative impacts, to minimise harm, and to optimise economic benefits. Ecotourism, a type of sustainable tourism, is usually conducted in largely untouched natural areas, which tend to be both environmentally and often socially sensitive so its potential impacts can be even greater, for good or ill. Ecotourism aims to extend the positive impacts, through a special focus on conservation, benefits for host populations, and the education of visitors.

Principles of Sustainabile Tourism

The principles of sustainability can be applied to any type of tourism mass or specialty; city, beach, or wilderness; large or small. They also can be applied to all sectors of the tourist industry: lodging, tours, agencies, ground operators, guiding, and transport. According to *Agenda 21 for the Travel & Tourism Industry*, "Sustainable tourism products are products which operate in harmony with local environment, community, and cultures, so that these become the permanent beneficiaries."

A large, conventional city hotel can be declared in 1988 that sustainable tourism is responsible, and so can a small ecolodge near a national park. This is one reason why many people see a growing need for internationally recognised, but locally adapted standards for sustainability.

In tourism, the triple bottom line can be critical, especially for those businesses and tours located outside of large cities. Hotels and tours in rural or natural areas depend on the good will of their local community for their survival. And towns, villages, and indigenous communities whose social fabric is damaged by tourism often lose their attractiveness for tourists. Businesses based on natural resources cannot survive if the resource is destroyed —this is why the clients are visiting in the first place.

The twelve aims for making tourism sustainable were described in "Making Tourism More Sustainable: A Guide for Policy Makers" as:

1) *Economic Viability:* To ensure the viability and competitiveness of tourism destinations and enterprises, so that they are able to continue to prosper and deliver benefits in the long term.
2) *Local Prosperity:* To maximise the contribution of tourism to the economic prosperity of the host destination, including the proportion of visitor spending that is retained locally.
3) *Employment Quality:* To strengthen the number and quality of local jobs created and supported by tourism, including the level of pay, conditions of service and availability to all without discrimination by gender, race, disability or in other ways.
4) *Social Equity:* To seek a widespread and fair distribution of economic and social benefits from tourism throughout the recipient community, including improving opportunities, income and services available to the poor.
5) *Visitor Fulfillment:* To provide a safe, satisfying and fulfilling experience for visitors, available to all without discrimination by gender, race, disability, or in other ways.
6) *Local Control:* To engage and empower local communities in planning and decision making about the management and future development of tourism in their area, in consultation with other stakeholders.
7) *Community Wellbeing:* To maintain and strengthen the quality of life in local communities, including social structures and access

to resources, amenities and life support systems, avoiding any form of social degradation or exploitation.

8) *Cultural Richness:* To respect and enhance the historic heritage, authentic culture, traditions, and distinctiveness of host communities.
9) *Physical Integrity:* To maintain and enhance the quality of landscapes, both urban and rural, and avoid the physical and visual degradation of the environment.
10) *Biological Diversity:* To support the conservation of natural areas, habitats, and wildlife, and minimise damage to them.
11) *Resource Efficiency:* To minimise the use of scarce and non renewable resources in the development and operation of tourism facilities and services.
12) *Environmental Purity:* To minimise the pollution of air, water, and land and the generation of waste by tourism enterprises and visitors

Ecotourism is a sector of tourism, based on nature travel and including the principles of sustainability. The International Ecotourism Society (TIES) defines ecotourism as:

> "responsible travel to natural areas that conserves the environment and improves the welfare of local people."

Whatever definition is used, ecotourism should have a *positive impact* on both natural areas and the local community.

Ecotourism is one kind of sustainable tourism, based on nature, and usually following a distinct set of principles and good practices. Ecotourism complements other types of tourism, as the diagram at right shows. Most visitors to Costa Rica, for example, participate in both conventional and ecotourism.

A major problem for trueecotourism businesses is apractice called greenwashing.This term refers to a business thatpresents itself as "sustainable",'ecological', 'green', 'responsible','ecotourist', etc., when it doesn'tcomply with generally acceptedstandards, or worse, it is incontradiction with them.

CERTIFICATION

Certification is a way of ensuring that an activity or a product meets certain standards. Within the tourist industry, different organisations have developed certification programs measuring different aspects of tourism:

i) quality, for the entire tourist industry,

ii) sustainability, also for all sectors, and

iii) ecotourism, for sustainable tourism that takes place in natural, protected, or fragile ecosystems, that may include indigenous communities, and that conforms to the definition above.

> Certification is defined as "a voluntary procedure that assesses, audits and gives written assurance that a facility, product, process or service meets specific standards. It awards a marketable logo to those that meet or exceed baseline standards."

Certification labels have a long history, dating back to the fifteenth century, when the Roquefort cheese label was regulated, and the nineteenth and early twentieth century, when French wines were first certified for origin and purity. The electrical industry has used certification as a way to ensure the safety of appliances and industrial equipment since the International Electrotechnical Commission (IEC) first established standards in 1904. Many other industry-specific certification standards were developed during the twentieth century, mostly to assure the reliability of products to wholesalers and industrial users. Most systems are known and recognised only within the industry, but a few have received consumer recognition.

The impetus for environmental certification began with the 1992 "Earth Summit," held under United Nations sponsorship in Rio de Janeiro. Among the many outcomes of this event was the "Agenda 21", with a call for environmental and social responsibility of all sectors of society in the world, including governments, non-governmental organisations, and businesses. Soon afterwards, environmental awards, prises, and certification systems began to be developed in agriculture and business, including bananas, flowers, fish, timber, and coffee.

Since 2000, there has been a growing recognition that most environmental certification programs have not seriously considered sociocultural issues, while social and labor certification systems have not considered environmental factors. In some areas, such as organic agriculture, this has led to cooperation between social and environmental certification programs.

A different evolution has occurred in tourism certification: quality certification has existed for decades, whereas environmental certification in tourism is relatively new and only since 1987. Sociocultural aspects have been added since about 1996 in the Americas and 2000 in Europe.

In tourism, certification has a long history. The American Automobile Association (AAA), the Mobil five-star system in the United States, the Michelin guides in Europe, and the worldwide five-star system of hotel quality have existed for most of the twentieth century. These systems have traditionally measured the *quality* of the tourist product as well as some aspects of *health*, *hygiene*, and *safety*. In recent years, negative environmental and social impacts of tourism have become obvious in many parts of the world, and some of these places have lost market position. As a result, some tourist industry leaders have started promoting the triple bottom line of sustainability as recommended business practice.

For tourism to survive over time, customer satisfaction can be likened to a three-legged stool: it will collapse if any of the legs is too weak. However, traditional tourism certification programs concentrated only on the first leg health, hygiene and safety. The third leg represents the triple bottom line. However the first "green" certification programs emphasised only part of the third leg without considering sociocultural and economic sustainability.

Environmental certification of tourism services began in Europe with the Blue Flag Campaign for beaches in Denmark, in 1987. The following year Austria established the "Silberdistel" label for lodgings and restaurants in Kleinwalsertal. Most were based in Europe, few took sociocultural factors into account, and all were voluntary. Only three of the programs in the study certified ecotourism. The vast majority of the programs evaluated lodging only, although some programs certified all sectors and aspects of tourism. By 2007, as many as 80 programs exist or are under development, although many smaller programs have ceased to certify new businesses.

Aware of the dangers of uncontrolled proliferation – confusion of the consumer, lack of brand recognition, and widely varying standards many of the most important sustainable and ecotourism certification programs met in 2000, in Mohonk Mountain House to begin to develop a common language and common minimum standards.

Following on this, a formal effort was established, entitled the Sustainable Tourism Stewardship Council (STSC) feasibility study. Consultation workshops were held worldwide, with contributing stakeholders from electronic list-servers, questionnaires, and direct communication with over 1,000 organisations and professionals in 26 countries.

Among the concrete results are the establishment of harmonised standards in Europe (the VISIT standard) and in the Americas. The member programs follow a set of agreed-upon minimum standards.

The movement towards establishing the STSC as an accreditation body was reinforced in 2005, and, as of 2007, an effort is underway to formally constitute this body.

As a consequence of these activities and studies, new and existing tourism certification programs have begun to take into account all aspects of sustainability: environmental, social, cultural, and economic—the triple bottom line. Many of these programs are designed to work in parallel with quality star ratings and government health and safety regulations.

Then we ask -why is Certification Important? Certification sets standards and helps distinguish genuine ecotourism and sustainable tourism businesses from others that make empty claims. This helps to protect the integrity of these concepts.

Certification is not an end in itself. It is one of a number of tools for motivating businesses and others to improve their environmental, social, and economic performance, while rewarding them for doing so. These rewards are sometimes tangible and sometimes not.

There are a number of other reasons why certification is important. They include:

Benefits for Certified Businesses

i) Certification helps businesses to improve themselves: going through a certification process is educational. Many certified businesses have stated that one of the greatest benefits of the certification process was to teach them the elements of sustainability in their operations and focus their attention on the changes they needed to make in their businesses.

ii) Certification tends to reduce operating costs. This has been found in almost every type of business certification. In tourism, it has been shown to dramatically reduce the costs of water, electricity, and fossil fuels, without reducing the quality of service, as in the graph at right.

iii) The process of implementing certification of sustainable tourism is often accompanied by easier access to technical assistance and financing for businesses to implement new technology.

iv) Potentially, certification can provide a marketing advantage to certified businesses, as consumers learn to recognise credible certification brands.

Benefits for Consumers

i) Certification provides tourists with environmentally and socially responsible choices – it helps consumers to know which businesses are truly socially and environmentally responsible and to make choices on this basis.

ii) Certification in general increases public awareness of responsible business practices.

iii) Certification can alert tourists to the environmental and social issues in an area, allowing them to act more respectfully or contribute to solutions.

iv) Certified businesses tend to offer better quality service.

Benefits for Governments

i) Certification helps governments protect their market niches as ecotourism or sustainable tourism destinations, especially when the credibility of the destination is threatened by greenwashing.

ii) Certification raises industry standards in health, safety, environment, and social stability.

iii) It lowers the regulatory costs of environmental protection.

iv) By requiring economic benefits to communities, certification can help reduce poverty, especially in rural areas.

Benefits for the Environment and Local Communities

Finally, certification of sustainable and ecotourism protects both the environment and the social and economic structure of local communities near the certified businesses.

i) Certification requires the businesses to protect the environment and do little or no damage to it.

ii) It requires businesses to respect local culture and provide real economic and social benefits for it.

iii) When the business is economically sustainable, and offers quality of service to ensure that, it is likely to continue offering benefits for the long term.

Different Types of Certification

There are many different types of certification systems, as well as related awards and ecolabels, and there is much confusion about how they differ.

First, we cover Common Elements to Most Tourism Certification Programs. Although well–designed certification programs can differ considerably, they almost all have some similar components. These are:

i) Voluntary enrollment by businesses

ii) Well-defined standards and criteria

iii) Assessment and auditing

iv) Recognition and awarding the use of a logo

v) Periodic follow up audits to renew the certification

vi) Continual improvement

vii) Transparency

viii) Participatory mechanisms to define standards

Ensuring Fairness and Objectivity

The technical aspects of ensuring the fairness and objectivity of a certification system can be very complicated. There are many definitions and rules that are accepted by most certifiers. A few of the most important are:

1) Nondiscrimination: certification should be available to all applicants who meet the standards and whose activities are covered;
2) Certification should be free of undue financial considerations and independent of size or membership in groups or organisations;
3) The certification standard should consist of clearly defined criteria, specifically related to what is being certified;
4) The certifying organisation should be able to make impartial evaluations and certification decisions, based on clearly defined criteria;
5) The certifying body should allow the participation of all parties significantly concerned with the activity being certified, with respect to the content and function of the certification system;
6) The person who evaluates a business or activity should be separate from the entity that decides whether to award the certification; both should be independent of whoever provides consulting service to help the business qualify;
7) The certification body should be free from commercial or financial pressures that might influence decisions;
8) The certification should award a logo and include a sunset clause that requires re-application after a given time period, to protect against greenwashing;
9) There should be established procedures for appeals, for revoking certifications, for revising and changing criteria and standards, and so on.

These and many other generally accepted guidelines and definitions for how to certify, are based on guidelines established by consensus among the members of the International Organisation for Standardisation (ISO), based in Switzerland.

An important cautionary note is to remember that ISO has issued hundreds of standards for everything from film speed to screw strength. The guidelines for how to *govern* certification programs are among the most widely accepted . But they should not be confused with the two most famous ISO *certification* standards, ISO 9000 for certifying quality management systems, and ISO 14001, for environmental management systems.

Eco–Labels

Some of the main distinctions among programs are

i) first, second, and third party certification,

ii) process versus performance–based systems,

iii) certification to minimum standards versus ecolabels, and

iv) multiple levels versus pass–fail awards. All of these systems usually follow generally accepted rules.

(i) First, Second, or Third Party Certification

First-party certification is self-evaluation. For example, when a company declares that its product meets certain standards but no one from outside verifies the claim.

Second-party certification is when a purchaser or industry body assures that the product meets the purchaser's standards.

Third-party certification is when a neutral, independent third party evaluates the compliance of the product with clearly defined standards.

(ii) Process or Performance

A controversial topic in certification is whether *processes* or *results* should be certified.

The most commonly used process-based systems are the ISO 9000 series for quality management systems and ISO 14001 for environmental management systems. They certify businesses that have established and documented *systems* for assuring the improvement of quality or environmental performance. They must show continuous improvement, but only compared to their own prior performance. Thus, for example, two hotels might both be certified with ISO 14001, while one might have excellent state-of-the-art water conservation systems and the other might have disastrous overuse of water, as long as each could demonstrate improvement from year to year of its own performance. In other words, it receives a certification of its effort, not its actual performance. For this reason, the consumer product of a process-based certification should not, under ISO guidelines, bear the certification logo, because there is no guarantee of the product's compliance with environmental or quality criteria. Only the business or activity is certified, not what it produces, which in the case of tourism, is lodging in a hotel room, a meal, a tour, or transportation.

(a) Process–Based Certification Programs

1) Environmental Management Systems (EMS): ISO 14001 and related programs
2) Management establishes systems for monitoring certain significant environmental aspects
3) Usually requires outside consultants; relatively expensive for small and medium businesses
4) Emphasis on internal cost savings & environmental impact mitigation
5) No universal standards: cannot compare across businesses
6) Logo given for setting up process, not for achieving fixed goals
7) Best suited for large businesses, where it is very cost-effective and offers economies of scale

Performance–based systems certify whether or not a business or activity complies with objective outside criteria.

In a number of ways, performance systems are better suited to small and medium businesses, which comprise some 80-90% of tourism businesses worldwide. They tend to be cheaper to implement than ISO 14001 or other types of environmental management systems, and they allow comparisons among businesses, since all are rated according to the same criteria.

(b) Performance–Based Certification Programs

1) Tangible criteria that permit comparisons among certified businesses
2) Measure achievement and results, not intent
3) Can include check list intelligible to both business and consumers
4) More transparent; less expensive
5) Can include environmental and socio-economic criteria within & without business
6) Can involve variety of stakeholders
7) Can offer different levels of logos reflecting different levels of performance
8) Suited for small, medium & large businesses

From this simple explanation, it might appear that performance-based systems are better than process-based systems of certification. However, the situation in real life is much more complex. Process-based management systems ensure that a company documents its performance, and more importantly, that it has the internal controls in place to continue to maintain good performance. Process-based systems tend to be very cost-effective for larger businesses, because they ensure that the mechanisms for improving quality and environmental performance become part of the structure of the business and its organisational culture. Finally, process-based systems can control and measure environmentally important aspects of the business's operations that might not even appear among performance indicators.

(iii) Certification or Eco–Label

The terms 'environmental certification' and 'ecolabel' are often used interchangeably, although they signify different things. Environmental certification is awarded to those businesses or activities that comply absolutely with a set of standards. Any number or all of the businesses in a sector can be certified, if they comply.

An ecolabel is an award that is given to a business or activity that has significantly better performance compared to the other businesses in its sector. Only the best performers, who show *exemplary performance*, according to the established criteria, receive the ecolabel. Ecolabels are based on comparison with the best performance (benchmarking), rather than compliance with baseline standards. Many certification systems in sustainable tourism incorporate aspects of both certification to minimum standards and the comparative requirements of an ecolabel.

(iv) Pass/Fail Certification or Classification to Different Levels

When a person graduates from a school, he or she is awarded a diploma that certifies compliance with minimum requirements. This is certification of compliance or not. However, to earn that diploma, the person received letter or number grades for each course, which are averaged to give a final grade. This is classification on a graded scale of best to worst.

It is often considered that a 'graded' certification scheme is better than 'pass/fail' because it acknowledges a range of differences within an acceptable sustainability framework, and it strongly motivates companies to work to improve their ratings in subsequent audits. A number of sustainable tourism certification programs have two to five levels of classification over and above the minimum requirements for certification. Many of the graded certification systems in sustainable tourism have characteristics of both certification and ecolabels.

Certification versus Accreditation

Following ISO definitions, certification applies to the awards given to businesses, products, processes, or services, while "accreditation" applies to the process of qualifying, endorsing and licensing entities that perform certification.

However there is some confusion in the use of the terms. In the United States, 'registration' and in Australia, Canada, and Fiji, 'accreditation', have also been used as synonyms for certification – the awarding of a logo to a business or a process that complies with certain standards.

Sustainable Tourism Certification Worldwide

The World Tourism Organisation, in a study published in 2002, identified over 60 sustainable and ecotourism certification programs around the world. A few programs operate worldwide, some are regional, and most are national or local.

i) To what degree do they take into account all three aspects of the "triple bottom line"– environmental, sociocultural, and economic sustainability?

ii) How well do they comply with international technical standards for certification programs – for example, with the well recognised ISO/IEC 17021:2006?

iii) Do they recognise the basic codes of conduct laid out in various documents for respecting the rights of indigenous and local communities?

iv) How well do they comply with the Mohonk Agreement, an informal agreement reached in 2000, by the principal certification systems for sustainable tourism and ecotourism about minimum requirements?

v) Are they in agreement with the Quebec Declaration and the Convention on Biological Diversity pronouncements on the certification of sustainable tourism?

vi) Do they follow the "Indicators of Sustainable Development for Tourism Destinations" of the World Tourism Organisation?

These technical studies, however, are not of much use to a business that wishes to be certified and doesn't want to become an expert on certification. Also, the sheer number of programs that exist has led to significant confusion about the relative benefits of each. Because of the scope of the project, it will take several years before this system is in operation. In the meantime, many businesses and organisations will want to certify their activities and will have to choose which certification program to use. This guide is an attempt to familiarise both business managers and certification program managers with the different options available, and how they might best fit their situation.

Chooseing aCertification Program

All sustainable tourism certification systems are voluntary. No business is required to be certified, nor can any one certification system be imposed on those businesses that want to be certified. The first step in certification then, is to determine which programs are available in your area and choose the one that best fits your needs. Or, if you are involved in creating a new program, you need to decide which model or models of existing programs to use.

First we have Decide between a Certification Program for Sustainable Tourism or Eco–Tourism. The first decision is whether to certify sustainable tourism or ecotourism. This depends on the nature of your individual business activities or the type of program you are trying to create. If your business does not involve close and direct contact with nature and some elements of interpretation of nature for visitors, you should choose a more general sustainable tourism certification. Your tourist board and national environmental organisations are probably familiar with the programs in use in your area.

Twelve of the principal European programs participated in the VISIT project and complied in 2003 with the VISIT standard as a set of 21 key requirements for ecolabels for tourism services. Seven programs belong to the VISIT Association, the umbrella organisation for tourism ecolabels in Europe.

In the Americas, nearly all of the certification programs belong to the Sustainable Tourism Certification Network of the Americas, and have also harmonised their requirements. Information and links to each program are at.

Process of Certification

Having selected a program and made contact with it, the next step is to determine how well your business complies with the criteria for sustainability. You should be prepared to determine your usage of water, electricity, and fossil fuels. You may be asked to examine how you process your wastewater and solid wastes. Do you reduce your consumption of disposable materials, like plastics and bottles? Do you recycle? If you are near a natural area, do you help protect it? These and a number of other environmental criteria are found in nearly all certification programs for tourism.

In the sociocultural realm, do you hire local people and pay them fairly? Do you offer training and upward mobility to lower-level employees? Do local people occupy management positions? Are working conditions safe, comfortable, and educational? Does your business respect local cultural norms? Was your property acquired in a just manner? Do you assist when needed in your local community? Do you offer outreach and educational programs to your guests? These criteria too are found in most sustainable tourism certification programs.

Then, Decide Whether or not you need Outside help to Improve the Sustainability of your Business. Once you have determined how well you are complying with sustainability standards, you may feel that you need outside help to improve your business. If the certification program you are interested in offers consulting services, be sure that the program does not require that you use its in-house services this may be an unethical conflict of interest. Most programs can be implemented without the use of outside consultants, by following the manuals and instructions.

Often governmental and international agencies can offer assistance and financing in implementing exemplary environmental practices, especially in water and energy conservation. These are called "benchmarking" programs, and are incorporated in a few certification programs, but are also available independently of certification. You can locate these programs, almost all of which charge a fee, by searching the Internet for "hotel benchmarking".

Benchmarks for water, energy, and waste in hotels and camping sites in Europe are available at based on over 450 datasets from 15 European countries. TourBench is online, for free, in 9 languages. EarthCheck has developed indicators for Asia Pacific,South America, and the Caribbean, as well as other countries. It is used for the benchmarking component of some certification programs. In addition to water, energy, and waste, EarthCheck considers social commitment and chemical use.

Very large businesses may find it cost-effective to establish an environmental or sustainable management department that works closely with high-level management or assign these functions to existing employees.

Once you are ready to be certified, the process usually consists of paying a fee to the certifier, filling in a series of documents and questionnaires, and evaluation by an auditor or some other mechanism of determining compliance. An auditor will usually meet with management or the owners, and then inspect the critical areas of the business that have been determined by the questionnaires. An auditor will also request to see documents, and although these may be confidential, the auditor should be legally bound to respect confidentiality. The certification program will then decide whether or not your business can be certified and will award your logo or inform you of the improvements you need to make.

Once you have been certified, the process does not stop. You will be expected to maintain the high standards that allowed you to be certified. The advantages will continue, however, and you should also be able to participate in cooperative advertising programs, receive preferential treatment from your government tourist office, and be listed by the certification program. You should *not,* however, expect to receive quickly an important increase in occupancy, because sustainable tourism certification programs do not yet have wide consumer recognition. After a period of one to three years, you should expect to renew your certification, with new questionnaires and inspections.

Limitations of Certification

Certification for quality in tourism has existed for nearly a century and has achieved great market recognition. The five-star rating system took decades to build, but today is accepted worldwide as a standard. Sustainable tourism certification has existed for less than 20 years. Professional market surveys indicate that there is a clear interest in the traveling public in choosing environmentally and socially responsible businesses, but that there is not yet recognition of credible brands of certification. So it will take time to build demand for certified tourism products.

In tourism, whether conventional, sustainable, or ecotourism, the success of the business depends on attracting and pleasing clients. But clients will not visit a place that is unsafe, unhealthy, inaccessible, or too highly priced for the quality offered. It is a grave mistake to think that your business will prosper if you offer environmental and social sustainability without giving your clients what they need in terms of a quality experience.

You should not think about certifying your business unless you are sure that you will meet or exceed the expectations of your clients in terms of safety, access, quality, and price. This does not mean that you should abuse the environment or your community to do so; you should certainly build your business with environmental and social responsibility from the very beginning.

Many businesses seek certification to increase their occupancy. While this may eventually happen, at present, most clients for tourist businesses do not use the sustainability of a business as a reason for choosing their destination. This is unfortunate, and may change in the future, as it has for organic agriculture. For this to occur, recognised programs must certify many more tourist businesses. In other words, there should be a critical mass of certified businesses with brand recognition of the certifying program. Right now, there has been a proliferation of certification programs and ecolabels for tourism, but none of them has more than a few hundred businesses certified. The result has been confusion for the few consumers who are aware of certification programs. The Sustainable Tourism Stewardship Council (STSC) initiatives hopes to accredit the most reliable programs and ensure that they meet minimum standards, as well as promoting the use of these programs.

Challenges of Sustainable Tourism

A primary challenge of local governance, both today and in decades ahead, is to steer increasingly external, global forces on local development so that development achieves the shared vision of the local population. In cities, towns and villages throughout the world, the primary responsibility for this steering process rests with the institution of local government and its diverse local authorities.

As providers of social services, builders of economic infrastructure, regulators of economic activity, and managers of the natural environment, local authorities have many direct instruments at their disposal to influence development. Only with such a facilitator can a community of diverse interests define a shared vision and act consistent with this vision.

The role of local authorities as facilitators in the development process is reinforced through municipal international cooperation

(MIC). These shared challenges of governance have instigated thousands of local authorities to establish municipal international cooperation projects and to join international local government organisations (LGOs) to advocate for local self-governance and control over the development process.

Even prior to the UN Conference on Environment and Development, but particularly since the adoption of Agenda 21, many local authorities and their LGOs have focused on the unique challenges of governance for sustainable development. At the local level, sustainable development is achieved by steering local development activities to simultaneously achieve three objectives:

i) Increased local social welfare;

ii) Greater, and more equitably distributed, local economic wealth; and

iii) Enhanced integrity of local ecosystems.

Thousands of local authorities, in partnership with their communities and supported by MIC activities, have instigated Local Agenda 21 processes to create a shared vision for local development that is consistent with the sustainable development concept. In response to these visions, local authorities have been adapting their practices and activities to steer local development along the sustainable development path.

Tourism is one of the many external forces influencing the direction and options for local development. The question of whether tourism can be sustainable is rightfully addressed in the context of the Local Agenda 21 process.

A truly legitimate and practical discussion on sustainable tourism must take place in and with the communities that are being influenced by tourist industry development. It must create accountability of the tourism industry to locally-defined development visions.

The true proof of "sustainable tourism" will be the sustainable development of local communities that serve as tourist destinations. Local authorities worldwide welcome the leadership of the UN Commission on Sustainable Development, and the interest of the tourism industry, to reduce tourism's negative impacts and to increase the positive contribution of tourism business and consumption activity to local sustainable development.

Industry Initiatives for Sustainable Tourism

Tourism is a recognised global industry—one of the largest industries in the world. Like any global industry, tourist business activities can have considerable impact on local development trends. The local impacts of the tourism industry are diverse and are often unique to the tourism sector.

Tourist activities, as traditionally defined by the tourism industry, fundamentally involve the transportation and hosting of the tourism consumer in a local community. No other global industry structures itself in such a way that the consumer is brought to the product, rather than the product being delivered to the consumer in his or her own community.

The primary product of tourism is not something produced by the industry. The product is often the heritage, wealth, and expected legacy of the community that serves as the tourist destination. The business activity of the tourism industry is to promote the "salable" or appealing aspects of the community, transport non-residents into the community, manage the hospitality for and guide the activities of these visitors, and provide them with goods and services to purchase during their stay.

Tourism activities can, in particular, degrade the social and natural wealth of a community. The intrusion of large numbers of uninformed foreigners into local social systems can undermine pre-existing social relationships and values. This is particularly a problem where tourism business is centred in traditional social systems, such as isolated communities or indigenous peoples.

Tourism in natural areas, euphemistically called "eco-tourism," can be a major source of degradation of local ecological, economic and social systems. These tourism-related changes are particularly deleterious when local residents rely on those natural areas for their sustenance. Resulting economic losses can encourage socially deleterious economic activities such as prostitution, crime, and migrant and child labour.

Solutions to adverse tourism impacts are to be found in the shared interest of local communities, tourism businesses, and tourism consumers to maintain the natural wealth and social heritage of the tourist destination. In the first instance, therefore, an institutional mechanism must be established, relative to each destination, to articulate and develop this sense of shared interest. To secure the legitimacy of these mechanisms, the participation of all interested local groups or interests must be guaranteed. Dialogue must take place in an open and transparent way.

Experience demonstrates that if dialogue among interested parties is to have a real impact on development, it must generate accountability among these parties with regards to future investments, practices and policies. Only through such accountability can interests maintain a commitment to continued dialogue and a common agenda for local tourism development.

Experience demonstrates that this accountability should be reciprocal between individual or private interests and societal or public interests. Without such reciprocal accountability, local communities are typically forced to choose, in conflict, between private and public benefits, even if ample "win-win" development choices exist. On the one hand, accountability requires that property owners are provided with opportunity to retain the economic value of their property, either through sale or income generating activity. On the other hand, private market relationships, including property ownership, do not provide sufficient basis for social accountability related to "public goods," including ecological integrity and social heritage. Excessive reliance upon private property ownership as a guide in development has in fact contributed to the deterioration of public goods.

Within such a framework of accountability, numerous instruments are available to guide local tourist development on a sustainable path. These instruments include:

i) Heritage preservation requirements for site developments and building designs;

ii) Programs to exchange land and development rights from non–suitable to suitable development areas;

iii) Private heritage and green space stewardship programs;

iv) Tax benefits accruing to property owners exercising sustainable development practices;

v) Tourism taxes and development fees to support construction and maintenance of required infrastructure.

However, without true commitment to the sustainable tourism agenda, these instruments are not themselves sufficient to prevent the steady erosion, by legally sanctioned private actions, of local natural wealth and social heritage.

Agents and Partnerships for Change

Fortunately, in more than 2,000 communities in 64 countries Local Agenda 21 partnership forums already exist to serve as a mechanism for sustainable tourism dialogue. Where these forums are weak or have not yet addressed tourism issues, the tourist industry, local government organisations (LGOs) and concerned NGOs can serve as a catalyst for dialogue. A particular opportunity exists in those countries where Local Agenda 21 national campaigns or where National Councils for Sustainable Development have been established. NCSDs can play a key role in providing country-level support to local review of the sustainable tourism agenda.

Of additional interest at the local level is the potential role of local tourism offices or Convention and Visitor Bureaus (CVBs) that have been created through public-private partnerships to promote local tourist attractions. Where motivated to support sustainable tourism development, the CVBs could serve as facilitators of working groups, within the context of Local Agenda 21 activities, on sustainable tourism development. Where CVBs or their related international body(ies) have made no express commitment to sustainable development, local authorities, as primary funders of CVBs, are in an excellent position to mobilise their awareness and support.

Consumer Behaviour in Sustainable Tourism

Tourism related consumption has three stages of impact. First, prior to departure, tourists purchase travel-related clothing and equipment, which may be produced under conditions that undermine the social and ecological sustainability of the producing communities. Second, when tourists travel long distances to tourist destinations, they create considerable atmospheric pollution and other impacts on the global environment. Third, upon arrival at the tourist destination, tourists often continue their accustomed habits of consumption, even though these destinations may not have the infrastructure required to manage those consumption patterns.

In addition to high altitude emissions from long distance air travel, air travel produces considerable negative local environmental impacts, including ground level emissions of VOCs and particulates, disposal of fuel, hasardous chemicals and solid waste, noise pollution, and wildlife and habitat disruption. Marine dumping of wastes from cruise ships is an increasing concern. However, with nearly 600 million international travellers in 1997, surprisingly little public information is available on the environmental and social impacts of long distance travel.

Following arrival at tourist destinations, the tourism industry typically strives to host tourists according to the standards and amenities of their country of origin. These hospitality standards mimic the high consumption lifestyles of developed countries. For instance, luxury hotel rooms, with high levels of energy and water consumption, are given the highest rankings or "stars" in international hotel rankings. These "luxury" consumption standards, using current technologies, are themselves globally unsustainable.

The most immediate observable impacts of introducing these high consumption practices into lower consumption communities are:

i) Degradation of local water and soil quality, with direct impacts on local health and economies, as a result of the lack of adequate water, drainage, waste water, and waste management infrastructure to manage the higher volumes of waste produced by higher levels of consumption;

ii) Reduced access by local residents to land, housing and marine resources through, among other things, reallocation of these community resources to foreign tourist residents and inflation of local prices;

iii) Destruction of traditional sources of income.

The most direct way to reduce the adverse impacts of tourism-related travel is to increase opportunities for people to engage in appealing tourism activities in their own cities, regions or countries. In various cities of the world, this local tourism concept is known as "green tourism." Green tourism—in contrast to "eco-tourism," which relies on travel to distant locations. While green tourism has the positive economic effect of stimulating local economic activity, it reduces the flow of foreign currency to developing nations. However, short of definitive actions by the tourism industry and host countries/communities to reduce the negative environmental impacts of foreign travel and the negative social impacts of foreign tourist enclaves in developing nations, green tourism advocates will continue to build support among tourism consumers.

Solutions to tourism-related pollution in the travel and tourism industry are technologically available. Overcoming economic barriers to their implementation may require government regulation, the development of economic instruments, and industry self-regulation.

The industry has every opportunity to institute voluntary initiatives and self-regulation to address green tourism advocates and those calling for government regulation. The growing effort among international hotel chains, for instance, to offer guests the option of reusing their bedroom towels and linens demonstrates the ability of the industry to respond in one area of impact. In this regard, the establishment of formal environmental management systems (EMSs) in each business establishment provides a way for tourism businesses to identify their adverse social and environmental impacts and to institute a programme for continuous reductions of those impacts.

Ultimately, the solution to adverse environmental impacts arising from local tourist consumption is the establishment of waste reduction programs and appropriate waste management systems and infrastructure, particularly in developing country destinations. Again a choice exists between voluntary and regulatory measures. National governments and tourism businesses, which receive disproportional economic benefits from tourism, share an interest in maintaining tourism-related hard currency inflows, and should either directly provide such infrastructure or ensure that funds are made available to local authorities for this purpose. Only through such economic instruments can the public costs of tourism activity be "internalised" in the local tourist economy.

Local revenue measures need to be carefully coordinated across municipal jurisdictions on a regional basis to ensure coordinated infrastructure development. Where statutory regional planning bodies do not exist to provide coordination, Local Agenda 21 forums may provide a flexible mechanism for multi-jurisdictional coordination.

Tourist businesses can make a significant voluntary contribution to resolving the social costs of tourism by:

i) Providing local resident employment and training opportunities, including in traditional trades and crafts;

ii) Establishing purchasing guidelines that favour local goods and services procurement;

iii) Making donations and investments in local recreational facilities, parks, cultural facilities and security operations;

iv) Establishing local profit–sharing arrangements.

Failing necessary voluntary measures, local governments can institute economic incentives and regulatory measures to reward best practices and prevent severe social impacts that need to be resolved at public expense. Ultimately, in the face of private establishments that demonstrate no long-term commitment to maintaining the preconditions for tourism local authorities need to use all powers available to protect the cultural and environmental wealth that make an attractive tourist destination.

Agents and Partnerships for Change

A partnership approach to addressing negative impacts of tourism consumption requires, above all, assumption of responsibility and voluntary action by the tourism industry. For example, within the framework of a voluntary EMS approach, partnerships can be established between local governments, airport authorities, regional air quality agencies, airlines, trade unions, NGOs and resident associations to develop an action programme to reduce local airport pollution. Following the model of the "Responsible Care" programme in the chemical industry, these partnerships could be supported by international travel and tourism organisations and related industry associations.

Of critical importance is the creation of mechanisms to inform and involve tourism consumers in making educated choices about their activities as tourists in distant tourist destinations. Ideally, these efforts would ensure that tourism consumers, as with industry, begin to recognise and understand tourist destinations as living communities that deserve their support and respect. International consumer advocacy organisations and trade unions can play an important role in informing consumers about tourism development activities that violate basic principles of sustainable development. Provision of such information to LGOs can facilitate local authority responsiveness to identified problems.

Promoting Sustainable Development through Tourism

Many of the technologies and measures required for sustainable development in the tourism sector are clear. Resources exist within the tourism industry-which annually generates hundreds of billions of dollars-to apply these technologies and to make development within the sector more equitable. However, as the experiences of hundreds of local authorities demonstrate, through their engagement in broad-based sustainable development planning through Local Agenda 21, the appropriate application of technologies and resources requires effective and truly accountable development partnerships.

In this respect, the primary barrier to sustainable development through tourism is an over reliance on market mechanisms to guide tourism development and consumption decisions. The market-which treats cultural and environmental wealth as free, "public goods" and which responds to degradation of this wealth as a "free rider"-provides instruments to guide development, but is insensitive to many requirements of sustainable tourism.

Sustainable tourism development requires a partnership among the stakeholders of the local tourist destination. This partnership must use both market and non-market instruments to implement a shared sustainable development vision. Without such a partnership, advocacy for sustainable development becomes a conflictive struggle between an industry which seeks to respond only to market forces and a public sector which, when accountable, acts to protect public goods and wealth for future generations.

Therefore, the key problem at this stage of the "sustainable tourism" debate is the creation of tangible, working local partnerships. These local partnerships must be encouraged and supported by national governments and industry, and not undermined by "higher level" agreements. Tourism businesses need to recognise and support the social conditions and the cultural and environmental wealth that make a community an attractive tourist destination.

The UN Commission on Sustainable Development has repeatedly recognised Local Agenda 21 planning as an effective partnership mechanism for implementing Agenda 21 in cities and local communities. Experience with Local Agenda 21 activities in hundreds of communities since 1990 has highlighted a number of principles for effective sustainable development planning. These partnerships can be established either within or independent from existing Local Agenda 21 activities.

The principles for Local Agenda 21 planning are as follows:

i) Participation and Transparency, that involves local residents, representing all major groups of society, in Local Agenda 21 planning and makes information about sustainable development easily available to the general public.

ii) Partnerships that build collective responsibility for planning, decision making, problem solving, project implementation and evaluation.

iii) Accountability that holds all partners answerable for their actions.

iv) Systemic Approach that addresses the underlying causes of social, economic and ecological problems in an integrated way, focusing on the entire systems that are affected, rather than only problem symptoms.

v) Ecological Limits, that are defined by Earth's carrying capacity and that serve as the limits for development.

vi) Equity and Justice, that are secured locally through the provision of equal opportunities and human rights, and globally through development cooperation partnerships between developed and developing nations.

vii) Concern for the Future, that requires long-term planning and action that addresses both immediate needs and long-term trends.

These principles can be applied, in working partnerships, to evaluate and improve efforts to address sensitive tourism development issues, such as:

i) Inequitable distribution of tourism revenues and "leakage" of revenues to foreign shores;

ii) Displacement of pre–existing local settlements by tourism developments;

iii) Equal access to local coastal and recreational resources and controversies over uses and long-term protection of those areas;

Concerns related to lack of foreign tourist sensitivity to cultural traditions and sites.

Agents and Partnerships for Change

The primary partnerships for sustainable tourism development will be local partnerships, addressing the unique development goals and needs of each community.

Notwithstanding the primacy of local partnerships, the transnational nature of tourism requires transnational partnerships to support sustainable tourism planning activities at the local and national levels. The Local Agenda 21 process has established a new mechanism for such transnational partnership, called "Local Agenda 21 Charters." Initiated by the Netherlands Ministry of Foreign Affairs, in cooperation with the International Union of Local Authorities, the International Council for Local Environmental Initiatives, and Towns & Development, the Local Agenda 21 Charters process provides a mechanism for local communities to factor issues of global responsibility within their Local Agenda 21 activities. Presently, 20 local authorities have established the first Local Agenda 21 Charters.

Ultimately, tourism consumers must be rallied to the sustainable tourism agenda, thereby shaping both the market and public policy. Tourism consumers in existing Local Agenda 21 communities may find the Local Agenda 21 Charters mechanism useful in supporting sustainable development in popular tourist destinations. Existing "twinning" or "sister city" relationships with cities that are located in tourist regions can provide the basis for a possible Local Agenda 21 Charters relationship.

Approach Coastal Impacts of Tourism

Economic development activities in any sensitive natural area pose a particular challenge for sustainable development. Coastal areas host the most productive marine ecosystems and serve as spawning grounds for the oceans.

Coastal zones are dynamic in nature, responding to daily tidal changes as well as long term events such as sea level rising. This dynamic quality offers a defence from extreme weather events.

Rigid infrastructure from coastal development can inhibit the ability of coastal ecosystems to respond to changes.

Since coastal areas are the most highly populated regions on Earth, their protection requires unique attention and the effective management of numerous competing interests.

In many coastal areas, tourism development is destroying or marginalising dwindling habitats for marine animals and spawning fish, as well as the livelihoods of traditional fishing families and villages. Unregulated water sport activities and machinery are adding to this toll. Excessive private tourist development is denying equitable human access to beaches and coastal waters, cutting off local populations from their coastal heritage. Inappropriate development in high risk storm areas is costing families, local economies and governments billions of dollars annually.

As a first measure towards the sustainable management of coastal areas, governments at all levels, working in partnership with private foundations and investors, should establish designated coastal areas where development will be forever restricted. Protection of these areas should be stringently enforced.

The reputation and viability of the sustainable tourism concept depends upon the definition and implementation of clear management objectives for each coastal area. These objectives should clearly designate ecologically and socially/culturally sensitive areas as well as high risk areas. Education programs should be established to inform tourists about these management objectives.

The aims of any sustainable tourism development in coastal areas should be to:

i) recognise the economic value of existing coastal ecosystems, towns and heritage sites by providing opportunity for local revenue-generation through managed tourist use of these areas;
ii) design tourism developments, in cooperation with local stakeholders, to suit the unique ecological and social characteristics of each coastal site;
iii) use tourism investment to develop and upgrade the watershed, solid waste and waste water management systems for coastal cities and towns;
iv) ensure equitable access to coastal areas by all people, with a specific emphasis on using tourism development as a means to upgrade and manage traditional social uses, for example, through the designation of special natural/cultural heritage sites.

In addition sound planning and management to achieve the above aims, the following opportunities for low-impact tourism development could be considered:

i) Application of low-impact building and transportation designs, materials and technologies;
ii) Control of waste production through recycling and efficiency measures;
iii) Co–investment by the tourism industry, government and local residents to upgrade existing settlements and urban infrastructure, including drainage and sewerage infrastructure.

Agents and Partnerships for Change

The planning and management of coastal development typically requires the cooperation of local stakeholders-including property owners, residents, local business groups, and local authorities-and government agencies at the national and sub-national levels. As coastal areas typically extend beyond the jurisdictions of individual local authorities, regional coastal management agencies are often established through inter-municipal cooperation or sub-national action to provide effective multi-jurisdictional coordination.

Under ideal circumstances, tourism industry representatives, including property owners, will be directly involved in coastal planning and management schemes. In such cases, the tourism industry, in particular transnational businesses, needs to make a good faith commitment not to circumvent local/regional planning and management discussions by directly lobbying national government for special permissions and considerations.

References

Butler , R. (1975). *Tourism as an Agent of Social Change.* Occasional paper 4. Trent University, Department of Geography, Peterborough, Ont.

Deller , S.C., D.W. Marcouiller, and G.P. Green. (1997) .Recreational housing and local government finance. *Annals of Tourism Research* 24(3): 687-705.

Dowling , R.K. (1999). Tourism and sustainability: principles to practice. *Tourism Management* 20(3): 379-381.

Faulkner , B. and C.Tideswell. (1997). A framework for monitoring community impacts of tourism. *Journal of Sustainable Tourism* 5(1): 3-28.

Gulumser , K. (1996).The relationship between tourism and environment. *Anatolia* VII/3-4: 38-41.

Haralambopoulos, N. and A. Pizam. (1996). Perceived impacts of tourism:The case of Samos. *Annals of Tourism Research* 23(3): 503-526.

Bibliography

Ap, J. and J.L. Compton. (1998). Developing and testing a tourism impact scale. *Journal of Travel Research* 37(2): 120-130.

Archer, B. H.(1973). *The impact of domestic tourism*. Bangor: University of Wales Press.

Bar kin, D. (2002). Eco tourism for sustainable regional development. *Current Issues in Tourism*. pp. 5(3–4):245–253.

Baumol, W.J., and W.E. Oates (1977). *Economics, environmental policy, and quality of life*. Englewood Cliffs, New Jersey, USA: Prentice Hall.

Bremner, Caroline (2010). "Trend Watch: Euromonitor International's Top City Destination Ranking". *Euromonitor International.*

Buckley, R. (1994). *Research Note, a framework for ecotourism*. Annals of Tourism Research. pp. 21(3):661–669.

Butler , R. (1975). *Tourism as an Agent of Social Change.* Occasional paper 4. Trent University, Department of Geography, Peterborough, Ont.

Cater, E. (1994). Cater, E., and G. Lowman. ed. *Ecotourism in the Third World —Problems and Prospects for Sustainability in: Ecotourism, a sustainable option?*. United Kingdom: John Wiley and Sons.

Cooper, Chris; et al (2005). *Tourism: Principles and Practice* (3rd ed.). Harlow: Pearson Education.

Crandall, Louise. (1994). The social impact of tourism on developing regions and its measurement. In. *Travel, Tourism and Hospitality Research*, second edition. J.R. Brent Ritchie and Charles R. Goeldner (eds). New York: John Wiley and Sons Inc.

Deller , S.C., D.W. Marcouiller, and G.P. Green. (1997) .Recreational housing and local government finance. *Annals of Tourism Research* 24(3): 687-705.

Dowling , R.K. (1999). Tourism and sustainability: principles to practice. *Tourism Management* 20(3): 379-381.

Elper-Wood, M. (1998). *Ecotourism at a Crossroads: charting the way forward.* Nairobi, Kenya: The final report from the Conference of Ecotourism at the Crossroads.

Faulkner , B. and C.Tideswell. (1997). A framework for monitoring community impacts of tourism. *Journal of Sustainable Tourism* 5(1): 3-28.

Frechtling, Douglas C. (994). Assessing the economic impacts of travel and tourism – Measuring economic benefits. In. *Travel, Tourism and Hospitality Research*, second edition. J.R. Brent Ritchie and Charles R. Goeldner (eds). New York: John Wiley and Sons Inc.

Gulumser , K. (1996).The relationship between tourism and environment. *Anatolia*VII/3-4: 38-41.

Gunn, C.A. (1988). *Tourism Planning.* Taylor and Francis, New York.

Hampton, M.P. (1998). Backpacker tourism and economic development. *Annals of Tourism Research* 25(3): 639-660.

Haralambopoulos, N. and A. Pizam. (1996). Perceived impacts of tourism:The case of Samos. *Annals of Tourism Research* 23(3): 503-526.

Hawkins, D.E. (Ed.). (1982). *Social and Economic Impact of Tourism on Asian Pacific Region.* Tokyo:Asian Productivity Organisation, p. iii.

Honey, Martha (2008). *Ecotourism and Sustainable Development: Who Owns Paradise?* (Second ed.). Washington, DC: Island Press.

Isaacs, J.C. (2000). The limited potential of ecotourism to contribute to wildlife conservation. *The Ecologist.* pp. 28(1):61–69.

Jacobson, S.K., and R. Robles (1998). Ecotourism, sustainable development, and conservation education: development of a tour guide training program in Tortuguero, Costa Rica. *Environmental Management.* pp. 16(6):701–713.

Johnson, Peter and Thomas, Barry (eds). (1992). *Choice and demand in tourism.* London: Mansell.

Kahraman, N. (1994). Sustainable development and tourism. *Anatolia* V/4: 73-77.

Laidlaw, Katherine (19 April 2010). "Vacationing a human right, EU chief says". *National Post.*

Lennon, J. John; Foley, Malcolm (2000). *Dark Tourism.* London: Continuum.

McLaren, D. (1998). *Rethinking tourism and ecotravel: the paving of paradise and what you can do to stop it.* West Hartford, Connecticut, USA: Kamarian Press.

Propst, D. B. (Compiler). (1985). Assessing the economic impacts of recreation and tourism: conference and workshop (64 pp.). Asheville, NC: U.S. Department of Agriculture, Forest Service, Southeastern Forest Experiment Station.

Sheldon, Pauline J. (1990). *A review of tourism expenditure research. In Progress in Tourism, recreation and* hospitality management. C.P. Cooper (ed). New York: Belhaven Press.

Theobald, William F. (1998). *Global Tourism* (2nd ed.). Oxford [England]: Butterworth–Heinemann.

Tuohino, A., and A. Hynonen (2001). *Ecotourism - imagery and reality. Reflections on concepts and practices in Finnish rural tourism.* Nordia Geographical Publications. pp. 30(4):21–34.

UNWTO World Tourism Barometer June 2009". *UNWTO World Tourism Barometer* (World Tourism Organisation) 7 (2). June 2009.

Vivanco, L. (2002). *Ecotourism, Paradise lost - A Thai case study.* The Ecologist. pp. 32(2):28–30.

Wight, P.A. (1993). *Ecotourism: Ethics or Eco-sell.* Journal of Travel Research. pp. 31(3):3–9.

World Travel and Tourism Council. (1993). *Measuring the size of the global travel and tourism industry.* London: WTTC.

Wurzburger, Rebecca; et al (2009). *Creative Tourism: A Global Conversation: How to Provide Unique Creative Experiences for Travelers Worldwide:* As Presented at the 2008 Santa Fe & UNESCO International Conference on Creative Tourism in Santa Fe, New Mexico, USA. Santa Fe: Sunstone Press.

Ziffer, K. (1989). *Ecotourism: the uneasy alliance.* Conservation International/Ernst and Young.

Index